Doing Pragmatics

Second Edition

PETER GRUNDY
Department of Linguistics and English Language, University of Durham

A member of the Hodder Headline Group
LONDON

Co-published in the United States of America
by Oxford University Press, Inc., New York

First published in Great Britain in 2000 by
Arnold, a member of the Hodder Headline Group,
338 Euston Road, London NW1 3BH

http://www.arnoldpublishers.com

Co-published in the United States of America by
Oxford University Press Inc.,
198 Madison Avenue, New York, NY10016

The advice and information in this book are believed to be true and
accurate at the date of going to press, but neither the author[s] nor the publisher
can accept any legal responsibility or liability for any errors or omissions.

British Library Cataloguing in Publication Data
A catalogue record for this book is available from the British Library

Library of Congress Cataloging-in-Publication Data
A catalog record for this book is available from the Library of Congress

ISBN 0 340 75892 9 (pb)

1 2 3 4 5 6 7 8 9 10

Production Editor: Anke Ueberberg
Production Controller: Priya Gohil
Cover Design: Terry Griffiths

Typeset in Times by Scribe Design, Gillingham, Kent
Printed and bound in Great Britain by Redwood Books, Trowbridge, Wiltshire

What do you think about this book? Or any other Arnold titles?
Please send your comments to feedback.arnold@hodder.co.uk

Doing Pragmatics

Contents

Preface (and how to get the best out of this book)

Some students find that learning pragmatics and learning syntax are mirror images of one another. Because pragmatic data consist of everyday utterances, the first impression of pragmatics tends to be that it is really quite easy: the examples and the ways in which they are described seem to accord closely with our intuitions about everyday talk. In contrast, when we study syntax for the first time, the formal representation of the examples often seems very challenging. But as time goes on, we realize that the underlying ideas in pragmatics are really very difficult indeed, whereas the underlying ideas in syntax have a simplicity and elegance that make syntax seem less difficult the more we study it. My main motive in writing the first edition of this book (which appeared in 1995) was to try and extend the sense felt in the early stages of pragmatics, that it's really a very accessible area of linguistics, to the second stage when we have to grapple with the more challenging underlying ideas. In the second edition, which you are holding in your hand now, I've also tried to widen the spread so that *Doing Pragmatics* now includes 'doing' linguistic pragmatics, including relevance theory, and studying talk from a conversation analytic perspective.

There are already a number of very good pragmatics textbooks available and new ones seem to be appearing all the time: for this reason I have recommended chapters from several of them in the suggestions for further reading which appear at the end of each chapter. If this book is different, I hope it is because you will feel that it is a genuine 'entry level' book with a wide coverage and that it justifies its title, *Doing Pragmatics*, which is meant to reflect its strong pedagogic orientation. Wherever possible I have also tried to use real examples of talk that I've collected over the years rather than rely on invented examples. A book about the use of language ought to work with 'live' examples.

The materials in this book have been extensively trialled over several generations of students at Durham. I have been fortunate to have had the opportunity to teach pragmatics at undergraduate and postgraduate levels for many years and to have benefited from large and extremely lively lecture groups where I've frequently been caught out and corrected by students at every level. And I have to admit that reading pragmatics essays and projects is often a learning experience too – students very frequently have insights and react to data in ways that I have found enlightening and shaming.

As well as all the faults that are owed to me, in this book you will also find many insights that are owed to generations of students. In particular I have acknowledged some by name in the text of the book: Laurence Brushi, Andrew Caink, Roger Maylor, Csilla Szabo, and especially Kelly Glover, who has contributed ideas and read and commented insightfully on parts of the manuscript of the first edition, thereby saving me from a number of mistakes. I also owe a considerable debt to Joanne Burdon and Susan Millington who have generously allowed me to use data for the second edition which they collected and analysed in particularly insightful ways. Several of my former colleagues in Hong Kong have also helped, both practically with data collection as well as with their insights, especially Annie Au, Phil Benson, Philip Bolt, Winnie Cheng, Hiroko Itakura, Yan Jiang and Martin Warren. But because this is pragmatics, I'm sure that as you read this book you will see things that I have missed and even got wrong – please write and let me know when this happens.

In fact, one of the real pleasures I've enjoyed since the first edition came out in 1995 has been receiving so many thought-provoking comments from readers and users. I've tried to act on all the helpful suggestions I've received for this edition and gratefully acknowledge them here. I must, however, correct one academic who wrote to ask whether I was having a relationship with our tea-lady following a misunderstanding of an example in the first edition that I've edited out of this edition.

I also owe a great deal to the several readers who commented anonymously on the proposal for this revised edition. I appreciate the real trouble they took. The new shape of this edition owes much to their helpful and generous work.

Although I've never had a colleague at Durham who was first and foremost a pragmaticist, I have been fortunate to work alongside stimulating colleagues in a department that takes its linguistics seriously and in which all our different interests and approaches have always been understood to be interdependent and yet to have the same ultimate goal. As with deixis, the point of origin has been important to this book.

I also owe a debt to my editors at Arnold: Lesley Riddle, who threw caution to the winds in allowing me to write this book in the first place; Naomi Meredith, who bore with me when the first edition took longer than it should have done and, for the second edition, Christina Wipf-Perry whose constant efficiency has shamed me into trying to match it and has given me real confidence at the same time. I have also been very fortunate to have benefited from the meticulous care of Anke Ueberberg, the production editor, and Lynn Brown who worked on the final proofs, as well as Susan Dunsmore, a copy editor whose indirect speech acts often enlivened what is sometimes a fraught process. Naomi also suggested the title, which is much better than the three previous ones I had toyed with – and which has often been praised by other pragmaticists.

How to get the best out of this book

As you read *Doing Pragmatics*, you'll notice that there is a movement from the study of short utterances in the early chapters to the study of more extended conversations in the later chapters. It's not only the data types that change, but the approach to pragmatics too. In the early chapters, you'll learn about the central areas of linguistic pragmatics. You can then use this knowledge in the later chapters as you develop the ability to handle larger pieces of data in a more 'empirical' way. You'll also notice that examples which we work with in the earlier chapters sometimes turn up again in the later ones. This gives you a sense of familiarity as you meet old friends again, but also shows that more than one way of accounting for a single example is often appropriate. As you'll see, things aren't always as simple as they appear at first sight.

Another motive in writing this book has been the hope that it may help you to do your own pragmatics. As explained below, there are three ways in which this book overtly addresses this motive.

As you read through, you'll find *Checking understanding* exercises at regular intervals. It's important that you attempt these exercises. Not only will they help you to confirm your understanding of what you are reading, but the section containing suggested answers often includes ideas which supplement those in the main text of the book. The section containing suggested answers to the Checking understanding exercises can be found at the back of the book, beginning on page 239.

Second, at the end of every chapter there are a number of *Raising pragmatic awareness* activities which you can try for yourself, or with friends, or in a tutorial group. These are sensitizing activities which involve you in tasks like eavesdropping on conversations and reporting your findings to your colleagues or writing entries for a dictionary of pragmatics. Each of these activities is meant to be do-able either as a task set by your lecturer or on a self-study basis.

Finally, *Project work*: Chapter 11 contains several suggestions about possible types of project and in particular gives advice on data collection and transcription techniques. It also contains a case study which shows how conversational data can be collected and analysed in the light of pragmatic theory. I hope this chapter will help you in planning and carrying out your project work.

I've tried to make this book a good read too – so sit back and enjoy yourself.

Peter Grundy
University of Durham
September 1999

1 Using and understanding language

'We all know what light is; but it is not easy to
tell what it is.'
(Sam Johnson in James Boswell's
Life of Johnson, 11 April 1776)

Keywords appropriacy, indirect meaning, inference, indeterminacy, context,
relevance, reflexivity, deixis, implicature, speech act

1.1 Introduction

In this first chapter I am going to write about some of the aspects of language
use that are of particular interest to pragmaticists such as you and me. At
several points in the chapter, I'll make suggestions about the essential
concerns of pragmaticists which will help you to define pragmatics.

Let's begin by eavesdropping on a fragment of conversation I overheard
in the corridor between two freshers queuing up to register at the beginning
of the academic year:

(1) P: What's your name by the way
     S: Stephen
     P: You haven't asked my name back
     S: What's your name
     P: It's Pat

I don't know if they are still together, but they each frighten me in their own
different ways. Let's look at some of the pragmatic effects of their utterances.

P: What's your name by the way
Pat's 'by the way' serves as a warning to Stephen that what she is saying now
is not quite as relevant to what went before as might be expected. 'By the

way' is not part of the way we ask someone their name, more a comment on the status of asking 'What's your name' at this stage in their conversation. Perhaps it suggests that corridor small-talk has gone far enough and that something more personal may now be risked. Pat's 'What's your name' is a conventional but indirect way of saying *Tell me your name* – indirect because, although it takes the form of a question, it's intended as a request. It's also more polite than *Tell me your name*, which we would not expect to occur in conversations between people of more or less equal status.

S: Stephen
Stephen's reply is so minimal as to seem almost rude. Why should this be when in fact he does comply with Pat's request to tell her his name? It seems that such a minimal answer may satisfy the request but does not satisfy the person making it, who expects more.

P: You haven't asked my name back
Pat then indicates that she does not consider that Stephen has fulfilled his conversational obligations, although strictly speaking, as we noted, he has complied with her request to tell her his name. 'You haven't asked my name back' is a genuinely indirect way of telling Stephen to ask her for her name. I call it 'genuinely indirect' because although it takes the form of a statement when it is intended as a request, it also requires Stephen to work out what she wants from him. Her utterance also seems to convey an attitude – perhaps she intends it as something close to a reprimand. Will Stephen draw the right conclusion, and will what Pat says have the effect she intends? Would the intention and effect have been any different if she had said not, 'You haven't asked my name back', but rather, 'You haven't asked me my name back'? And why, one might reasonably ask, didn't she simply tell him her name?

S: What's your name
Notice how inappropriate it would have been at this stage in the conversation for Stephen to ask Pat her name in the same way that she had asked his ('What's you name by the way'). If he had used exactly her words just three turns later in this short conversation, what sort of effect might it have had?

P: It's Pat
The 'It' in 'It's Pat' is anaphoric, a term linguists use to describe a word that refers back to an earlier item or 'antecedent', in this case 'name'. This use of 'It's' establishes a cohesive link between her utterance and his – they are beginning to co-construct the conversation. It also gives her utterance the typical information structure we find so often in utterances, that of proceeding from the known (the *It* of 'It's') to the unknown or new, the word 'Pat'.

Such simple observations about some of the pragmatic properties of this brief, trivial exchange show how subtle even the most apparently straightforward uses of language are. Pragmatics is about explaining how we produce and understand such everyday but apparently rather peculiar uses of language. In the subsequent chapters of this book we will explore this in more depth.

Checking understanding (1.1)

Before we move on, perhaps you would like to try your hand at coming to some conclusions about what is going on in a simple conversation of the kind we have just examined together. Try to come to some conclusions about the following short exchange which occurred when I asked for a particular brand of cold capsule at the chemist:

(2) PHARMACIST: Do you usually have this sort
     PETER: Yeh I think so
     PHARMACIST: They make you drowsy mind
     PETER: Oh are there others that don't

If you want to check your ideas against my suggested answers, look at the answer section at the back of the book.

The more you work on conversations like (1) and (2), the more you come to see that it is not so much what the sentences literally mean that matters when we talk as how they reveal the intentions and strategies of the speakers themselves. This point is very well made by Atkinson, Kilby and Roca, who define pragmatics as being to do with 'The distinction between what a speaker's words (literally) mean and what the speaker might mean by his words' (1988: 217).

In the rest of this chapter I am going to discuss some of the features of everyday language use which are of particular importance in pragmatics. When we get to the end of the chapter I shall be more systematic and make a number of observations about the properties of a single utterance with the aim of signposting our way through the first few chapters of this book. Meanwhile, the first feature I want to discuss is appropriacy.

1.1.1 Appropriacy

Not very long ago my wife and I went out for lunch with two other couples, both a bit older than us and both slightly more important at work. We had a drink in the bar first and ordered our meal. In due course the waiter came back and announced that our lunch was ready, a communication which we all ignored. Four or five minutes later one of the more important members of the group said

(3) I think we could go in now you know

whereupon we all duly stood up and began the awkward transition from bar to dining room. The point is that in choice of words, in moment of speaking and in status of speaker this utterance was absolutely appropriate to the situation.

Similar examples are easy to find. At one stage in my career I had a senior colleague who had the bad habit of saying

(4)   Are we all here

at exactly the moment a meeting was due to start and only if he could see that we were not all there. His utterance was perfectly attuned to the situation and always had the same effect, that of causing a younger member of our department to get up and go on a missing colleague hunt. And just recently when we were waiting for a colleague without whom a meeting couldn't start, another colleague said to the person sitting next to her

(5)   Shall we go and get Mike

whereupon the person addressed dutifully got up and went to look for him.

Or when I begin a lecture I usually call for attention by uttering loudly

(6)   Right, shall we begin

which I take to be the most appropriate utterance in the context. When I am feeling mischievous I sometimes begin a first-year pragmatics lecture by saying

(7)   May I speak English

This always causes a moment of consternation when the students think their lecturer really has gone bonkers at last. But this beginning enables me to make the neat point that 'May I speak English' is not the appropriate way to begin a pragmatics lecture in Britain. And to make the still neater point that when I say 'May I speak English' in a shop in Italy, the commonest response (I know, I have done the research) is

(8)   A little

This response indicates that the addressee, struggling with limited English, takes me to be saying the more appropriate or expectable 'Do you speak English?'

And then there used to be a service manager at the garage where I take my car for servicing, who could never remember my name and knew he should, so he signalled it every time I went with

(9)   What's your name again

Now that they have a computer, they ask your car number first and the screen obligingly tells them who you are. But the new service manager is much more efficient than his predecessor and has begun to say

(10)   What's the number again

as though he knows that he should be able to remember it.

And when I stayed for two nights in a bed-and-breakfast recently and had the same waitress each morning, she used two different ways of asking me whether I'd like tea or coffee. You can surely guess which of the following utterances she used on the first morning and which she took to be more appropriate on the second:

(11) Is it tea or coffee

(12) Would you like tea or coffee

And what is the most appropriate way of getting my fun-loving Australian friend out of the pub when I want to get home to my family before they've all gone to bed and left the milk bottles out in revenge formation on the doorstep where I'm bound to send them flying? I tried the rather feeble

(13) How are you doing

to which my friend obligingly replied

(14) Am I ready to go do you mean

Being rather a cowardly person, I of course protested that that wasn't what I meant, but I soon made it clear by bored stares at the wall and lots of posture shifts that I was getting itchy, so that it wasn't long before my friend said

(15) You're in a hurry

and since she had initiated the conversation this time, I judged it OK to reply

(16) No, well, yes I am

I cite these few examples because they are immediately recognizable as appropriate ways of using language to get business done. One of the features of language use that is of interest to pragmaticists is its appropriacy in relation to those who use it and those they address.

1.1.2 Non-literal or indirect meaning

As well as being appropriate to the contexts in which they occurred, many of the utterances in the last section were also indirect in the sense that their literal meanings were not all the speakers intended them to convey. So

(4) Are we all here

and

(6) Right shall we begin

both purport to be questions in terms of the forms in which they are expressed, yet both are clearly intended to have other functions. Indeed, I would be rather cross if someone took 'Shall we begin?' as a real question and replied with a negative rejoinder. It would have been similarly inappropriate for my Australian friend to have replied 'I'm doing just fine' to my indirect hint that I was ready to go.

Sometimes the literal meaning is very far removed from the indirect meaning. Thus you would have to have seen the television programme *Fawlty Towers* to know that

(17) He's from Barcelona

is a way of saying that someone is stupid and undeserving of sympathy. But usually the indirectness is much more subtle than this, so that it takes a bit of working out to realise that

(18) Radion removes dirt AND odours

is an indirect way of saying that other washing powders are good at getting the dirt out but leave your clothes smelling bad. And when the BBC referred to

(19) The campaign group called the Freedom Association

the listeners had to do quite a lot of work to come to the conclusion that the BBC was indicating indirectly that it did not necessarily share the philosophy of the Freedom Association and that the name 'Freedom Association' might give a false impression. Or what about the infamous headline in the *Sun* on the day after 'Black Wednesday', the day when the pound left the European Exchange Rate Mechanism:

(20) Now we've ALL been screwed by the Cabinet

This headline was an indirect reference to the personal behaviour of a Government Minister who had resigned shortly before, after having an extra-marital affair, as well as an indirect way of saying that the Government had made a mess of things.

It is also remarkable that we are so clever at interpreting indirectness. I once had a Head of Department who showed me the draft of a letter which he had written to the Dean. The draft contained the sentence

(21) Meanwhile, Peter Grundy has just told me of his long conversation
      with you earlier today

I asked for 'long' to be removed from the sentence because 'long conversation' is a marked, or unexpected, description and might seem to the Dean to be an indirect way of referring to what had in fact been a disagreement between us.

So we see that indirectness too is typical of real-world language use, and that literal or stated meaning is only one aspect of the meaning conveyed in an utterance.

1.1.3 Inference

One question worth asking is how we get from a string of words that appears to have a literal meaning (for example, *long conversation*) to an understanding of its indirect meaning (i.e. *a disagreement*). We obviously have to draw inferences or come to conclusions as to what the speaker is intending to convey. So although we are not told that other washing powders leave our clothes smelling bad, we can work out that this is a conclusion we are meant to draw from the stress on 'AND' in

(18) Radion removes dirt AND odours

In a similar way 'called' in

(19) The campaign group called the Freedom Association

triggers an inference. Why, we ask ourselves, did the BBC not say 'The campaign group, the Freedom Association', or, more simply still 'The Freedom Association'? 'Called', we decide, must be telling us something about the title 'the Freedom Association', and so we infer that it is slightly suspect.

This suggests that communication is not merely a matter of a speaker encoding a thought in language and sending it as spoken message through space, or as a written message on paper, to a receiver who decodes it. This is clearly insufficient – the receiver must not only decode what is received but also draw an inference as to what is conveyed beyond what is stated.

Sometimes this inference is quite dramatic and much more interesting than the literal meaning itself, as when one of my colleagues said

(22) I'm a man

Nothing remarkable in that one might think, except that the speaker was a woman. Here the meaning she intended to convey was much more important than the literal meaning of her utterance. In fact, when you think about it, if someone says something that's obviously true (for example, a man says 'I'm a man') or obviously false (for example, a woman says 'I'm a man'), they must intend us to infer a hidden meaning.

Sometimes the inference just repairs a message that is in some way unclear. So that there's a supermarket chain in Britain which specializes in selling frozen food and whose carrier bags say

(23) If you want it Fresh, buy it Frozen

Think about it! Or there's a car showroom next to the building I work in which advertised a particular car like this

(24) If you want a cheaper drive, visit the golf course

It's also interesting to notice how some speakers feel that when they are speaking metaphorically, they sometimes need to use the term 'literally'. It's as though language really were a matter of literal meanings that could be encoded and despatched by the speaker and received and decoded by the addressee with any inference being required. I heard a nice example of this on the *Today* programme on BBC Radio 4 when a reporter said

(25) The conference trade has literally helped turn Brighton around

In fact, every utterance seems to invite an inference, so that the addressee has to determine whether an utterance such as

(26) I really like your new haircut

is sincere or ironical.

Sometimes there does not even seem to be much point in what people say, until one draws an inference. I was recently working on a short course with several colleagues, all of us spread out around various classrooms. For the first few days, the course members found it all a bit confusing. One morning as we were waiting to go into our classroom, one of them addressed me with the apparently redundant

(27) Are you here Peter

I didn't think she was mad, but merely drew an inference as to what she wanted to confirm.

1.1.4 Indeterminacy

Regarding some meanings as matters of inference has one important consequence. It implies that the utterances we hear are in some ways unclear, or, as linguists sometimes say, 'under-determined'. By this we mean that an utterance might typically have one of several different possible meanings and that the inferences we draw determine which of these possible meanings is the one the addressee thinks the speaker is intending. Good examples of under-determined utterances in the previous section are

(22) I'm a man

(26) I really like your new haircut

and

(27) Are you here Peter

In each of these cases, we need to draw inferences that determine which of a number of different possible understandings is the right one.

In her book *Understanding Utterances*, Diane Blakemore (1992: 83) very interestingly draws our attention to how under-determined the possessive is in English and gives a long list of examples which, although they share the same grammatical form, are all determined quite differently. Her list includes

(28) I have borrowed *Jane's car*
I would hate to have *Simon's job*
Yesterday's events really shocked the *country's president*
Jane's father has bought her a car

There are many other structures besides possessives that are typically under-determined. I remember that my daughter was very upset when she first noticed the sign 'Pet mince' outside our local butcher's shop. Indeed butcher's signs are a rich source of such indeterminacy: how fortunate it is that a *Family Butcher* does not do to families what a *Pork Butcher* does to pigs!

When the sculpture 'The Angel of the North' was first erected on a hilltop near Gateshead, a road sign appeared beside the road which runs past it. The message on the road sign was 'Angel parking'. Were passing motorists being advised that there was an angel parking? Or that there was a parking place for angels? Or that there was a place where motorists could park to view the sculpture of an angel?

Sometimes the problem is to do with determining which word in a two-word phrase is the head word, so that although *a child actor* is a child who acts, the meaning of *a child psychiatrist* cannot be determined by analogy. Similarly, in *additive free* the headword is *free*, whereas in *50 per cent extra free*, *50 per cent extra* is head.

In my capacity as an external examiner, I once found myself writing an examiner's letter which, on re-reading, I saw contained one particularly pompous sentence that might be understood in either of two quite different ways. The sentence was

(29) There must therefore be a very good case for not allowing anyone to proceed to Year 3

The word that gave the trouble was clearly 'anyone' – it was meant to mean *a particular person* rather than *every person*. A similar problem occurs with 'the team that won in mid-week at Everton' in the following sentence which I heard on BBC Radio 4's *Today* programme:

(30) Wimbledon are playing the team that won in mid-week at Everton

Were Wimbledon to play against the team that won at Everton? Or are they the team that won at Everton and intending to field the same players against their new opponents?

I once had an interesting intercultural experience of this sort. It was at the time when I first went to live in Germany and was a couple of lessons into my German course. Arming myself with a phrase book and a good deal of misplaced confidence, I took myself off to a bar for a drink. Although I seemed to order my first beer with some success, I was less successful with the second one, which involved consulting my phrase book for the German word for *another*. In English *another* is indeterminate between *another the same* and *another different*, but in German these two notions are represented by different expressions. This explains why when I thought I was ordering 'another beer', the barman gave me a very dirty look and a beer that was distinctly different from the previous one.

And I cannot resist telling you about a party where someone was telling a story about her holiday. The story contained the sentence

(31) We were woken up at three o'clock in the morning by a drip in our bedroom

Of course, she meant that water was dripping into her room. But if you know that *drip* is a British English slang expression for someone of little character, then you'll appreciate why we found the indeterminacy entertaining.

Sometimes the context helps us to determine the meaning. When most people say

(32) I've just finished a book

we take them to mean that they have just finished reading a book. But when a university lecturer says 'I've just finished a book', they usually mean that they have just finished writing one. So knowing who the speaker is will help us to determine what is meant. A colleague of mine once made what we thought was a very funny joke when someone at lunch one day said that a particular member of his department had just finished a book, and my colleague asked, 'Reading one or writing one?'. This would only be a joke in a context where the determination of *has just finished a book* could be problematical. And in fact, another of Diane Blakemore's examples is

(33) Should I read *your book*

where *your book* is clearly ambiguous between the book you own and the book of which you are the author.

And just the other day I had an interesting experience where the developing context affected the way I determined the meaning of a poster I saw beside the road. I was looking for a particular pub buried deep in the Kent countryside, and my attempt at map-reading took me down a very narrow country lane. About 100m down the lane, I came across the following poster:

(34) No houses at Brogdale

Oh no, I thought, this lane is only a farm track to Brogdale and I'll have to turn back and retrace my path. But then I saw a second poster, and a third, and a fourth, and I realized that the posters were part of a campaign against building new houses at Brogdale.

Although we may often think that what we say has one clear, determinate meaning, the examples above show us just how indeterminate our utterances actually are. Pragmatics is partly about trying to account in systematic ways for our ability to determine what speakers intend even when their utterances are so dramatically under-determined.

1.1.5 Context

In the paragraph before last we discussed how context can help in determining the meaning of an utterance. Another way to think through this issue is to think of all the contexts in which you might utter the same words. Take the case of the utterance

(35) I'm tired

If I say it late at night, it may count as a way of excusing myself and getting off to bed before my wife. Or she may take it as a hint that I want her to come to bed too. Either way it means that I want to go to bed. But if I say *I'm tired* when the alarm clock goes off at ten to seven the next morning, it probably means that I do not want to get out of bed and perhaps might be interpreted by my wife as a hint that she should get out of bed and make the coffee. In fact we could think of as many meanings for *I'm tired* as we could think of contexts in which it might be uttered; or put another way, as many contexts for it as meanings that it might have. The same point could be made about

(36) I've got a flat tyre

In a garage, this might be taken to mean that I need help; or if addressed to a friend with a car, that I need a lift; or as a response to a request for a lift from a friend without a car, that I can't give them a lift; or indeed a wide range of other things in all the other contexts in which you might imagine it being uttered.
   Similarly,

(37) Can you open the door

is usually taken as a polite, indirect way of requesting someone to open a door for us. But imagine a non-typical context: you and I are robbing a bank and you are struggling with an oxy-acetylene torch while I am keeping an anxious look-out. If I were to say *Can you open the door* in such a context, it would obviously be a genuine question rather than an indirect request.
   I found myself thinking very hard about the context when I had to give a lecture in a university in China on 4 June, the anniversary of the Tiananmen Square massacre in Beijing. The title of my talk, which was about second language learning, was *Listening to Learners*. I began with this sentence

(38) I suppose today it's especially important to be thinking carefully
        about what our students say to us

There was a perceptible tension as the audience struggled for a moment to determine whether *today* was a reference to 4 June specifically or to the more general contemporary language teaching methodology scene. I let them consider which of the two contexts was most appropriate for a fraction of a second before going on to explain why listening to our learners is important in language teaching. Had I referred to the Tiananmen context? For some people, perhaps yes; for others, perhaps no.
   Sometimes it's interesting to try and guess the context of an utterance. Someone once said to me

(39) Have you got a plastic bag?

Can you guess the context? The same utterance may well have been addressed to you on some occasion in the past. I was once foolish enough to ask a lecture theatre full of students to try and supply the context in which this utterance occurred. Someone shouted out, 'You'd just had a colostomy?'

In fact, the real context was much more interesting. It was seven o'clock one Saturday night in Warsaw at the time of military rule. I was with a Polish colleague who was looking after me and we were on our way to a party. I suggested that we should buy a bottle of wine to take with us, which caused her to say rather pityingly, 'You must be joking!' She explained that General Jaruszelski, the then President, did not approve of drinking and so had decreed that no alcohol was to be sold after 5 p.m. on Saturday afternoons, not even in the hotels where at every other time of the week hard currency could buy you alcohol. So we hit upon the idea of playing the stupid foreigner in town. Entering the restaurant across the road, I asked whether they spoke English (no) or German (nein). So I explained that I would speak English and that my friend would translate: 'Translate please, Maria,' I said, which she duly did. I then explained that I had had a meal in the restaurant two days before and had enjoyed a bottle of most excellent wine. Again Maria translated. As we were going to the birthday party of a very special friend, I was wondering whether it would be possible to have another bottle of their excellent wine to take as a present. Maria translated again, and this time the lady behind the bar obligingly replied

(39) Have you got a plastic bag?

Luckily I had, and passed it across the bar. Her reply is especially interesting because in the context in which it occurred it counted as an agreement to break the law, and could in theory have landed her (and perhaps us) in quite serious trouble.

My daughter provided another nice example of how context helps us to determine what an utterance means. When she began to be too big for her first pony, I suggested that she should sell the pony and get a bigger one. She replied

(40) I'll never sell her

It took me several months of persuasion, but in the end we put an advertisement in the paper. After two or three time-wasters had been to see the pony, my daughter said once again 'I'll never sell her', but of course she meant something entirely different this time.

The postmaster in our local post office is an endless source of pragmatically interesting utterances. One morning a customer complained that the money he had been given was dirty. The postmaster leaned forward and said

(41) Be careful you don't trip over the step on your way out

What was really interesting about this utterance was that there isn't a step on the way out of our post office. Once you have this little bit of contextual information, you can begin to think about what the postmaster meant by what he said.

Another way in which we try to make the way we say things reflect context is in our use of politeness strategies. We know that

(42) Could I just borrow a tiny bit of paper

is a way of lessening our request and much more likely to be acceded to than

(43) Give me a sheet of paper

Not all contexts are real-world ones – some are linguistic too. I read a recent newspaper report which included the sentence

(44) People living nearby said Mr Neale would go away on 'lengthy business trips'

I expect your interpretation of this sentence is quite different when you know its linguistic context. The previous sentence was 'Neither would the police comment on whether Mr Neale had recently served time in prison.'

I recently received a long letter from a life insurance company explaining in tortuous terms that it would be paying a lower bonus to policyholders. The last sentence of this letter was

(45) I felt it important to write at some length on this rather important matter

which we all recognize instantly as an apology. In principle it might equally have been a congratulation or an appeal for a donation but in fact we all know that it invokes a quite different context from either of these two theoretically possible ones. In this sense we might almost argue that it is language which creates context and not context which determines the language we use.

In fact, the relationship between context and language is central in pragmatics. One of the things you'll have to make up your mind about as you study pragmatics is whether the context determines the way we use language or whether the way we use language determines the context. Let me give you an example to illustrate what I mean. My daughter used to take a teenage magazine for girls called *19*. One morning at breakfast she asked me if I wanted to hear my horoscope, and taking silence to mean yes, read out

(46) You are obsessing about a lad but you don't know how to show him how you feel

I said that it wasn't a very appropriate horoscope but she defended it on the grounds that I might be 'going gay'. For me, the context was given – *19* was a teenage magazine for girls and I didn't want to hear the horoscope because I knew it wouldn't be appropriate to a 52-year-old male. But Eleanor, on the other hand, tried to find a context which would make sense of what was written.

Because pragmaticists are interested in the meanings of utterances, they are also interested in the contexts in which utterances occur, since, as we have seen, these contexts help us to determine the meaning of what is said to us.

1.1.6 Relevance

In the previous section we showed how understanding

(38) I suppose today it's especially important to be thinking carefully
      about what our students say to us

depended on choosing the most relevant of two possible meanings. Deciding
on the most appropriate reference for *today* is really a matter of deciding
whether the reference to 4 June as the anniversary of the Tiananmen
massacre or the reference to present times in general is the more relevant.
Usually it's a fairly simple matter to decide on the most relevant way to take
an utterance, so that in case of *I'm tired*, we can readily discount all but two
or three of the possible pragmatic meanings, on the grounds that none of
others could be relevant to the situation obtaining at the time of the utterance. And usually it's relatively easy to tell which of the two or three possible meanings is the most relevant.

   We know that relevance is important to understanding because there are
mechanisms that enable us to check that we have achieved the most relevant
understanding. For example, shortly after half-term in my son's first term at
secondary school, he said one day

(47) I'm enjoying school much more now

I was unclear about the reference of *now*. Did he mean that he was enjoying the second half of his first term at secondary school more than the first
half, or did he mean that he preferred secondary school to primary school?
Because I could see no way of determining which was the more relevant
understanding, I had to ask him to clarify.

   Relevance has been seen by Sperber and Wilson (1995) as the most important principle in accounting for the way we understand language. Since we
take every utterance as relevant, we understand utterances in whatever way
will make them as relevant as possible. Thus for weeks there was a broken
chair in our corridor at work with a notice pinned to it which said

(48) Sit down with care
      Legs can come off

It was obviously more relevant to assume the legs belonged to the chair than
to the person sitting down.

   Sometimes we change our minds about how to take an utterance. A nice
example occurred when I worked in Hong Kong. One of the Hong Kong
radio stations invented a little jingle

(49) Hong Kong's original channel, 567, Hong Kong's Radio 3 – is there
      anything else

Whoever thought it up obviously intended 'is there anything else' to be most
relevantly understood as an assertion that there couldn't be anything else as
good to listen to. But as the weeks went by people began to make jokes

about it and roll their eyes heavenwards while saying 'is there anything else'. Their despairing tone indicated that 'anything else' would be better than Radio 3. Not long after, the jingle ceased to be broadcast.

1.1.7 Reflexivity

Frequently one part of what we say provides some sort of comment on how our utterance fits into the discourse as a whole or on how the speaker wants to be understood. For example, *therefore* in

(29) There must therefore be a very good case for not allowing anyone to proceed to Year 3

tells the reader how this sentence relates to the one(s) before. Or *I suppose* in

(38) I suppose today it's especially important to be thinking carefully about what our students say to us

advises the audience that the speaker isn't absolutely certain that what he says is right.

At the beginning of the academic year, I saw two first-year students in conversation in the corridor. One was listing the courses she was taking. She mentioned courses with conventional titles like 'Twentieth-century drama', and then said

(50) and er is it Knowledge and Reality

Her 'er is it' convey to the hearer that she isn't at all sure that she's got the title right.

Or Bill Clinton's statement of 18 August 1998 contained the following sentence:

(51) Indeed, I did have a relationship with Ms Lewinsky that was not appropriate. In fact, it was wrong.

Notice how 'Indeed' and 'In fact' tell you of Clinton's commitment to the truth of what he is saying, as does the emphatic use of 'did'. And notice how 'it was wrong' glosses 'that was not appropriate' and how both comment on the 'relationship'. Clinton simultaneously tells us something (that he had a relationship), comments on what he tells us (that it was wrong) and assures us of his veracity (the function of 'in fact').

When speakers advise us of how they want us to take what they say, they make the task of understanding easier. This is why reflexive uses of language are so common.

1.1.8 Misfires

There was the wonderful Admiral Stainforth who nominated the independent candidate Ross Perrot for the American Presidency in 1992. He began his nominating speech with the weedy shriek

(52) Who am I? Why am I here?

and must have been astonished at the howls of laughter that greeted what seemed to his audience to be all too real questions. He had made a calculation that this ringing start to his oration would have a particular rhetorical effect, which unfortunately for him it did not have. It was a kind of pragmatic 'misfire'. Pragmatic misfires are important because they tell us that there are expected norms for talk by showing us the effect of not achieving the norm. If you think back over the last few hours, you will probably be aware that several of your utterances did not have quite the effects you would have wished, or at least so it seems when you judge from the reactions of those you were addressing.

A misfire I rather enjoyed occurred at a dinner when someone said to an important professor sitting across the table from me

(53) Will you have some more chocolate

None of us had realized up till then that when the chocolates had come round the first time he had somehow got missed out, but he made us all too aware of it with his petulant reply

(54) I didn't even have any to begin with

What seemed to make him particularly angry was that 'some more chocolate' presupposed that he had already had some 'to begin with'.

And then there was one of the secretaries who works in the same building as me who, in the days before the building became a no-smoking zone, put a notice on her office door which read

(55) Thank you for not smoking

This was taken rather amiss by one or two people who should have known better but who clearly did not like being ordered about by the secretary.

This reaction suggests that misfires are a kind of pragmatic failure which results from language being used in a way that is not felt to be appropriate to the context. Thus the last sentence of the letter from the optician reminding me that I was due for an eye test would have been perfectly appropriate from anyone else. The sentence was

(56) We look forward to seeing you soon

Or the video I watched at Newcastle airport would have been fine if it had been signed as well as spoken

(57) Some airport staff have been trained in British Sign Language and requests for assistance should be made at any time of day

Or what is written on the toothpaste dispenser in front of me as I write this would be fine if a little bit more care had been taken over expressing the intended message

(58) After brushing bacteria build up on your teeth and can
cause

      Cavities   Plaque   Tartar

      Gum Disease   Bad Breath

Summary

What have we said so far? We have listed a number of features of talk which are at the heart of pragmatics. They include the notions of appropriacy and relevance on the one hand, and our liking for non-literal and indirect meaning on the other. We have seen that there is a crucial relationship between what we say and the context in which it is relevant. This is made possible to some degree by the indeterminacy of language and the role of inference in language understanding. Frequently, speakers use language reflexively to indicate how they want what they say to be understood.

Although for convenience I have treated each of these features as distinct, it is already apparent that they are really a bundle which typically appear together. Take the case of the utterance

(59) Now I've done it

which is indelibly etched in my memory after one particular occasion when I heard it used. I was watching a group of American visitors on their first morning in China trying to eat fried eggs with chopsticks. Somehow one of them managed to snap a chopstick clean in half, and as he picked up the two broken pieces and proceeded to treat them as the next best thing to a knife and fork, he said despairingly to his colleagues

(59) Now I've done it

His utterance seemed perfectly appropriate to a situation that could not have passed without some comment. It was certainly an indirect way of conveying whatever message it does convey (perhaps that he wasn't expecting to be able to eat anything for his breakfast after this mishap). And it obviously requires an inference to be drawn to determine just how it is relevant in just whatever the context seems to be.

Checking understanding (1.2)

Consider how each of the following utterances relates to the notions of appropriacy, indirectness, inference, indeterminacy, context, relevance and reflexivity discussed in this chapter:

(60) Even Presidents have private lives (Bill Clinton, 18 August 1998)

(61) I don't know how you say this in English but for me it was ooh-la-la-la (the French jockey, Olivier Peslier, after riding the winning horse in the Prix de l'Arc de Triomph, 6 October 1996)

I am now going to try and round off this chapter in the more systematic way promised all those pages ago by looking at the pragmatic properties of a single utterance. As we will see, it's one thing to describe the pragmatic properties of utterances, but quite another to explain how we understand under-determined utterances more or less in the way the speaker intends.

The utterance

(62) I'm here now

which Kaplan (1978) discusses in his long and difficult paper on demonstratives, looks superficially innocuous. But for a pragmaticist it has three very problematical properties.

Deixis   The first of these is to do with an indeterminacy that can only be resolved when we look at the context, and particularly at three aspects of that context: *who* the speaker is and *where* and *when* the sentence is uttered. This indeterminacy stems from the speaker's use of the words *I*, *here* and *now*. Although the meaning of the word *I* is perfectly clear and not at all problematical, the reference that is effected each time it is uttered clearly depends on who utters it. In this respect *I* is a quite different kind of description from *Agatha Christie*, which always refers to the same person. Just the same point could be made about *here*. Its meaning is clear enough but its reference depends on the location of the speaker when the sentence is uttered, so that *here* might refer to *Durham* or *Durban* or *Marks & Spencer* or the speaker's kitchen. Similarly the reference of *now* is determined by the time at which the sentence is spoken. This property of a small set of words like *I*, *here* and *now* to pick out an aspect of the context in which they are uttered is called **Deixis**.

Utterances as Speech Acts   The second problematical property of *I'm here now* stems not only from the natural indeterminacy of the utterance and from the context, but also from considerations of what it most appropriately counts as doing. So if I had heard that a relative had been injured and taken to hospital, I might race there as quickly as possible and say 'I'm here now', which would count perhaps as a comforting reassurance. On the other hand, if I get home from work and see my children larking about instead of getting on with their homework and say 'I'm here now', it counts as a stern warning. Or if I were to arrive late for a meeting and knew that I had kept my colleagues waiting, uttering 'I'm here now' might count as an apology. Utterances not only convey an invariant meaning (such as, the person speaking is in the same location as the addressee at the time of speaking) but also count as *doing* something, be it reassuring, warning, apologizing or whatever. This is why we call them **Speech Acts**. After all, there isn't much point in saying *I'm here now*, which must be readily apparent to all and sundry anyway, unless you intend to do something by saying it.

Implicature   The third problematical property of *I'm here now* stems not only from the natural indeterminacy of the utterance but also from the context and from considering what inference ought to be drawn to make the utterance maximally relevant. Imagine the utterance being used by two different students talking to themselves on the day they arrive in Durham to begin their Linguistics degree course. The first student comes from Southampton and uses *here* to refer to Durham; the second student comes from Singapore and had been looking forward to studying overseas for several years – for this student *here* refers to Britain. The point is that both references for *here* are equally consistent with any correspondence the sentence might be thought to have with states of affairs in the world. But knowing which is the right one is a matter of working out which understanding is the most relevant and might be thought to be the one being implied by the speaker. A similar point could be made about *now*, which for one speaker might refer to a particular date and for another might mean something more like *at last*.

But this isn't all: sometimes 'I'm here now' conveys something like *There's no need to worry any more* (the hospital context), sometimes something like *Stop messing about and get on with your homework* (the kids larking about context) and sometimes something like *I'm sorry I've held you up* (the meeting context). And of course these three meanings are only a tiny subset of the possible meanings that a speaker saying 'I'm here now' might be intending to convey. Thus one of the properties of language is that in addition to expressing an invariant meaning, propositions also frequently convey an implied meaning which the addressee must infer. This kind of meaning is called an **Implicature**.

To sum up, pragmaticists study the way in which language is appropriate to the contexts in which it is used. Fortunately, language is under-determined enough to allow us to infer the way in which an utterance is to be understood in the context in which it occurs. Often speakers comment reflexively on what they say (as I did with *fortunately* in the previous sentence) so as to assist hearers in determining how to take utterances. In the rest of this book, we will investigate the crucial relationship of language use and context which is the essential subject area of pragmatics.

Checking understanding (1.3)

In the next four chapters we will be looking at Deixis, Speech Acts and Implicature in more detail. Meanwhile, you might like to think about one famous utterance within this framework. Consider President Kennedy's announcement in Berlin at a time of great tension shortly after the Berlin Wall was erected, in which he intended to say in German that he was a Berliner:

(63) Ich bin Berliner
    I am Berliner
    (I'm a Berliner)

But because of his speech writer's limited knowledge of German he managed instead to say that he was a kind of cake or doughnut:

(64) Ich bin ein Berliner
      I   am   a   Berliner [doughnut]

Despite his mistake, his audience of course understood what he wanted to say and applauded loudly.

   Can you identify the deictic property of this utterance, what speech act is accomplished by saying it and any implicatures it contains? In coming to these conclusions, take the context into account, try to work out what indirect meaning President Kennedy was trying to convey, and draw whatever inferences you need to to make proper sense of his utterance. In short, how do you get from the under-determined utterance 'I'm a Berliner' to the most relevant understanding of it?

Raising pragmatic awareness: using and understanding language

1. This exercise works well if you do Step (a) individually and Steps (b) and (c) in your tutorial or with a group of friends.
   (a) Write a very short dialogue between two imaginary characters.
   (b) Dictate each utterance to your colleagues. As you dictate, they write down not what you say but the contexts in which they imagine each utterance being spoken.
   (c) Ask each person to read out what they have written down and discuss the pragmatics of the utterances in relation to the contexts which have been imagined for them.
2. This exercise works best in a tutorial or with a group of friends. Choose an item from the following list and brainstorm all the contexts in which you could utter it: *I'm tired, I'm sorry, Is it me, I thought so, Don't.* Why do you think a single proposition can function as so many different speech acts?
3. Get together with a few friends. Each person should recall something surprising which someone once said to them. The other members of the group try to guess the context by asking Yes/No questions.
4. This exercise works best in pairs. You and your partner each find three or four sentences from different newspaper stories or captions for newspaper photographs which invite the reader to draw an inference. (For example, 'The husband of the doctor who disappeared last week refused to comment. Meanwhile, the police continued digging in his garden.') When you have each found your sentences or captions, see whether your partner draws the same inferences as you and try to work out what triggers them. (Acknowledgement: this is Andrew Caink's idea.)
5. This exercise works well in a tutorial group. Before the tutorial, cut out three or four magazine pictures and pin instructions to them which test pragmatic skills. For example, if you cut out a picture of a romantic couple looking out over the sea at night, your instruction might be 'Ask these two for a cigarette/if they've lost a pen you've just found/where they get their hair done'; or if you cut out a picture of someone with a gun, the instruction might be 'Ask her/him for the gun'; or a picture of a toddler, 'Get this person to admire your shoes/to call your Mummy'. Take the pictures and instructions to your tutorial and ask the other members of your group how they would carry out the instructions.

Further reading

Blakemore, D. (1992: 3–23); Levinson, S.C. (1983: 1–5); Mey, J. (1993: 3–17); Thomas, J. (1995: 1–23); Yule, G. (1996: 2–3).

2 Deixis: the relation of reference to the point of origin of the utterance

The car you saw today and intend to buy
tomorrow, somebody saw yesterday and
intends to buy today.
(Sign displayed in a Mazda showroom)

Keywords deixis, context, indexicality, reference, demonstrative, person deixis,
honorific, anaphora, place deixis, time deixis, deictic centre, point of origin,
deictic change, membership, common ground

The chapter you are about to read consists of three main sections, each of
which contains several sub-sections. The first section, Deictic reference,
discusses the properties of deictics and the way we understand deictic reference. The second section, Deixis in the real world, describes a number of
actual uses including several typical of Hong Kong contexts. The third section,
The limits of indexicality, discusses the wider indexical properties of language.

2.1 Deictic reference

2.1.1 Indexical signs

Two scenarios: In the first, you ring my doorbell, and I open the door and
say

(1)   Do come in

In the second, we approach my house together. I take out my key, open the
door and, standing aside, say to you

(2)   Do go in

In both cases you are going to go from the same point A to the same point B. But my instruction differs in each case because the relationship between where I stand and where you are to go differs. In other words, there is a common element of meaning which *come* and *go* share, but they differ in the way in which they encode the context – although you are to move to the same place, in the case of (1) you are to move towards me and in the case of (2) you are to move away from me.

In this chapter we will be exploring the way in which a small number of words, such as *come* and *go*, and *I* and *here* and *now*, require an addressee to be able to pick out a person, place or time relevant in understanding how the word refers. Because *I*, *here* and *now* identify particular referents, pick them out to refer to if you like, we call these words indexical and this function of language **deictic**, borrowing the Greek word meaning *pointing* to or *picking out*. Thus the property of language we are studying is called **indexicality**, and the lexical items which encode context in this way are called **deictics**.

A third scenario. Imagine you finally get through the front door and into my house. As you stand in the hall, this is what you see:

(3)

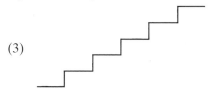

Figure 2.1

leading to the floors above. But unlike the case of *come* and *go*, the word you might use to describe what you see, *stairs*, does not depend on where we are each standing. And it doesn't matter whether you use the word, *stairs*, or draw the diagram above, in each case I will know what is referred to. The philosopher Peirce drew a distinction between 'signs' like the one you see in Figure 2.1, which he called 'icons', and signs like the word *stairs*, which he called 'symbols'. As well as icon and symbol, Peirce also identified a third sign type which he called an 'index'. Imagine we are in the hall of my house and you have come to stay with me. I might say to you

(4)   Let's go upstairs and I'll show you your room

The sign *upstairs* is rather problematic because unless you happen to be in a particular place, such as my house, you cannot know which location is picked out by it. In your house, for example, the indexical sign *upstairs* does not pick out the same location as in my house. In this chapter we will be studying indexical signs like *upstairs*, to add a further example to the five we already have – *come* and *go*, and *I* and *here* and *now*.

2.1.2 Indexicals: the role of context in helping to determine reference

Consider the following:

(5)   I know you'll enjoy reading the chapter

(6)   When I say you have to read the chapter, I mean YOU have to read it and YOU have to read it and YOU have to read it

(7)   You never know whether to read every chapter or skip one or two

In (5) *you* picks out a particular but different person on each separate occasion when the sentence is read. On this occasion it is, yes, you, my friend, who is picked out to be the referent (or person referred to). (And if by any chance there are two of you out there working together in a team reading the book aloud and saying things about me the author, then on this particular occasion *you* picks out and refers to both of you.)

Similarly, if in a lecture I were to deliver (6), the three stressed *yous* in the second part of the utterance would be accompanied by gestures and/or eye contact of some kind. Each would pick out a different referent whose identity would be known only by those present at the time of my utterance.

But in

(7)   You never know whether to read every chapter or skip one or two

you has a much more general reference. In fact, being present when the sentence was uttered would not help you to identify a referent. Thus this generalized use of *you* is sometimes said to be **non-deictic**.

These three uses of *you* can be represented diagrammatically as in Figure 2.2.

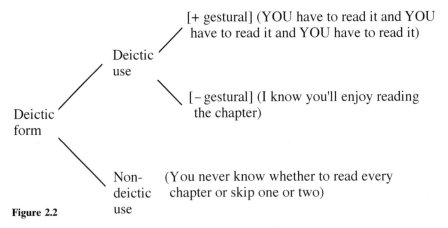

Figure 2.2

Now consider the more problematical case of

(8)   You just have to read this chapter

Sometimes this use of *you* might be thought to pick out the addressee(s) and identify him/her/them as the referent. In this case, the use of *you* would clearly be deictic. But what about those times (8) is taken as a general exhortation implying that the chapter is well worth reading? Although it's difficult to know precisely who is referred to by *you*, it's also clear that the utterance wouldn't be used when talking to just anyone. It's as though the addressee is taken to belong to a particular group, perhaps people who appreciate chapters of the kind the one the speaker is reading at the time. This suggests that the notion that demonstratives like *you* can be used non-deictically may be problematic – a suggestion that we'll pick up later in the chapter when we look at real uses of deictics in extended talk.

The use of *you* is frequently problematical in intercultural communication when native speakers of English think they are using it non-deictically, but their non-native speaker addressees take it deictically to refer to themselves. Utterances like

(9)   You don't want to go to London

(10) You're not supposed to say that

are guaranteed to bewilder in such encounters.

Finally in this section, notice that deictics are demonstratives, words that point to people, times and places. So when we were wondering about the status of *you* in (7) and (8), we were really asking whether it is possible to use the demonstrative form *you* non-demonstratively.

Whereas determining quite how *you* is used seems rather problematical in some situations, there are certainly cases where it's easy to distinguish deictic use from what is usually called 'intrinsic' use. Thus in

(11) How long ago did the last bus leave

the last bus is a deictic used to refer to whichever bus had left most recently before the time of speaking, so that the expression could in principle be used to refer to every bus throughout the day. This use contrasts with the intrinsic

(12) The last bus leaves at 23.30

Here *The last bus* always refers to the same timetable slot in a non-demonstrative way and can be interpreted without knowing the time of the utterance.

Checking understanding (2.1) ───────────────

1. Try to think of utterances in which the following words *this*, *now*, *behind*, might be used (a) gesturally and deictically; (b) non-gesturally and deictically; (c) non-deictically.
2. Write five or six sentences containing either the word *that* or the word *then* which you could place on a cline from very obviously deictic to non-deictic.
3. If you were reading a chapter in a linguistics book and came across the phrase *the last example*, under what circumstances would it be (a) a deictic and (b) an intrinsic use?

2.1.3 Deictic types

At this stage we need to consider a number of difficult questions.

1. How many deictic words are there in a language and to what extent
    can these words be used both deictically and non-deictically?
    Simple answer: Deictics are a closed class, i.e. there is a limited set of
    such words; some of them can be used non-deictically.
2. Is there any way of categorizing these words?
    Simple answer: It is possible to categorize them according to semantic
    criteria such as person reference (e.g., *I*), place reference (e.g., *here*)
    and time reference (e.g., *now*).
3. Why should this small set of lexical items have this property?
    Simple answer: Speakers will always find it useful to have a limited
    set of indeterminate lexical items (such as *you*) whose references are
    determined in the context of face-to-face interaction and which act as
    a shorthand for a potentially infinite number of descriptions (such as
    the names of all the people one would ever address).

Many pragmaticists would doubt whether any of these simple answers is truly
adequate, but if we treat them as working hypotheses for the moment, this
will enable us to establish a familiarity with a set of deictic terms.

2.1.4 Person deixis

We have already seen how *you* can be used both deictically (when the
context is required to determine the reference) and non-deictically (when the
reference is general rather than to particular identifiable persons). *You* is
also used in English in a much wider range of social contexts than would be
represented by a single second person reference term in most other
languages. For example, most languages have at least two forms, an informal one for use when talking to friends and a more formal one used for
showing respect to the person addressed, typically because they are older or
more important than the speaker. In many languages the second person
plural form (*vous* in French) or the third person plural form (*Sie* in German)
has this honorific function, so that in German

(13) Ich danke Ihnen
      I thank them (dative)
      (Thank you)

is a formal way of thanking and at the same time showing respect to the
person one is speaking to. In discussing this 'honorific' use of language,
Levinson (1983: 90), following Comrie (1976), points out that deictics like
vous and *Sie* are oriented to a referent (person being referred to) rather than
to an addressee (person being addressed). This explains why it makes sense
to describe the person we are talking to as *you (plural)* or *they* without
appearing contradictory: we address our equals and refer to our superiors.

To a native speaker of English this may seem exotic at first; but of course there are similar strategies in English, such as saying *Shall we do x* or *We could do y* to someone more important than yourself who you are steering towards some course of action. Here the interrogative form and the use of the modal auxiliaries *shall* and *could* convey respect to the addressee too. In Polish, it would be usual for a ticket collector to show respect to a passenger in the humiliating position of being ticketless on a train by including him/herself in the reference as a sign of respect:

(14) Nie mamy biletu
      not have (1st pl) ticket
      (You haven't got a ticket?)

In English this inclusion of self in a reference (so we haven't got a ticket) is usually sarcastic rather than respectful.

Although English appears to have only one deictic address word, *you*, the use of *you-all* (for example, by teachers when talking to groups of students) suggests that speakers do indeed want to make distinctions that are impossible when there is only a single form available to them.

Just as *you* (and the possessive forms *your* and *yours*) are typically deictic, so too are the first person pronouns *I* and *we* and the possessives *my*, *mine*, *our* and *ours*. Notice that in the utterance

(15) What are we supposed to do

the deictic *we* would typically include the addressee in the reference if the speaker was one student asking another about an assignment, but exclude the addressee from the reference if two students were asking their tutor for instructions or advice. Many languages grammaticalize exactly this distinction between addressee inclusive and addressee exclusive uses of *we*.

The third person pronouns, *he*, *it*, *she* and *they*, are not usually used deictically but rather refer anaphorically to objects or persons already mentioned in the discourse (antecedents). A typical example of anaphoric reference would be *it* in (6) whose antecedent is *the chapter:*

(6)   When I say you have to read the chapter, I mean YOU have to read it and YOU have to read it and YOU have to read it

All pronouns require identification with some other point for their reference to be effected. In the case of third person anaphors, the reference is determined in relation to an antecedent in the co-text; in the case of deictics, the reference is determined in relation to a *demonstratum,* something that can be pointed to or picked out, in the context.

Checking understanding (2.2)

Here are some problems to puzzle over.
1. Spend a few minutes trying to decide whether *we* and *our* can be used non-deictically.

2. (a) Do you agree that all third person pronouns are non-deictic?
   (b) What do you make of *him* and *it* in

(16) Let him have it, Chris?

3. When the *fatwa* was pronounced on the author Salman Rushdie following the publication of his novel *The Satanic Verses*, he made a written
   statement apologizing for the distress his book had caused. Consider the
   following sentence taken from this apology:

(17) Living as we do in a world of so many faiths, this experience has
     served to remind us that we must all be conscious of the sensibilities
     of others.

Try to decide whether you think he meant to use we and us inclusively
or exclusively – or even non-deictically.

2.1.5 Place deixis

Consider (8) again:

(8) You just have to read this chapter

The reference of the demonstrative description *this chapter* can only be
determined if the context indicates which of several potential possible
chapters is being picked out. This makes it different from non-deictic descriptions like *the second chapter*. For most but not all speakers of English, there
is a 'proximal' demonstrative, *this* (pl. *these*), and a 'distal' demonstrative,
that (pl. *those*). Each may be used either as a pronoun or in combination with
a noun. Although demonstratives encoding two degrees of proximity to the
speaker, as in English, is the commonest pattern across languages (Diessel,
1999), three degrees of proximity is by no means uncommon, with some
languages distinguishing proximity to the speaker and to the addressee.
   Other place deictics include

> *here* (proximal), *there* (distal), *where* (and the archaic *hither, hence,
> thither, thence, whither, whence*)
> *left, right*
> *up, down, above, below, in front, behind*
> *come, go, bring, take*

The extent to which context is involved in determining the reference of these
items is well illustrated by what happens when Literature students climb the
stairs to the floor in the building where I work, and to their surprise find the
Linguistics Department office at the top of the stairs directly facing them.
They then typically ask our secretary where the Literature office is.
Sometimes she replies

(18) Just along the corridor on your left

and sometimes

(19) Just along the corridor on your right

This isn't because she wants to be difficult – quite the contrary in fact, but because she thinks (18) is more helpful for students who are standing in the doorway facing her directly with the Literature office down the corridor to their left (as in Figure 2.3)

Figure 2.3

and (19) more helpful for students who look through her door over their right shoulders with the Literature secretary's office further along on the right-hand side of the corridor down which they are already facing (as in Figure 2.4).

Figure 2.4

Checking understanding (2.3)

1. What is the difference between saying

(20) I'm going to London

(21) I'm coming to London

2. Under what circumstances would it be appropriate to say

(22) I'm going to John's party

(23) I'm coming to John's party

3. You are looking at a school photograph with Mark in the middle (see Figure 2.5). If I described one of the other people as being

(24) to the left of Mark

(25) on the left of Mark

(26) on Mark's left

   in which cases would the use be deictic and why?

Figure 2.5   SUE   MARK   DAVE

4. I was recently having a conversation with someone in a place about ten miles from Durham. During the conversation he said

(27) I just live yon side of Durham

   What would you have taken him to mean?

5. You may have noticed that several location demonstratives include body-part terms – *ahead*, *in front* (*front* is an archaic term for *face* or *forehead*), *behind*, *back*, *right-/left-hand side*. Think about any other languages you know and whether they exhibit the same phenomenon. Can you explain why body parts should be used in this way?

2.1.6 Time deixis

Here is a list of some of the deictic items whose reference can only be determined in relation to the time of the utterance in which they occur:

> *this/last/next Monday/week/month/year*
> *now, then, ago, later, soon, before*
> *yesterday/today/tomorrow*

Although making such a list is relatively simple, the use of time deictics is not always so straightforward. For example, if I say to my daughter at the beginning of September

(28) I hope you're going to do well this year

she knows that *this year* refers to the school year. If I say the same thing on 1 January, it refers to the calendrical year. And if I say it on 20 April, her birthday, it refers to the year up until her next birthday. A related phenomenon occurs in the case of utterances including the deictic item *today*. If I say

(29) Today's always a bad day

as I get out of bed on a Monday morning, *today* refers to *Monday*. But if I say

(30) I'll see to it today

or

(31) I filled up with petrol today

today refers to some unspecified moment in that portion of the day that remains unexpired (30) or has already passed (31). (A similar effect in the case of location might occur with

(4)   Let's go upstairs and I'll show you your room.

Being an observant person, you would have noticed from the outside that our house has three storeys. And, therefore, knowing which location I refer to when I say *upstairs* also depends on whether we are talking in the hall or on the landing at the top of the first flight of stairs.)

Back to time: the use of *yesterday*, *today* and *tomorrow* is also privileged over the use of the name term for the days, so that we cannot say

(32) I'm going to finish this book on Thursday

if either today or tomorrow is Thursday. English has only a three-member set of single-word, pre-emptive terms of this sort, although we also use the phrases *the day before yesterday* and *the day after tomorrow*. In a discussion initiated by Jan Tent on the *Linguist List* in 1995, it turned out that 23 of the 48 languages of which the contributors had knowledge had a five-member set of terms and no language had fewer.

Another important time deictic is the tense system. In fact, almost every sentence makes reference to an event time. Often this event time can only be determined in relation to the time of the utterance. Thus when Alf Ramsey, the former manager of the England football team, said repeatedly in 1965 and 1966

(33) England will win the World Cup

he was referring to an event which he thought would be accomplished in 1966. Half-a-lifetime later, it only makes sense to refer to that event with a past form such as

(34) England won the World Cup

or to make the utterance non-deictic by saying

(35) England won the World Cup in 1966

Checking understanding (2.4) ──────────────────────

Some weeks after his first wife died, Thomas Hardy wrote the poem *After a Journey*. It included the line apparently addressed to his deceased wife

(36) What have you found to say of our past

or more accurately it included this line and the word 'now' – but I am not telling you where he placed *now*.

1. How many grammatical positions can you find for *now* in this line?
2. Consider each position and decide whether *now* is used deictically or non-deictically, and if deictically whether it is used gesturally.
3. Can you draw any conclusions about the relationship between where *now* is placed in the line and deictic usage in general?
4. In the paragraph before this set of Checking understanding exercises, you read a sentence beginning with the words 'Half-a-lifetime later ...'. In the first edition of *Doing Pragmatics*, the sentence began 'Now ...'. Why do you think I made this change?
5. In Britain, the police often place notices beside the road appealing for information about traffic accidents. Usually these notices say 'Accident' and then give the date and appeal for witnesses. In one road safety campaign, there was an advertisement showing a traffic accident with a notice erected in front of it which read

(37) Accident tonight

   If you find this anomalous, can you say why? What effect does the advertisement have?
6. List all the examples of person, place and time deixis you can think of.

2.1.7 Meaning and deictic reference

It's important to distinguish the invariant meaning of a deictic like *here* or *now* from its variable reference. Thus, Hanks suggests 'the region immediate to you' as one of the principal meanings of *here* and 'the time immediate to this utterance' as one of the principal meanings of *now* (1992: 52). It isn't these propositional meanings that change when a deictic occurs, but the place or time picked out or referred to which shifts as the context changes – hence the name 'shifter', which is sometimes applied to deictics. So when we look at the sign in the Mazda showroom with which this chapter began

(38) The car you saw today and intend to buy tomorrow, somebody saw
       yesterday and intends to buy today

we realize that the person who saw the car yesterday and intends to buy it today referred to what is now today as 'tomorrow' when they made the decision to buy the car. Thus knowing which day is picked out or referred to by deictics such as *yesterday*, *today* and *tomorrow* depends upon knowing the time of utterance – and gives rise to the adage *Tomorrow never comes*.

You may have noticed that I have been using slightly opaque descriptions, such as 'picked out or referred to', when discussing the function of deictics. This is because we probably need to distinguish the demonstrative act of indicating from actually effecting reference.

At one time it was thought that merely uttering a deictic effected a reference, so that to say *this chapter* was to refer to the chapter indicated. More recently, however, Nunberg has rejected the index-referent identity hypothesis that 'the referents of indexicals are the very things picked out by their linguistic meanings, or by their meanings taken together with the demonstrations that accompany their use' (1993: 6). Instead he proposes a theory of **deferred reference** which distinguishes between the index (what is indicated) and the interpretation (what is referred to). Or, if you prefer it in Latin, between the *demonstratum* (what is actually pointed to) and the *demonstrandum* (the reference that needs to be effected). An example may help: imagine that after you have made yourself comfortable in the spare bedroom in my house, you come downstairs and join me in a glass of wine. In the course of our conversation I point at the wine bottle and say

(39) These are on special offer in the supermarket at the moment

I point to a single bottle (the night is yet young) and use a plural form, *these*. The *demonstratum*, what I point to, is the bottle in front of us, but clearly it is not the referent. What I want to refer to, the *demonstrandum*, are the bottles on special offer in the supermarket. The interpretation you reach depends upon instantiating the index pointed to into the interpretation in some way.

And later if we watch television together, we may see repeated the advertisement I saw the other day

(40) You can get this superb all leather football

These are obvious examples of deferred reference, but Nunberg argues that all deictic reference works in this way, so that the deictic index must first be identified and then instantiated into an interpretation.

2.1.8 The deictic centre

When we hear a deictic we typically make a number of assumptions about the context. So when we hear an utterance like

(41) The postbox is on the left

for example, we have to decide whether the postbox is on the left in relation to the speaker (who may perhaps be talking about her local post office) or the hearer (who may perhaps be listening to directions). The default deictic centre is the speaker's location at the time of utterance but as we saw in

(18) Just along the corridor on your left

and

(19) Just along the corridor on your right

the deictic centre has shifted. How does this happen?

The use of *on your left* and *on your right* is deictic since the same location is being indicated by two different descriptions and can only be determined by knowing the context – in this case, the direction in which the addressee is facing. But the co-text associated with *left* and *right*, the lexical item *your*, advises the addressee that the spatial deictic centre has shifted from the unmarked norm (the location of the speaker) to a marked alternative (the location of the addressee). Sometimes a shift is accomplished without co-text, the context itself being sufficient to prompt the addressee to draw the inference that their location rather than the speaker's is the deictic centre. If I am the hider in a game of hide-and-seek, for example, I might decide to give the seeker a clue by calling out

(42) Behind the tree

It's to be hoped that the seeker would draw the inference that I was behind the tree in relation to themselves rather than in relation to myself!

It is also very common for a speaker to update the deictic centre in more extended discourse. So that if I am giving you directions, I may punctuate them with expressions like *after the traffic lights* or *when you get to the post office*. These are signals to you to update the deictic centre and to interpret succeeding directions in relation to this new centre. We do the same with time when we say things like *and then* and *after that*, which provide a new temporal deictic centre in relation to which subsequent utterances are to be understood.

In the phrase

(28) I hope you're going to do well this year

knowing which of the three possible referents – school year, calendrical year, year from birthday, is intended is determined by knowing which of the three possible deictic centres or points of origin of the utterance obtains. So that when an addressee knows the point of origin, they will be able to infer which reference is intended by the speaker.

2.1.9 Competing deictic centres

We all know how annoying it is to come across a back-in-ten-minutes notice. Our annoyance stems from not being able to calculate precisely when the writer will return because we don't know the deictic centre. I was on a train recently (there, I've done it too with *recently*); I was on a train where the announcer said that there were empty seats *at the far end of coach C*. Of course, identifying *the far end of coach C* would depend upon whether you were approaching from coach B or coach D – a case of competing deictic centres. Or another example: on 7 September 1997 I was listening to the radio when the announcer said of a panel game that was about to be broadcast

(43) This edition was recorded last summer

Was *last summer* the summer of 1996? Or was the summer of 1997 already over in England by 7 September I wondered as I looked through the window to see what the weather was like that day. What I was trying to do, of course, was to identify a context that would help me to determine the deictic reference, just as we do, but with fewer problems, when we hear deictics like *you* or *tomorrow*. In fact, understanding pragmatic meanings is always a case of identifying a context that will make sense of an utterance.

Or to take another case of problematic context identification, when General Pinochet was arrested in London in October 1998, the BBC broadcast an interview with the British Ambassador to Chile who was speaking from Santiago. One of the answers he gave to a question the interviewer asked began

(44) What many people maybe don't realize in this country

When he said *in this country*, was he referring to Chile (where he was speaking from) or to Britain (where his audience was situated)? If you listen carefully for examples like (44), you will often be surprised as you listen to the succeeding discourse to find that the deictic centre isn't as you'd expected.

Although it may be annoying when we can't identify a deictic centre or distinguish between competing potential deictic centres, there are times when the confusion has to be avoided. A prime example is in the theatre, where the left side of the stage to an actor is the right side of the stage to the director watching the rehearsal. So there is a convention that *stage-left* and *stage-right* mean left and right from the actor's perspective. Similarly, the expression *local time* is intended to clarify reports of news stories that occurred at, say, midnight. So *at midnight* is assumed to be at midnight in relation to the time in the country where the news is being broadcast, and *at midnight local time* refers to midnight in the country in a different time zone from which the news story originates. So as the world shrinks, it's possible to conceive of several different 'midnights'. This perhaps explains why a BBC radio reporter interviewing an official in the Japanese foreign ministry at 8.57 British Summer Time began:

(45) Good morning Mr Yakamata – good evening to you

This seems a neat way of getting both the audience's and the interviewee's deictic centres into a single greeting.

2.1.10 Deictic change

As you probably know, English once had a *tu/vous* honorific system. Modern English has dispensed with the familiar second person *thou*. Location-denoting forms like *hence* and *yonder* are also largely archaic. Some of the deictics which are no longer used in face-to-face interaction have, however, found a place in the interaction that goes on between a writer and a reader. *Hence* and *thence*, for example, like *now, then, earlier, later, in an earlier chapter, above, in the paragraph above, already, next, in the next section*, are frequently used to point a reader up and down a text in relation to a deictic centre, the current place in the discourse. It seems that the spread of literacy and the use of the written form in everyday communication means that redundant face-to-face deictics such as *hence* find a new role in written communicative discourse.

2.2 Deixis in the real world

Because we use deictics to encode a relationship between persons, times, places and ourselves as speakers, we should expect individual uses to vary. For example, if you are a student, you may sometimes use *we* to refer to the university of which you are a member. What you are doing when you use *we* in this way is encoding membership or affiliation. Similarly, when you say *this is problem* you almost certainly mean that it appears to you to be more of a problem than when you say *that's a problem*. Glover (2000) reports a planning negotiation in which two suggested routes into a proposed housing development are both referred to as *this way*, indicating their problematic status from the speaker's point of view, when we might have expected *this way* and *that way*, indicating their relative proximity to the speaker:

(46) I mean if you come this way you're into there's a road here and
      there's a circulating ring road and if you come this way there's a very
      tight corner here

If individual uses vary, we should also expect intercultural variation in the way that speakers encode the relationships of themselves to the world around them. In this section, I'm going to share a number of uses of deictics I encountered in English utterances in Hong Kong which I found surprising as an outsider, I think because they encoded relations between speakers and context that were different from those I was accustomed to.

2.2.1 The dining room example

(47) Please do not enter the dining room unless you are going to eat there

Nothing surprising about this, you might think – just the kind of notice you might expect to find in the lobby of a hotel. But I saw it on the dining room door in the United Services Club in Hong Kong when I was taken there once by a member. What I found odd was this: if the notice had been displayed in the lobby, I'd have taken *there* as anaphoric and *the dining room* as its antecedent. But standing right in front of the dining room, I found myself thinking that *here* would have been more appropriate – in other words, I was trying to take *there* deictically, but it wasn't working. So here's my hypothesis: members of the club had decided that the dining room should only be used for those wanting to eat, and a member of staff had been given the delicate task of enforcing this rule. The situation may have been complicated by the members consisting mostly of influential expatriates and the staff being mostly local. Perhaps (47) had been tried on the notice-board, but still non-eating members persisted in using the dining room, and a sign on the dining room door became necessary. In choosing (47) rather than

(48) Please do not enter the dining room unless you are going to eat here

the staff member had tried to state a general rule rather than a particular prohibition. However, the notice felt slightly anomalous to me in its dining room door location. I suppose I had stumbled on a cultural practice which reflected a local social context with which I was unfamiliar and which encoded indirectly the differing statuses of the local staff and the expatriate club members.

2.2.2 The railway announcement example

I encountered another deictic use on my very first day in Hong Kong which kept me thinking for months. I was travelling south on the overground commuter train (the KCR) on my way into work and heard the following announcement:

(49) The next station is Kowloon Tong. Passengers may change there for
      MTR trains

All I noticed the first time I heard it was that it was unlike what was at that time the default announcement in Britain:

(50) The next station is Newcastle. Passengers for Sunderland,
      Middlesbrough, Carlisle and the Newcastle Metro should change here

Some days later, I noticed that the announcement occurred at the beginning of the two-and-a-half minute journey before the train entered the tunnel that takes it under the Lion Rock. So perhaps *there* was appropriate because the announcement was made a long way away so as to avoid it being drowned out by the noise of the train in the tunnel. And perhaps the announcement reflected the notion that the next station was the other side of a mountain.

And then one day as I was travelling home, i.e. approaching Kowloon Tong from the opposite direction, I realized that although I had heard the announcement many times before, I hadn't registered that it was the same when travelling north, although there was no tunnel and no mountain, so bang went my hypothesis.

Figure 2.6: The KCR

And when I asked my Chinese colleagues, I discovered that the Cantonese announcements also used *there* rather than *here*.

And then another idea occurred to me: the KCR is the overground train linking China with Hong Kong. It brings people from the country areas known as the New Territories into Kowloon (see Figure 2.6). And at Kowloon Tong there is an interchange with the underground (MTR), hence the announcement. In fact, Kowloon Tong is the MTR's northernmost station. The MTR runs in a huge circle and serves Hong Kong Island, the rich international business area (see Figure 2.7).

Figure 2.7: The KCR and the MTR

So another way of looking at the two systems is to see the KCR as the country boys' line and the MTR as the city slickers' line. This made me wonder whether the KCR announcement might be encoding psychological rather than physical distance. So what announcement would I hear on the MTR if I took a train to Kowloon Tong?

Try to imagine my excitement as the MTR got closer and closer to Kowloon Tong and I was hoping that I would hear the announcement clearly over the babble of passenger talk. This is what I heard:

(51) The next station is Kowloon Tong. Passengers should change here for KCR trains

So it seems that approaching Kowloon Tong is a different experience for the passengers on the two railway networks, and my second hypothesis, that it's scarier for country boys to approach the interchange with the MTR than for city slickers to approach the interchange with the KCR, may hold.

Checking understanding (2.5)

Compare the three versions of the announcement: KCR, default British and MTR. What conclusions do you draw? Do you think there's a possibility that *there* in (49) and *here* in (50) and (51) are anaphoric rather than deictic?

2.2.3 The newspaper headline example

Another example of a deictic use that surprised me as I crossed cultures (and which I must admit that I didn't notice until one of my colleagues drew it to my attention) concerns the use of *local*. Nunberg calls *local* a 'contextual' (1993: 36) because sometimes it requires knowledge of context to be interpreted (i.e. it works like a deictic) and sometimes it doesn't (i.e. it's used intrinsically). Imagine a crime story appearing in a newspaper under the headline

(52) New York murder – local man arrested

Would you expect the man arrested to be from New York (the intrinsic use) or from whichever town the newspaper was printed in (the deictic use)? I suppose the answer partly depends on the newspaper, so that in a strictly local newspaper you would perhaps expect the deictic interpretation and in a national newspaper you might expect the intrinsic interpretation. So if I were reading *The Times*, I would expect the man arrested to be American rather than British. But in Hong Kong, *local* in this sort of headline is almost always deictic. Does this mean that Hong Kong newspapers are local rather than national? Or does the compactness of Hong Kong favour a reading consistent with the strong sense of community that the deictic reading implies? Or is there such a strong sense of Chinese ethnicity that events are interpreted where possible as involving compatriots? Who knows the answers to these questions, but once again I was surprised by a deictic use that from my cultural perspective seemed unexpectable and which tells you something about the culture in which it occurs.

2.2.4 The bare past example

One Sunday afternoon I was at a country bus terminal in Hong Kong and saw this sign displayed on a sandwich board:

(53) Last bus had departed

It struck me as strange that the past perfect rather than the expected present perfect had been used, but at the time I put it down to the ideolect of the writer and thought no more about it. But then I began to notice other written public address messages where the past was used rather than, to me, the more expectable present. Here are two more examples, the first a sign displayed at a KCR station and the second a sign displayed beside some road works:

(54) This section of the platform had been cordoned off. Sorry for any inconvenience caused.
      Vivien Lok
      Station Manager
(55) This lane was closed temporarily

As I thought more about these uses, it occurred to me that the more expectable present implies that whoever wrote the sign has some responsibility for the message it conveys – perhaps they put up the sign because they have closed the platform or started to mend the road. But the Hong Kong cases seems to imply that the event has occurred before the notice is displayed – therefore the writer of the notice can disclaim responsibility for any inconvenience. If this analysis is right, we might want to draw conclusions about the attitude to accepting individual responsibility in different cultures. Once again, we see how a deictic use, here tense, indicates cultural membership. (For further discussion, see Grundy and Jiang, forthcoming.)

2.2.5 The radio interview example

The point established in this section of the chapter is that in encoding a relation between speaker and context, deictic reference inevitably tells you something about the membership status of the speaker, and the degree of their affiiiation to the culture as a whole and to sub-groups within the culture.

The last example is taken from a radio interview recorded and transcribed in Hong Kong for the *International Corpus of English*. In the broadcast, a Chinese interviewee, Annie Wong, is asked to describe how to make the special kind of dumpling eaten during the Dragon Boat festival. Here is a typical example of the way Annie Wong talks about making the dumplings:

(56) you wash and you soak it for about two hours and apart from that
      one other thing that we like especially the Chinese kong shin chong
      [leaf-wrapped steamed dumplings] is that we like to have the shelled
      green beans right and you take about uh half ...

What's noticeable about the way Annie talks is that she constantly switches
from non-deictic *you* to an exclusive deictic *we* that refers to the Chinese
community (as opposed to the expatriate community who are her overhearing audience). It seems that *you* is favoured for general instructions and *we*
for the particular practices of the expert dumpling makers. Notice also how
the first switch from general instruction to particular practice is signalled by
'apart from that one other thing' and the switch back to a general instruction is signalled by 'right'. What Annie does is to show two kinds of affiliation: with her use of non-deictic *you* she affiliates to her overhearing
audience and with her use of deictic *we* she shows her affiliation to the
Chinese community.

2.3 The limits of indexicality

Most of this chapter has been about the deictic properties of a closed class
of demonstratives that include determiners like *this* and *that*, personal
pronouns and possessives, and some time and place adverbials. The social
relation encoded in *tu* or *vous* raises a question about the extent to which
language typically encodes a social relation and whether non-demonstrative
lexical items are also indexical.

   Not only must speakers choose between *tu* and *vous* but also between an
infinite number of possible ways of conveying the proposition or essential
idea that underlies the actual utterance they will decide upon. Think for a
moment about your reaction to one of the earlier examples in this chapter:

(5)   I know you'll enjoy reading this chapter

Try to recall how you felt about the relationship that was assumed between
yourself as reader and me as writer when you read it. You can tell that I was
assuming a relationship between us – a kind of common ground if you like –
precisely because, as you think about it now, you may or may not be feeling
happy with the relationship that I was assuming. I don't suppose I would have
conveyed the proposition in the same way if the addressee had been a
member of the Royal Family – or even a member of my own family, come
to that. This suggests that utterances themselves have indexical properties in
that they invoke (i.e., they create or presuppose) a shared understanding of
the speaker–addressee social relation.

Checking understanding (2.6) ───────────────────

Could lexical items ever have indexical properties, in the sense that the use
of any particular lexical item assumes a common ground between speaker

and addressee? Heritage (1984) describes the way in which the word *nice* in

(57) That's a nice one

exhibits indexicality. Think of a range of contexts in which it would be appropriate to say 'That's a nice one' and try to work out what you would expect an addressee to understand by *nice* in each case.

2.3.1 Common ground and indexicality

The deictic use of language we have been considering in this chapter has two clear properties: (a) it picks out a referent, and (b) relates this referent to a kind of common ground that exists between speaker and addressee. In the case of deixis, what is referred to and the point from which the reference is made are typically, although not necessarily, encoded in a single word: thus *you* picks out a referent and relates this referent to a particular point, typically the speaker's location at the time of utterance. This property of linking what is referred to to a background or context is what causes us to categorize deixis, and indexicality generally, as pragmatic: indexicality provides clear evidence that language is not just an autonomous or self-contained phenomenon but that aspects of context are organized as grammatical systems.

What then is the nature of this common ground in relation to which a referent is identified? One very important point is that there are far fewer options for elaborating the common ground than for elaborating the description of the referent. This is to be expected when we recall that the common ground is a speaker/hearer shared phenomenon and that referents are variable figures. Consider one of the sentences you read much earlier in the chapter:

(58) And if by any chance there are two of you out there working together in a team reading the book aloud and saying nasty things about me the author

It is readily apparent that the referential element of the deictic *out there* can be elaborated much more easily than the common ground element. Thus I might have written

(59) out there in the real world

(60) out there at your desks

(61) out there in a library

I would have been much less likely to have written

(62) ?out there miles away from me

(63) ?out there in relation to me

The fixedness of the common ground is indicated in situations where we use different descriptions to refer to the same referent from different common ground perspectives. Thus if at this stage in the chapter 'two of you out there' were to decide to write me about some point, you might begin the letter like this:

(64) There are two of us here who ...

My *two of you out there* and your *two of us here* pick out an identical referent. The different lexical items we each choose indicate the different points of origin of the two descriptions. When two people say to each other

(65) I love you

each uses *I* to pick out the referent that the other picks out with *you*. Again the referents are identical, but the deictic centres are different. And when I think I am kissing you on your left cheek, you think I'm kissing you on your right one.

   The fixedness of the deictic centre poses a particular problem when we want to quote what others have said to us. Imagine my son says to my daughter

(66) Why don't you want to come to the cinema with me, Eleanor

When she reports his utterance to me, she has a choice of several ways of representing its deictic properties. She might say any of the following:

(67) Eddie said, 'Why don't you want to come to the cinema with me?'

(68) Eddie asked why I didn't want to come to the cinema with him

(69) Eddie complained that I didn't want to go to the cinema with him

In (68) the deictic centre is partly projected from Eddie's original perspective to Eleanor's – she encodes this projection in her use of *I* and *him* and *didn't* while her retention of *come* is still faithful to the deictic centre of Eddie's utterance. Reported speech, and especially fully projected examples of reported speech like (69), are important evidence of the existence of an unmarked deictic centre, which, as (66) and (69) show, is that of the speaker's perspective even when the speaker is representing the speech of another person.

   Our identification of this fixed deictic centre reveals an important pragmatic principle – that we are able both to assume shared knowledge and to foreground what is new in each particular utterance, so that what is new appears as a kind of figure in relation to the ground.

   Because of the role of assumed knowledge in determining reference, deictic referents are typically denotations with limited descriptive power. Thus the pronouns *you* and *me* and *us* are semantically empty tokens in the sense that they lack the descriptive power that the names of the people they refer to have. In English, only third person singular pronouns are marked for gender and, significantly, stand in anaphoric rather than deictic relation to an antecedent. Notice too that many place and time deictic adverbials are reductions of preposition phrases. Sometimes these reduced preposition phrases are deictic while their non-reduced parents are both descriptions with more semantic content and, frequently, non-deictic:

deictic	non-deictic
up	up the hill (note *up the street*, which may be either deictic or non-deictic)
upstairs	up the stairs
down	down the pipe, down a rabbit hole
above	above John, above the water-line
below	below the window
in front	in front of Mary, in front of the children
behind	behind my house (but not *behind Rover, behind the tree*, which are deictic)

It is also significant that these are all noun-reduced preposition phrases (i.e., their nouns are gapped) and therefore more semantically reduced than preposition-reduced phrases such as *today* (reduced from *on today*), *right* (as in *turn right*, reduced from *to the right [side]*). The deictic status of preposition reduced adverbials is not altered by reconstituting them as whole phrases by adding the gapped prepositions (i.e. by saying *on today* or *to the right*).

2.3.2 Grammaticalization and deixis

Leading on from the discussion of grammatical phenomena at the end of the previous section, in this section we illustrate Hanks's view that deictics 'constitute key points of juncture between grammar and context' (1992: 47).

Consider examples (33) and (34) again:

(33) England will win the World Cup

(34) England won the World Cup

Each of these statements encodes two moments in time, the time of the utterance and the time of the event. The first, the time of the utterance, is the deictic centre. This is the present, as we would expect. The second is the time of the event referred to – in the case of (33) some time in the future and in the case of (34) some time in the past. The following sentence is slightly more complicated:

(70) Because England had won the World Cup in 1966, they were granted an automatic place in the 1970 finals

In this sentence, we can distinguish three points in time: the time of utterance (present); the time of the first event referred to (longer ago in the past than the time of the second event – in fact, 1966); and the time of the second event referred to (a past time intermediate between the time of utterance and the time of the earlier event referred to – in fact, 1970). In this way the highly grammaticalized system of tense and aspect auxiliaries in English enables the speaker to refer from a present deictic centre to events at two points of distance in time.

Of particular interest in (70) is the time of the second event, expressed by the use of the past tense. This is also the time of the other events which the speaker will refer to in the continuing discourse:

(71) ... they were granted an automatic place in the 1970 finals, but were knocked out by Germany who came from behind to win

Example (71) shows that the 'second event' time in (70) is actually the time the speaker refers to in the continuing discourse, a kind of discourse time rather than event time. This suggests that even in a sentence like

(72) I'm reading

which describes a present event, there are in fact three different time types encoded, even though in this utterance they are all present time: the time of the utterance; the time of the event referred to; and the time the speaker refers to in the discourse. In case 'discourse time' is an unclear idea, imagine adding *now* to (72) to give

(73) I'm reading now

Clearly this use of *now* indicates that the speaker is referring to the present. This is even clearer when we consider the function of the present perfect. In

(74) I've read most of the chapter now

we can distinguish the utterance time (present), the event time (past, indicated by *read*) and the discourse time that the speaker refers to (present, indicated by *now*).

Summary

In this chapter we have seen how single lexical items such as *I*, *here* and *now* are part of a highly grammaticalized system and assume addressee knowledge of the identity (in the case of *I*), the spatial location (in the case of *here*) and the temporal location (in the case of *now*) of the speaker in order to identify referents in relation to this point of origin. Crucially, the references effected (i.e., to person, place and time) can only be understood by an addressee who is able to reconstruct the speaker's viewpoint. When this reconstruction occurs, the intersubjectivity attained is a kind of common ground that speakers and addressees share. Pragmatics is precisely about accounting for the ability of speakers and addressees to invoke a common context in relation to which a very wide range of language uses can be interpreted. This kind of interpretation is necessary because basic, literal meanings are radically under-determined.

Final directions

Well, you've just about made it to the end of the chapter. I hope you enjoyed reading it. So, as your visit's over, let me show you to the door of my house. To get to the bus stop, you need to turn left, and then right at the T-junction.

But if I lived in Beijing, I'd be telling you to go south and then west. In Britain, for the most part, we use deictics such as *left* and *right* when we give directions, although some people still talk about *going up to London* from whichever direction they approach it, as though it were a central hub. But in some cultures, absolute terms such as points of the compass rather than deictic terms are used to give directions. Whichever system you are familiar with, the other takes a bit of getting used to.

Raising pragmatic awareness: the relation of language to its point of origin

1. Form a small group which includes at least one person with a good knowledge of a language other than English. Ask this person to translate utterances containing a range of deictic phenomena into their other language and explain any problems or differences to you.
2. This exercise works well in tutorial groups. Ask each member of the group to come with two consecutive sentences chosen from this book or some other whose indexical properties they are prepared to discuss.
3. This makes a good vacation task. If you get the opportunity to travel, watch out for uses of deictics that surprise you, as I did in Hong Kong. If you aren't able to travel, try to mix with unfamiliar groups and see how they use *we* to show membership, or listen out for uses of *this* and *that* to encode psychological distance. Try to note down exactly what you heard or read and then report it to your tutorial group at the first meeting of the new term.
4. Identify an occasion when you might expect to hear a variety of deictic ways of communicating what appears to be the same message – in Britain since the privatization of the railways, announcements on trains are particularly interesting as each company, and even individual announcer, tries to encode their own notion of the common ground you and they share. Note down what you hear and present an analysis to your tutorial group.

Further reading

Primary text: Hanks, W.F. (1992: 43–76).
Textbooks: Levinson, S.C. (1983: 54–96); Yule, G. (1996: 9–16).

3 Speech acts: language as action

'Suit the action to the word, the word to
the action.'
(*Hamlet* III.ii.20)

Keywords speech act, intention, literal meaning, sentence and utterance,
proposition, truth value, locutionary act, illocutionary act, perlocution,
(explicit) performative, felicity condition, entailment, truth-conditional
semantics, indirect speech act, form and function, idiom theory,
inference theory

Sunday evening at home and I'm sitting at the kitchen table preparing for
my pragmatics class. My then eighteen-year-old son is sitting at the top of
the table turning the pages of the newspaper apparently looking for pictures.
My then thirteen-year-old daughter is sitting opposite me with nothing better
to do than think, and kick the underside of the table from time to time. All
of a sudden, she speaks: 'Why don't we get a parrot?' My son and I ignore
her. She speaks again, and looking up from my work, this time I reply:

(1)   ELEANOR: They're as intelligent as three-year-olds
      ME: Some are as intelligent as eighteen-year-olds

My son continues to turn pages as though he hasn't heard.

She is not only telling me something about parrots, she is trying to
persuade me that we should get one. I understand both what she says and
what she does, or tries to do, by saying it.

For my part, I'm not only telling her something (doubtful) about parrots,
but I'm also turning down her suggestion and insulting my son in a typical
father–daughter bonding exchange. She understands both what I say and
what I do by saying it.

For his part, my son, who is partly the target but not the addressee of what I say, feigns deafness. My daughter and I both understand what he means by not saying anything.

Later, I wish I'd said, 'Some eighteen-year-olds are as intelligent as three-year-olds.'

At the end of the first chapter we saw how, depending on the context in which it was uttered, *I'm here now* might be taken as a comforting reassurance, a stern warning or an apology. This chapter explores the property that utterances have of counting as actions, such as the actions of persuading, refusing, reassuring, warning and apologizing.

3.1 Language as a representation of intention

3.1.1 Language and action: understanding the phenomenon

Our butcher once asked why farmers have long ears and bald heads. When I obligingly said I didn't know, he took the lobe of one of his ears between thumb and forefinger and, pulling it downwards, said 'How much?' Next he ran his hand through his hair, saying 'Cor' as he did so. This neat joke shows how language (saying 'How much?') and action (pulling your ear lobe downwards to indicate that you can't believe what you've just heard) can be co-incident. Of course there are times when actions are preferred to words, such as when flagging down a bus or a taxi; or times when either actions, or language, or both may be used, such as when greeting someone in the street; or times when both language and actions are required, as in the complicated ritual of introducing people to one another. These examples show that there is no clear-cut boundary between using actions to count as actions and using language to count as actions.

In fact, we usually realize that we are doing something with words when we talk. When my son was two years old he came into the bathroom one day when I was bent double scrubbing out the bath and said in a particularly jaunty and self-satisfied way

(2)   It's me again

This struck me as a rather peculiar utterance. The sentence was an accurate description of a state of affairs in the world – indeed, it was a statement of the obvious. But when we use *It's me again* as an utterance, it is usually to apologize for troubling someone a second time. This did not seem to be my son's intention on this occasion. I wasn't able to explain his utterance to myself until I recollected that on the previous occasion when he had come into the bathroom as I was scrubbing out the bath, I had turned to him in exasperation and said

(3)   It's you again

He had evidently understood the semantics but not the pragmatics of my utterance and had assumed that to get in first with *it's me again* was the appropriate pragmatic strategy in the bath-scrubbing context we found ourselves in.

This simple example illustrates the difference between the literal meaning of sentences like *it's me again* and *it's you again* and the use of such sentences as utterances. Knowing the literal meaning of the sentences is not enough to determine what they count as doing, what speech act is performed, when they are used.

Checking understanding (3.1)

1. Although the following utterances all express the same proposition and are therefore true under just the same conditions, they are each used to perform a range of different acts. Try to list some of the situations in which each might be used and decide what speech act would be effected in each case.

(4)   Sorry

(5)   I'm sorry

(6)   I am sorry

2. A former student once sent me an e-mail beginning

(7)   Remember me

What speech act did she intend? And what speech act did Hamlet's father's ghost intend when he said the same thing?

3. Can you think of other examples of a single proposition being used for a variety of speech acts? Begin with my daughter's use of

(8)   I'll never sell her

mentioned in Chapter 1.

4. One day my colleague Hiroko and I had lunch together in the staff restaurant. When it was time to pay, Hiroko discovered that she had forgotten her purse. Our conversation went like this

(9)   H: I haven't got any money
      P: It's all right I've got money
      H: I'll pay you back later
      P: It's OK

Later I was surprised to find that Hiroko had put the cost of her lunch in my pigeonhole. What had gone wrong?

3.1.2 Locution, illocution and perlocution

A year or two back, I was a passenger in a car travelling through Uzbekistan. At one stage in our journey, we passed a man standing by the roadside with his arms spread wide. Seeing my puzzled look, the driver explained that the man we had seen was selling fish (which made sense as we were passing a lake at the time). Notice that we can distinguish three aspects of this semiotic act:

- first, its literal 'meaning' – a man stands arms akimbo
- second, what it counts as doing (for those in the know) – offering fish for sale
- third, the effect it has – presumably sometimes cars stop and a negotiation takes place (the actor's probable intention); occasionally a foreigner is puzzled (presumably not intended by the actor).

Notice that the same three aspects of meaning can also be distinguished in the utterance

(2)   It's me again

First, it conveys the proposition that the speaker has returned to a place he/she was in on a previous occasion. In saying this we are regarding *It's me again* as a sentence with a truth value. (In fact, it's very difficult to think of any circumstances under which this sentence could be uttered without being true.)

Second, when this sentence is used as an utterance, it usually has the force of, or counts as, an apology. Thought of in this way, it does not make any real sense to ask if the sentence is true or not – rather, the utterance represents the intention of the speaker to apologize.

Third, the utterance will have effects or consequences that are not entirely foreseeable. Presumably, the speaker hopes it will mollify the addressee, but there will be occasions on which it has some other effect, such as making the addressee angry.

In *How to do things with words* (1962) Austin called the first of these aspects of meaning – uttering a sentence with determinate 'sense' (i.e. non-ambiguous meaning) and reference – the **locution**. He called the second – performing an act by uttering a sentence, the **illocution**. And he called the third – the effect the utterance might have, the **perlocution**.

Checking understanding (3.2) ———————————————

1. Thomas draws attention to *Interflora's* neat slogan *Say it with flowers!* (1995: 101). Can you determine the literal 'meaning' of this act, the kinds of things giving someone flowers might count as doing, and the kinds of effects it might have?
2. Identify the locutionary, illocutionary and perlocutionary acts typically associated with saying

(3)   It's you again

3.1.3 Language and action: Austin's theory of Speech Acts

The distinction between the meaning that sentences have as a result of our knowing whether they are true or false and the meaning that utterances have as a result of our understanding what they count as doing was first described in *How to do things with words*. Austin drew attention to the 'performative' or action accomplishing use of certain language formulas. A good example is

(10) Pass

as uttered by contestants in the television general knowledge contest, *Mastermind*. We call this use explicitly performative because the action of 'passing' is accomplished just by saying *Pass*. In fact, uttering *Pass* counts as forfeiting the right to supply an answer: it is not a statement (true or false) about the world. Moreover it is only 'felicitous' to utter *Pass* under narrowly defined circumstances, such as when taking part in *Mastermind* or at particular moments in the bidding sequence of a game of bridge. Try walking down the street nodding at people and saying *Pass*, and it will only be a matter of time before someone makes a telephone call and you get taken away in a van.

In the previous paragraph, we used the term 'explicitly performative' to denote the use of an expression that accomplishes an action merely by virtue of being uttered. Thus by uttering

(11) I call upon these persons here present to witness that I, AB, do take thee, CD, to be my lawful wedded wife (or husband) (UK *Marriage Act*, 1949)

the speaker both makes those present witnesses and marries the person addressed. Some years ago, this form of words was superseded by the less formal but no less performative

(12) I [name] take you [name] to be my wedded wife (or husband) (UK *Marriage Ceremony (Prescribed Words) Act*, 1996)

Checking understanding (3.3) —————————————————————

I hereby pronounce you man and wife counts as performing an action – we might say that it is explicitly performative. *I sneeze* is not. Make a list of as many explicitly performative utterances as you can think of and in each case think through the conditions under which it would be appropriate to utter them.

Yet as Austin points out, utterances do not need to contain an explicitly performative verb to be performative. For example, saying *Pass* on a football field is not explicitly performative, although as a call for the ball it is clearly performative.

Or take the case of promising. It would be distinctly odd for me to say to my wife

(13) I hereby promise to pick you up at eight o'clock

Even

(14) I promise to pick you up at eight

would only be natural if I'd failed to honour such an agreement on a previous occasion. It would be much more natural to say

(15) I'll pick you up at eight

Although the explicit performative *promise* does not occur in (15), the utterance certainly counts as promising. Or I can reassure my wife of the reliability of what I commit myself to by saying

(16) I'll pick you up at eight, don't worry

or I can use pitch prominence

(17) I WILL pick you up at eight

Even saying

(18) Shall I pick you up at eight

or

(19) Would you like me to pick you up at eight

commits me to the promised action in the event of my offer being accepted. Only the first two of these seven ways of promising use the explicit performative verb *promise*. The last two examples are interrogative and (19) even embeds what is promised within an interrogative sentence. Yet all of them count as making a promise. That is to say, they all share a common set of what Austin called 'felicity conditions', in this case, conditions which make it appropriate to make a promise. Would you agree that these include minimally

- that what I offer is in my power to deliver
- that it is desirable to the person to whom I make the promise
- that what is promised was not going to happen anyway?

Thus we see that non-explicit, even very implicit, ways of using language performatively are the norm. The implicit nature of many speech acts means that they are doubly pragmatic: they are pragmatic first of all because they convey meanings (illocutionary force) that are not entailments, and at the same time they are typical of other pragmatic phenomena in that these meanings are frequently conveyed indirectly in implicit ways.

This is well illustrated by the case of

(2) It's me again

when used by speakers other than my son at the age of two. Typically this utterance counts as apologizing. But

(3)   It's you again

expresses irritation. Yet neither contains any explicit performative verb. One has the force of an apology, the other of an expression of annoyance, and both have literal meanings of a quite different kind.

More usefully, we might ask how *It's me again* comes to be understood as an apology when, as my son demonstrated in understanding only its semantics and not its pragmatics, this is not a necessary assumption. Since the proposition conveyed in the utterance is already obvious without being uttered, the speaker must have some further reasons for saying it since, if it were intended only to convey its literal meaning, it would lack sincerity or usefulness. It therefore conveys an implied meaning, perhaps an implied meaning that it shares with *It's you again*, namely that the person indicated (*me*, *you*) is imposing on (the territory of) the other party in the exchange. This implied meaning then enables the speech act, in the case of *It's me again* that of apologizing and in the case of *It's you again* that of expressing irritation, to be determined.

At this stage we need to be clear about some basic distinctions.

- It is important to distinguish: from:
  sentences that describe states of   doing things with words
  affairs in the world

  Thus
  (2) It's me again
  describes a state of affairs in   and constitutes an apology.
  the world

- It is important to distinguish: from:
  the truth or falsity of sentences   the felicity of utterances

  Thus when President Kennedy said
  (20) Ich bin ein Berliner = Ich bin Berliner
  it may not have been literally true   but it was felicitous.

- It is important to distinguish: from:
  Truth as a way of determining   Performative effect as a source
  meaning   of meaning

  Thus it is reasonable to ask whether the meaning of
  (21) This is a no smoking zone
  when addressed to someone smoking in a prohibited area, consists more
  in knowing that it happens to be   or in understanding the intention
  true as a description of the area   of the speaker in uttering it and
  referred to   the effect that it is likely to have
  on the addressee.

- As Austin noted,
  it is important to distinguish:
  The locution (uttering a sentence with determinate sense (= unambiguous meaning) and reference

  from:
  The illocution (performing an act by uttering a sentence), and the perlocution (the effect the utterance might have).

  Thus saying
  (22) I'm going on holiday next week conveys the proposition that the speaker will be on holiday at the time indicated

  and, when the addressee is the milkman, instructs him to suspend milk deliveries; if overheard by a thief, one of the effects might be to cause the speaker's house to be burgled.

- It is important to distinguish:
  Propositional content

  from:
  Force

  Thus in the following exchange between the Lord Mayor of London and a resident of an old people's home reported in *The Sunday Times* (14 March 1999)

  (23) Lord Mayor: Do you know who I am
       Resident: No dear, but just ask a sister – she'll tell you

  the Lord Mayor expresses the open proposition that his identity may or may not be known to his interlocutor

  the Lord Mayor's open proposition has the force of indicating that he is an important person (although the perlocutionary effect is no doubt unforeseen).

The left-hand column in this list of distinctions treats meaning in the manner of truth-conditional semantics – if you know when a sentence is true or false, then you know what it means. Thus, to take Tarski's classic example,

(24) Schnee ist weiss

will be a true sentence if and only if snow is white. (I'm following the usual practice of using one language [here German] for the sentence and another [here English] to describe the state of affairs the sentence purports to describe so as to avoid a confusion between sentence and state of affairs in the world.)

    Working down the left-hand column above, (24) is seen as a description of a state of affairs in the world whose meaning derives from recognizing the truth of the proposition it expresses. This way of understanding the meaning of (24) is to be contrasted with the speech act perspective set out in the right-hand column. Under this account

(24) Schnee ist weiss

would be uttered for some purpose, such as giving information to a child or convincing a Saudi who had never seen snow. It would be felicitous in such contexts (only), would be meaningful as an act of informing or convincing, and would be likely to have effects which would be only partly predictable.

Checking understanding (3.4)

How does Speech Act theory help you to understand the cartoon strip (Figure 3.1)?

Figure 3.1: Mr Logic. *Copyright House of Viz/John Brown Publishing. Reproduced with permission.*

3.1.4 Language and action: direct and indirect speech acts

We have already noticed that many speech acts are doubly pragmatic: they are pragmatic not only because they convey meanings that are not entailments but also because these meanings are frequently conveyed indirectly.

So when we say

(2)   It's me again

we are being indirect. In fact, we are stating one of the felicity conditions (returning with a purpose that implies an imposition on someone else) that would make it appropriate to apologize.

And if I say to my wife

(19) Would you like me to pick you up at eight

I am promising indirectly to pick her up by asking about one of the felicity conditions on doing it – that it is desirable to her.

President Kennedy is promising to support Berlin by stating one of the felicity conditions

(20) Ich bin ein Berliner = Ich bin Berliner

that would usually have to obtain for someone to commit themselves to the future of Berlin.

And if I say

(21) This is a no smoking zone

I am stating one of the felicity conditions that would need to obtain for me to be in a position to (attempt to) prevent someone from continuing to smoke.

And when I say to the milkman

(22) I'm going on holiday next week

I am stating one of the felicity conditions on suspending the milk delivery.

And when an important person asks

(23) Do you know who I am

they are asking about a felicity condition on being important (that people know who they are), and therefore indirectly asserting that they are important.

And when Mr Logic asks whether one of the felicity conditions for buying stamps is in place with the utterance

(25) Do you sell postage stamps

he is assumed to be asking to buy a stamp.

All these examples show how it is sufficient for a speaker to state or ask about a felicity condition on an action to imply that they are performing the action itself.

Consider again the butcher's joke about farmers which you read on p. 49. When we don't hear part of an utterance clearly, one strategy open to us is to request the speaker to repeat what they said. We often do this indirectly, by asking a question which indicates that we didn't hear properly. So if we didn't hear the price of something clearly, we might say 'How much?' or 'Did you say £100?'. Of course, the joke here turns on the suggestion that the price mentioned was so high that it couldn't have been right and the farmer must have misheard. We get this effect because the farmer implies a felicity condition (that he didn't hear what was said) on the need for the speaker to repeat the original utterance. (And perhaps he calculates that the perlocutionary effect will be that when the speaker repeats what was said, the price will be lower!)

Relatedly, one very interesting way of expressing strong feelings is to state that you do not know how to express these feelings. So that when we hear someone else's distressing news and want to express sympathy, we might say

(26) I don't know what to say

Thus we perform an illocutionary act by stating that we can't express the meaning we want to convey as a literal meaning or locutionary act. It's as if a felicity condition on having strong feelings to express is not having the words to express them with. Thus a witness to the Oklahoma bomb explosion in the USA said in a television interview

(27) There's got to be fatalities over there – I'm speechless – I've never seen anything like it

And Bill Clinton, on being re-elected president of the USA, expressed his thanks to those who had voted for him in the following way:

(28) I am more grateful than I can say

3.1.5 Sentence types, and direct and indirect speech acts

Imagine you had the misfortune to attend one of my pragmatics lectures and that after half-an-hour in which I had been particularly difficult to follow, I said

(29) I know this isn't very clear. Can anyone do any better

You might be very uncertain as to the illocutionary force associated with *Can anyone do any better.*

If you were very bold, you might treat it as a genuine question and tell me that several of my colleagues had done better earlier in the week. Or if I held out a piece of chalk as I said it, you might take it as an invitation to come and have a try yourself. Or if you thought I was being sarcastic, you might take it ironically as an assertion that no one else could do any better.

The bold reading takes my utterance as a direct speech act in which the interrogative form is used to ask a question. The chalk-offering reading takes it as an indirect speech act in which I ask about one of the felicity conditions that would need to be in place to make it worthwhile inviting someone else to come and have a try. I am thus understood to be implying that someone should come and do just that. The ironical reading takes it as an indirect way of asserting that no one can do any better, which is inferred if you assume that I am asking what appears to be a Yes/No question to which the only correct answer is no.

This example shows us how a sentence with interrogative form can be taken not only as a question, but also as an indirect request/order or as an indirect assertion.

English is fortunate in having one set of terms for sentence form

- *declarative* (subject + verb order)
- *imperative* (no overt subject)
- *interrogative* (verb + subject order [with some exceptions])

and another matching set for utterance function

- *assertion*
- *order/request*
- *question*.

This metalanguage makes it easy to distinguish form and function. When form and function match, we call the effect a direct speech act as in

(8)   I'll never sell her (declarative used as an assertion)

(30) Don't ever sell her (imperative used to give an order/make a request)

(31) Will you ever sell her (interrogative used to ask a question)

When form and function do not match, we might say that the illocutionary effect is conveyed as an indirect speech act (Searle, 1975), as in the following examples.

(32) I wonder when the train leaves (Declarative form functioning as a question = *do you know when the train leaves*, or as a request = *tell me when the train leaves*)

(33) (to a child) You'd better eat your dinner fast (Declarative form functioning as an order)

(34) Have a good journey (Imperative form functioning as an assertion = *I hope you have a good journey*)

(35) Tell me why it's a good idea (Imperative form functioning as a question)

(36) Who cares (Interrogative form functioning as an assertion = *No one cares*)

(37) Can you open the door for me (Interrogative form functioning as a request)

Some of these examples are slightly awkward, but the point stands that every sentence type can be used for every utterance function. And in fact when we make a request or give an order, we almost always do it indirectly by using an interrogative sentence. This raises the question of whether it's appropriate to think of sentence forms as having prototypical functions, an issue to which we will return in the second part of the chapter.

Notice also that in the last paragraph I once again linked making requests and giving orders. I did this because of the difficulty of pinning down just what force is prototypically associated with imperative sentences. Because they are reflections of our intentions, speech acts are notoriously hard to define – as you will discover as you work through the Checking understanding exercises that follow.

Checking understanding (3.5) ─────────────────────

1. What do you make of the following conversation I overheard at breakfast in a hotel involving a middle-aged couple and a waitress.

(38) HIM (to waitress): Could we have some more coffee
     <waitress goes away>
     HER (to him): You should say may we
     HIM: Why
     HER: Because it could mean are you able
     HIM: That's what I meant
     HER: Of course you didn't

2. I stopped at a garage to fill up with petrol one evening on the way home and when I went to pay, the person at the cash desk said

(39) Do you know about our offer on oil

     What are you supposed to do when this happens?

3. We have a no smoking policy in our building. I have taken it upon myself to try and enforce this policy when I come across smokers polluting our corridor. What do you make of the following three brief encounters?

(40) PETER: You're in a no smoking zone
     FEMALE STUDENT: Am I
     PETER: The whole building's a no smoking zone
     FEMALE STUDENT: Thanks very much (extinguishing cigarette)

(41) PETER: This is a no smoking zone
     MALE STUDENT: Is it (getting up)
     PETER: Outside only I'm afraid
     (Male student extinguishes cigarette)

(42) PETER: Excuse me you're in a no smoking zone
     MATURE, PIPE SMOKING, MALE STUDENT: Ah is it sorry (puts lighted pipe in his pocket)

4. What speech act is conveyed by each of the following?

(43) Have you seen that room of hers (My wife talking to me and referring to our daughter's bedroom)

(44) You are on my right (Spoken by the chairman of a meeting. He had just introduced two speakers and explained that the one on his left would speak first. The one on his right then began to speak.)

(45) ELEANOR: Dad, are you in a good mood today
     PETER: Why, do you want to put me in a bad one

3.1.6 Syntactic reflexes of indirect speech acts

Requests are often marked by the use of pre-verbal *please*, as in

(46) Please pick me up at eight

However, pre-verbal please is ungrammatical in utterances such as

(47) *When do you please want to be picked up

and

(48) *I'll please pick you up at eight

One might be tempted as a first reaction to suggest that this constraint is formal and that only imperative, but not interrogative or declarative, sentences allow pre-verbal *please*. But this is not correct as

(49) Will you please pick me up at eight

and

(50) Perhaps you could please pick me up at eight

show. Both (49) and (50) prove that pre-verbal *please* is grammatical just where the function is to order or request.

Sometimes *please* is attached as a sentence-adverb to mark the illocutionary function of the utterance. Thus

(51) Please, I hate that music

is a request to stop playing the music, and

(52) Please, why do you hate that music

is a request to explain your view of the music.

The importance of these data cannot be overstated. What we are seeing is a syntactic reflex of a pragmatic phenomenon. In other words, what is grammatical is determined not within an autonomous syntax but in relation to the function of the utterance.

Summary

In the first part of this chapter we have seen that language is used performatively. In fact, the performative nature of language is explicitly encoded in a limited number of lexical items, such as the verb *promise*. When we use this predicate, it counts as performing the action of promising. However, there are many other, implicit, ways of promising. Indeed, all uses of language are performative. Thus sentences are grammatical objects which describe states of affairs in the world (snow is white) or in possible worlds (I'll pick you up at eight) and may be thought of as verifiable in the relevant real or possible world. But when those sentences are used as utterances, it is not their truth value that determines what they mean so much as whether we understand what they are used to do.

As well as the formal properties of sentences (they may be interrogative, for example), sentences also have functional properties (when interrogative sentences are used as utterances, they are prototypically used to ask questions). However, not all interrogative sentences are used to ask questions; sometimes interrogative sentences are used indirectly to give orders/make requests

(53) Why don't you leave me alone

or to make assertions

(36) Who cares

This raises an issue only briefly touched on in the first part of the chapter, that of how we understand utterances whose intended meaning (e.g., that no one cares) appears to be at odds with their literal meaning (e.g., is there someone who cares).

3.2 Literal meaning and indirect speech acts

The first part of this chapter described one phenomenon, indirect speech acts, which raise a problematic issue: what is the status of the literal meaning of a sentence like

(36) Who cares

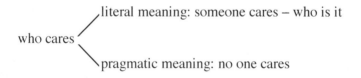

who cares
    literal meaning: someone cares – who is it
    pragmatic meaning: no one cares

3.2.1 Idiom theory and indirect speech acts

One way of dealing with this problem would be to say that *who cares* is an idiom, meaning *no one cares*. This was a favoured solution at one time and neatly bypasses the problem of literal meaning simply by claiming that *who cares* has idiomatic meaning (Sadock, 1974). Thus *can you x*, as in *can you pick me up at eight*, is an idiomatic way of saying *do x*. One objection to this solution is that idioms are supposedly untranslatable, yet *can you x*, unlike true idioms such as *kick the bucket*, occurs widely across languages as an indirect way of making a request or giving an order. A still more serious objection to the idiom account is raised by examples like

(29) Can anyone do any better

and

(54) Who likes fish

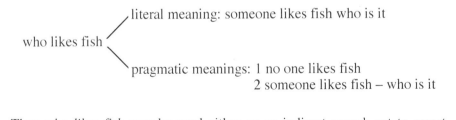

who likes fish

literal meaning: someone likes fish who is it

pragmatic meanings: 1 no one likes fish
                    2 someone likes fish – who is it

Thus *who likes fish* may be used either as an indirect speech act to assert that no one likes fish or as a direct speech act to enquire as to the identity of those who do like fish. It is obviously unsatisfactory to have to claim that an expression is sometimes an idiom and sometimes not. And anyway, an idiom theory of indirect meaning would not be sufficient since an inference theory of some kind would be needed so that a hearer could determine whether *who likes fish* was intended idiomatically (i.e. indirectly) or not.

The two possible ways of understanding (54) raise the problem at the heart of speech act theory, that of how the illocutionary force of an utterance is determined.

3.2.2 Literal meaning and conventional understanding

Inference theories necessarily preserve the literal meaning as part of the calculation of the intended force of the utterance. To ask the question posed by Morgan in his paper 'Two types of convention in indirect speech acts', is it really credible to suppose that in the case of utterances like

(55) Can you pass the salt

so complicated a mechanism is required to arrive at the most relevant under-standing (1978: 261–80). Morgan argues that the indirect request in (55) is calculable but not calculated. If you accept that (55) has become so conven-tionalized as not to require an inferencing procedure like that required to determine the force of (54) and you deny that *can you x* is an idiom, you are forced to the conclusion that there is little difference between

(55) Can you pass the salt

and

(56) Pass the salt

and that therefore the notion of literal meaning is to some degree problem-atic.

However logical this argument may be, we are obviously reluctant to abandon the notion that literal meaning is a stable, consistent component of sentences and utterances. Moreover, whatever its meaning status, there is clearly a difference between (55) and (56), at least in terms of their politeness status.

3.2.3 Literal meaning as a feature of sentences but not of utterances

In this section I am going to argue that even sentences are under-determined and therefore make a relatively arbitrary contribution to the understanding of utterances. In Chapter 1 we saw how the sentence

(57) May I speak English

is taken in some contexts to be functionally equivalent to the quite different sentence

(58) Do you speak English

Thus in such contexts, producing the sentence, i.e. actually saying *May I speak English*, counts as enquiring whether the addressee speaks English. Put another way, it has the same force, in the particular context described, as saying *Do you speak English*.

I want to try and persuade you that, in understanding utterances in our mother tongue, contrary to our common-sense expectation, we behave rather like non-native speakers with limited knowledge of a language, a lot of context and people who say things like (57) to us. We actually know much less of the meaning of our language than we think we do, precisely because what any token of our language means is much less determined than we tend to think it is. We let the context do the work for us so that, looked at alongside the contextual knowledge we take into account in determining what is meant by what is said, words and sentences make a relatively less important contribution to our understanding than we tend to think they do. In fact, I challenge you to go back to Chapter 1 and find a single example in which the speaker intended to mean only what they said literally.

Meaning is a relative phenomenon anyway. This is because lexical items have syntactic function as well as semantic content and in each case the balance between syntactic function and lexical salience has implications for the extent to which their meaning is arbitrary. So we find a strong meaning attached to nominals or naming words like *substance* or *general*. And we can particularize them with determiners to give expanded phrases such as *a substance* and *the general*. But when these words acquire a secondary syntactic function, that of modifying other naming words as denominal adjectives, their lexical salience declines; so the meanings of *substantial* or *general* as adjectives are less concrete than the meanings of the base nouns from which they are derived. And if you apply the productive morphology of English to mark a further derived syntactic function, the adverbial function of modifying adjectives or verbs, then we see that the adverbs *substantially* or *generally* are much less lexically salient than their original nominal forms. As we shall see in Chapter 5, when used as sentence adverbs, expressions like *substantially* and *generally* lose their conceptual salience and frequently acquire a pragmatic, or procedural, function.

This arbitrariness of meaning is especially obvious in the case of prepositions, which are notoriously difficult to translate across languages. Thus the single preposition *mit* would occur in German in contexts where English would use *by* (*mit dem Flugzeug* = by plane), *of* (*voll mit* – full of) and *with* (*mit einem Freund* – with a friend). And in fact if you listen carefully to native speakers, you will find that their choice of prepositions is often much more arbitrary than you might suppose. When I first noticed this consciously, I was listening to an important person giving a talk about his work overseas. I heard him say in rapid succession

(59) a number of factors which seemed to militate towards an unbiased approach

(60) the findings from the particular questionnaire

(61) I hope some of you here will find some relevance for what I want to talk about

And then just afterwards I heard a trade union leader on the *Today* programme on BBC Radio 4 say

(62) There are 67 options and someone somewhere has to make sense into it

And then I went to a function and heard a senior police officer say

(63) The standard is very very high both on behalf of the pupils and of the teachers

and

(64) I want to thank them for the entertainment they're going to provide to us

Although we may not think we talk like this ourselves, actually we sometimes do; and the point is that it does not matter much because the choice of prepositions, although very interesting from a cognitive perspective, is relatively arbitrary, as you may confirm for yourself by trying to justify your choice of *be in sympathy with*, *feel sympathy for* and *be sympathetic to/towards*.

The last two paragraphs have taken us away from the problem of literal meaning in speech acts, but have made the important point that the semantic component of language is much more less fixed or predictable than we sometimes realize. This indeterminacy allows us the freedom to determine what is meant by the literal language speakers use in the wide variety of contexts in which they use it. But as it turns out, this indeterminacy isn't confined to the level of lexical items. If we take a step back and think for a moment about the phoneme, we see that these basic components which combine together in morphemes and words are themselves essentially meaningless segments. Thus none of the separate phonemes [a], [p], [t] has meaning until they come together to make [apt] or [pat] or [tap]. Phonemes are like bricks, in the sense that they represent nothing but bricks until assembled as a wall or a house.

A phoneme is the smallest unit in language's 'visible spectrum', a visible spectrum which includes at least the phoneme, morpheme, lexical item (word), sentence, utterance and discourse. So a sentence is to the lexical items which constitute it what a morpheme is to the phonemes which constitute it. Sentences may be regarded as syntactic structures or as semantic representations. As a syntactic structure, the sentence

(54) Who likes fish

consists of a *wh*-proform as subject, with a predicate consisting of a tensed verb and a noun phrase. But it only attains the status of a sentence when these separate parts – *wh*-proform, verb, noun phrase – are grouped as constituents. In a similar way the three separate words – *who*, *likes* and *fish* – are separate forms whose function, to invite an addressee to complete the open proposition *x likes fish*, results not from their status as three separate forms, or bricks, but from their combination into a meaningful structure.

That words have meaning is not in dispute, of course, but the argument I want to put to you is that their meaning results from the combination of forms, phonemes or morphemes, that constitute them; and that they in their turn are forms that constitute a higher unit, a sentence, whose meaning is more and other than the meaning of its constituent segments. In fact, in the truth-conditional semantic account, the meaning of a sentence is determined according to its correspondence to a state of affairs in a real or possible world and may be expressed as a truth value – this is clearly not the way the meaning of a word or morpheme is determined.

Thus the constituent parts of a word (phonemes, morphemes) have a function in combination as a word, but words are forms when in their turn they are the constituent parts of sentences. And at the next level up, it will resolve our literal meaning problem very neatly indeed to argue that sentences have a function as a combination of constituents, but are forms which combine with a set of felicity conditions and pragmatic presuppositions appropriate to a context to give meaningful utterances. And in their turn an utterance has a function as a combination of a sentence and knowledge about the world. But when organized sequentially as a series of 'forms' in a containing speech event, utterances combine in regular, expectable ways to give a conversational sequence that has a function, as is shown in my exchanges with would-be smokers.

In this way we can have our cake and eat it because we are treating a sentence as two objects – as a combination of constituent forms which function as a sentence, and as a form which in combination with other contextually derived propositions (including felicity conditions and the encyclopaedic knowledge of the hearer) constitutes an utterance. This point is well illustrated by utterances like

(65) That was a wonderful meal

which is frequently false as a sentence, at least in Britain, but would typically be considered appropriate as an utterance (and would be unlikely to have the effect of deceiving).

Similarly, the salutation which began a letter I once received from a would-be overseas student, *My pleasant dear*, is a perfectly grammatical expression and entirely expectable in some cultures, but rather unconventional as a speech act in the culture in which it was received. It is at the heart of language to be able to recognize this arbitrariness of meaning which is the result of seeing the simultaneous relation of an item both to the level below and to the level above in the 'visible spectrum' of language.

We are now ready to return to the specific problem posed by *who likes fish*.

Under the account of language suggested above, we can see that, when viewed as a combination of lexical items or syntactic constituents,

(54) Who likes fish

functions as a sentence expressing an open proposition. At the same time, this sentence may also be thought of as a formal component of relatively indeterminate meaning, which, together with other premises, allows a hearer to infer the function of the utterance to which it contributes. These premises would be likely to include perceptions of aspects of the surrounding situation. If choosing from a menu in a restaurant was an aspect of the surrounding situation, one utterance function would be inferred, if talking about food people do not like was an aspect of the current situation, a different utterance function would be inferred.

These arguments are tantamount to dissolving the difference between so-called 'direct' speech acts and so-called 'indirect' speech acts. This would be a welcome advance on postulating two classes of speech act, which seems to obscure the generalization that all speech acts are understood in relation to a context. Nor is this distinction syntactically motivated, since pre-verbal *please*, to take just one example, is blind to differences in the supposed direct or indirect status of speech acts, as we saw at the end of the first part of this chapter.

3.2.4 Speech act choice

The explanation suggested here of how the force of an utterance is determined in a specific context is not intended to obscure the fact that speakers do have choices to make in how to encode illocutionary force. It is intended rather as a more logical explanation of why sentences appear to have two levels of meaning, the literal (what our words mean) and the understood (what we mean by our words) (Atkinson, Kilby and Roca, 1988: 217). As we noted above, there is certainly a difference between

(55) Can you pass the salt

and

(56) Pass the salt

In our discussion of politeness in Chapter 7, we will see that the expectation of the addressee is a crucial factor in determining which of two alternative utterances such as (55) and (56) is chosen by the speaker. As it turns out, the choice between many different locutionary means of requesting that someone pass one the salt, the real issue is what societal or individual attitudes motivate the way the illocutionary act is performed on any particular occasion and the perlocutionary effects this choice is calculated to bring about.

Finally, speech acts might be seen as a prototypically pragmatic phenomenon in the sense that they challenge the notion that there is a one-to-one correspondence between a form and its function. It is simply not possible to argue that interrogative sentences, to take one example, have a single function. In fact the function of an interrogative sentence when used as an utterance crucially depends on an essentially pragmatic phenomenon, how the context assists the addressee in determining what is meant by what is said.

Raising pragmatic awareness: speech acts

1. You will need a partner for this exercise. Working separately, you and your partner each choose one short extract from a contemporary play and copy it out without the original punctuation. The best extracts are those where two speakers are holding an emotional conversation over about ten turns and each of their turns is very short. Then exchange texts: you each invent your own punctuation using either conventional symbols or any new ones that you need to invent to capture illocutionary force. When you have completed the exercise, explain your suggested punctuation to your partner.
2. Working individually, either listen out for or recall occasions when a speaker responds, as Mr Logic does (in Figure 3.1), to the propositional content rather than the illocutionary force in the previous utterance. Television comedies and family arguments are good sources of data. Share and explain your examples in your tutorial group.
3. Choose an emotion such as anger or a behaviour such as showing tenderness or criticizing someone. During the next few days, see if you can provoke this emotion or behaviour in someone else. Report your strategies and your interlocutor's exact utterances to colleagues in your tutorial group.
4. Find a partner and together choose a picture of a couple from a colour magazine. Each of you should take the role of one of the people in the picture. Decide who will speak first and what proposition they will convey. The speaker should then try several different ways of conveying the agreed meaning – each time the person addressed gives it a score out of ten for effectiveness.
5. What is the relationship between language and touch? Out of class, note the occasions when language accompanies touch. Note down what you observe carefully and report it in your tutorial group.
6. How do people express disagreement? Out of class, listen out for disagreements. Note down what you overhear and report it in your tutorial group.

Further reading

Primary texts: Austin, J.L. (1962, 1971); Morgan, J.L. (1978); Searle, J.R. (1965, 1969, 1975).

Textbooks: Levinson, S.C. (1983: 226–83); Mey, J. (1993: 109–75); Schiffrin, D. (1994: 49–96); Thomas, J. (1995: 28–54); Yule, G. (1996: 47–56).

4 Implicit meaning: Grice's theory of conversational implicature

Words are like leaves; and where they most abound,
Much fruit of sense beneath is rarely found.
(Alexander Pope, *An Essay on Criticism*, 309–10)

> *Keywords* (conversational) implicature, entailment, context, inference, conventional meaning, cooperative principle, maxim, flout, hedge, truth value, generalized and particularized implicatures, relevance, scalar implicature, defeasibility, historical pragmatics

4.1 Entailment and implicature

This chapter begins with a problem: how is it that we understand

(1)   It's the taste

in the Coca-Cola advertisement to mean that the taste is good? By itself, *It's the taste* means very little – in fact, we are not even told what the taste is or what it does. And yet we understand a meaning that is not explicitly stated at all. And more puzzling still, when my daughter comes home from school and starts her destructive journey through the biscuit barrel, and I ask her why she didn't eat her school dinner, and she replies *It's the taste*, I understand her to mean exactly the opposite: that the taste is not good. How can the same sentence be understood to convey two meanings that are the opposite of one another and neither of which is explicitly stated by the speaker? This is the problem addressed in this chapter.

You might at first think that there could be something special about *It's the taste*. But this isn't the case at all. For example, we would probably all understand the theatre critic talking about the opening night of the musical *Heathcliff* in the same way. What she said was

(2)   I looked at my watch after two hours and realized that only twenty
        minutes had passed (*Today*, BBC Radio 4)

Although she didn't say that the show was boring, we understand her to
mean that it was. But how?

Let's go back to an example from Chapter 1 and our entertaining postmaster. This is the context of the mind-the-step utterance. A customer is
complaining about the notes he'd been given:

(3)   CUSTOMER: These aren't very clean – I gave you clean ones last time
        POSTMASTER: Be careful you don't trip over the step on your way out

Notice that he didn't tell the customer that he was a fussy old idiot, but he
certainly conveyed it. And if the customer didn't get the message at the time,
he would certainly have realized it as he left and found that in our post office
there isn't a step on the way out.

One Saturday morning I went in when the post office had just opened:

(4)   POSTMASTER: It's a nice morning isn't it
        PETER: Not bad
        POSTMASTER: It'll be better at one o'clock

I understood him to mean that he'd be happier when the post office had
closed, but again, he never explicitly stated this.

The only time I heard anyone get the better of him was when an elderly
lady, who was hardly as tall as the counter, went into a long description of
what had happened the day before, which she found unsatisfactory. The
conversation went like this:

(5)   CUSTOMER: I gave you a pound yesterday, etc., etc.
        POSTMASTER: My it's early in the morning isn't it
        CUSTOMER: It's too early for you

Although the postmaster didn't actually tell the customer that he thought she
was talking rubbish, he certainly conveyed it. And although the customer
didn't actually tell the postmaster that he was stupid, he became unaccount-
ably silent all of a sudden.

So the problem is this: how is it that in almost every utterance we can
distinguish between what is said and what is meant? By the end of this
chapter, you should have a better idea about how to answer this question.

For the present, it's sufficient to notice that the context is very important
in determining what someone means by what they say. For example, the two
contexts in which *It's the taste* occurs help us to decide what the speaker
means by saying it on each occasion. Or in

(2)   I looked at my watch after two hours and realized that only twenty
        minutes had passed

the first part of what is said establishes a context with which the second part
is inconsistent. And whether or not there is a step to trip over makes a big

difference to understanding what is meant by saying *Be careful you don't trip over the step on your way out.* And knowing that the post office closes at one o'clock on a Saturday enables us to understand what is meant by saying *It'll be better at one o'clock.* And because it's part of our culture to believe that people find it hard to think properly early in the morning, we understand why *it's early in the morning isn't it* conveys that the postmaster couldn't follow his customer's line of reasoning and therefore it had to be tortuous. Given different contexts, we would have understood each of these utterances quite differently.

Thinking of context, you may recall that in each of the three previous chapters I've suggested that understanding pragmatic meaning involves identifying a context that will make sense of an utterance. In various different ways this holds good for deixis, speech acts and, what we are going to explore in this chapter, implicature. A single example (whose context I won't tell you right away) will illustrate this point well:

(6)   A: Are you working this afternoon
      B: I'm going back to the office

Deictic context   Unless you know the speakers involved in the exchange, you don't know who *you* and *I* refer to. Unless you know whether the exchange takes place in the morning or once the afternoon has already commenced, you don't know whether *this afternoon* picks out the whole of the afternoon or the remaining part of it. And unless you know on which date the exchange takes place, you don't know which afternoon is referred to.

Speech act context   If A and B are a couple, A might be requesting B to do some shopping; or if A is B's boss, A may be hinting that it's time B went back to work; or if A knows that B has two workplaces, the question may count as a request to be told where B is working; or if B has a car and A works near B's office, A might be asking for a lift. In other words, there are as many potential speech acts as there are contexts.

Implicature context   In fact, I was A and B was someone I'd never met before who I got talking to at a publisher's lunch. Other important elements of the context are that we had been given several glasses of wine to drink and it was a Friday. The lunch was in London and B knew I came from Durham and therefore wouldn't be working in the afternoon. My question was intended to imply that I would feel sorry for him if he had to go back to work. I took his reply to mean that, although he would be going back to his office, he didn't expect to be doing any work there.

Once again, this example shows how important context is in helping us to understand utterances. In the case of deixis, context helps us to resolve matters of reference, and in the case of speech acts to determine the speaker's intentions. In the case of implicature, context helps us to determine what is conveyed implicitly but not explicitly stated by the speaker. In this and the next chapter, we will explore just how this kind of a meaning is recovered.

4.1.1 Grice's theory of conversational implicature

In order to solve the problem of how we understand speakers to mean things that they don't actually say, we need first to draw a distinction between what the linguistic philosopher Paul Grice (1967a) called the 'natural' and the 'non-natural' meanings of utterances like

(7)   Manchester United won.

The natural meaning is that Manchester United scored at least one goal more than the team they were playing against. We call this kind of meaning an entailment, a meaning that is present on every occasion when an expression occurs. So when you are talking about football, you can never say that a team 'won' without it entailing that they scored at least one goal more than their opponents. Unlike the entailment, the 'non-natural' meaning is variable and on different occasions (7) could convey the meaning that Manchester United played particularly well or only rather modestly. This 'non-natural' meaning is only sometimes associated with the sentence from which it may be inferred and is therefore not part of the entailment.

Grice argued that speakers intend to be cooperative when they talk. One way of being cooperative is for a speaker to give as much information as is expected. So an addressee who knew that Manchester United were playing a top team in a European competition might be expecting the speaker to say that they had done reasonably well considering the circumstances. Since *Manchester United won* would be more than was expected, the speaker would imply that they had done brilliantly. Conversely, an addressee who knew that Manchester United were playing a non-league side might be expecting the speaker to say that they had scored several goals or that they had wiped out the opposition. Hearing only *Manchester United won*, less than might be expected, the hearer would draw the inference that they had played rather poorly. Because *Manchester United won* in the first context is more than the addressee was expecting and in the second less, in each case it gives rise to a non-conventional meaning. This kind of meaning was called an 'implicature' by Grice. He deliberately chose this word of his own coinage to cover any meaning that is implied, i.e., conveyed indirectly or through hints, and understood implicitly without ever being explicitly stated.

Checking understanding (4.1) ——————————————

What implicatures are associated with the following utterances?

(8)   Some people believe in God

(9)   The plumber made a reasonable job of fitting our new boiler

(10)   I've got £100 to last me until the end of the month

(11)   Maurice Greene can run 100m in 9.8 seconds

Grice formalized his observation that when we talk we try to be cooperative by elevating this notion into what he called 'The Cooperative Principle'.

The Cooperative Principle   Make your conversational contribution such as is required, at the stage at which it occurs, by the accepted purpose or direction of the talk exchange in which you are engaged.

Within this Principle, he suggested four maxims.

1. QUANTITY

(a)   Make your contribution as informative as is required (for the current purposes of the exchange).

(b)   Do not make your contribution more informative than is required.

Thus

(12) The students are making progress

being all the information the speaker provides, gives rise to the implicature that the students aren't doing brilliantly, and

(13) I don't drink

invites the implicature that the speaker doesn't drink alcohol.

2. QUALITY
Try to make your contribution one that is true

(a)   Do not say what you believe to be false

(b)   Do not say that for which you lack adequate evidence

Thus

(14) Pragmatics is difficult

being assumed to be well founded, gives rise to the implicature that the speaker believes or has evidence that it is, and

(15) When will dinner be ready?

being assumed to be a sincere question, gives rise to the implicature that the speaker doesn't know, has a reason for wanting to know, and thinks the addressee does know.

3. RELATION
Be relevant. Thus

(16) You've got up to here now

gives rise to the most relevant implicatures, viz for *here*, page 74 (rather than Grice's third maxim, etc.) and for *now*, at this stage in your Pragmatics course (rather than today, since 1979, in the twentieth century, etc.).

4. MANNER
Be perspicuous

(a)   Avoid obscurity of expression
(b)   Avoid ambiguity
(c)   Be brief (avoid unnecessary prolixity)
(d)   Be orderly

Thus

(17) They washed and went to bed

being an orderly representation of the world, gives rise to the implicature *in that order*, and the following opening sentence of a letter from a life insurance company

(18) As one of our policy holders, I hope you'll already know that
        creating products which provide excellent value is our aim at
        Scottish Widows

is taken to convey the less obscure implicature that the recipient of the letter rather than its writer is the policy holder.

Checking understanding (4.2)

Grice observes that we are cooperative in other endeavours besides talk. Imagine two people working together on a single task such as cleaning a car, or building a wall, or changing a light bulb. Can you think of any cooperative strategies they might use that are like those that apply in talk?

4.1.2 Flouting maxims

The implicatures that arise from examples (12)–(18) arise because the addressee assumes that the speaker is abiding by Grice's maxims, i.e. (12) is as informative as required, (14) is well founded, (16) is maximally relevant in its context and (18) is to be read in a way that assumes its perspicuity. But the thought has probably already gone through your mind that speakers do not always abide so rigorously by these maxims. For example, if I say, as I frequently do:

(19) It's just Coco being Coco

(you should know that Coco is a horse who doesn't always do exactly what you want), I am clearly not abiding by the maxim of Quantity in that the information I give does not appear, at least superficially, to be informative to the expected degree. However, you don't have any difficulty knowing what I mean.

    On one occasion I just stopped myself in time from responding to a complaining student with

(20) Well, it is a university

Although (20) flouts a maxim, notice that there is still an implicature. The addressee will assume that, despite flouting a maxim, the speaker is essentially cooperative and must therefore be intending to convey a meaning. I cannot sensibly be intending to convey the entailment of *Well, it is a university* since this meaning is already known to the addressee.

In fact, whenever a maxim is flouted there must be an implicature to save the utterance from simply appearing to be a faulty contribution to a conversation. In the case of (20), the addressee will try to work out what I am intending to convey in addition to the information that was already known to them (i.e. that we are in a university) – perhaps that there is no point in complaining since what the complainant has noticed is to be expected. This is the implicature, what is implicit in (20) but nowhere explicitly stated.

When you stop to think about it, it's obvious that statements that are self-evidently true or self-evidently false must be uttered for some other purpose than to convey merely their stated meaning. Such utterances will be especially obvious invitations to look for an implicature. As we noted in Chapter 1, utterances like

(21) I'm a man

whether spoken by a man (self-evidently true and therefore a flout on Quantity) or by a woman (self-evidently false and therefore a flout on Quality) will alert the addressee/s to an implied meaning.

Checking understanding (4.3)

1. Is it possible to flout all four of the maxims? Decide whether the following utterances are flouts, and, if so, of which maxims:

(22) It's part of the culture – it survives because it survives (Commentator on the Miss American competition, BBC Radio 4)

(23) Have you seen that room of hers

(24) PETER: Have you done your homework
   ELEANOR: Joanna had her ear pierced today

(25) Dogs take lead from owner (headline in *The Times*, 21 July 1997)

2. The following rhetorical strategies have been considered flouts of Gricean maxims. Which maxim do you think each flouts?

Tautology
(26) At the end of the day the Church can only afford to pay the number of people it can afford to pay (a bishop speaking on the *Sunday* programme on BBC Radio 4 when asked whether there would be job cuts in the Church)

Metaphor
(27) Money doesn't grow on trees but it blossoms at our branches (Lloyd's Bank advertisement)

Overstatement
(28) Now we've ALL been screwed by the Cabinet (*Sun* headline)

Understatement
(29) This is not a man who would have been a natural member of the Liberal Democrats (Paddy Ashdown, former leader of the Liberal Democrats, following the death of the Chinese leader Deng Xiao-ping, *Today*, BBC Radio 4)

Rhetorical question
(30) How many divisions has the Pope (attributed to Stalin)

Irony
(31) The world's most exciting politician (said of the unglamorous Bob Dole, the Republican candidate in the 1996 American Presidential election)

3. Advertisements often flout Manner. Can you say in which way each of the following advertisements does this?

(32) Ahead of current thinking (National Power advertisement)

(33) In cordless technology we have the lead (Black & Decker advertisement)

(34) The best 4 x 4 x far (Land Rover advertisement)

(35) The best 4 x 4 x PHONE (Land Rover advertisement)

(36) First and fourmost (Land Rover advertisement)

(37) In a glass and a half of its own (Cadbury's chocolate advertisement)

(38) We take the mega*hurts* out of buying a PC (newspaper advertisement for computers)

(39) Walter Wall Carpeting (the name of a chain of carpet stores)

(40) They say beauty is in the eye of the beholder. But no eyes are more critical than yours (advertisement for an optician on suburban trains in Dublin)

(41) You just can't help yourself (written message accompanying a television advertisement for McCain pizzas in which the cook takes a piece of pizza for herself before serving her guests and then tries to make it look as though the pizza is still intact)

(42) BA better connected person (British Airways advertisement)

(43) Acts on the spot (advertisement for an acne preparation)

Why do you think this sort of flout is so common in newspaper headlines and advertisements?

4. Are you now able to explain why *It's the taste* gives rise to the implicatures suggested at the beginning of the chapter?

Summary

There are guiding principles which govern cooperative talk. Knowing these principles (maxims) enables an addressee to draw inferences as to the implied meanings (implicatures) of utterances. Every utterance, whether it abides by or flouts the maxims, has both 'natural' meaning (entailment) and 'non-natural' meaning (implicature). Flouting a maxim is a particularly salient way of getting an addressee to draw an inference and hence recover an implicature. Thus there is a trade-off between abiding by maxims (the prototypical way of conducting a conversation) and flouting maxims (the most salient way of conveying implicit meaning).

4.1.3 Hedging maxims

Sometimes when we talk we simply make assertions like

(44) Smoking damages your health

But if you listen carefully when people talk, you notice that speakers are frequently reluctant to make bald statements like this, instead preferring an utterance like (45), which might be taken to indicate that the speaker does not want to engage in further argument:

(45) All I know is smoking damages your health

In this utterance, the speaker is making the assertion that *smoking damages your health*. But by prefacing it with *all I know is*, the speaker simultaneously advises the addressee that the quantity of information being conveyed is limited. So the speaker makes an assertion and at the same time advises the addressee of the extent to which they are observing the maxims. Thus the maxim of Quantity is 'hedged' – in the same sense that we can talk about 'hedging' a bet.

If the speaker had said

(46) They say smoking damages your health

they say would be understood as a hedge on the maxim of Quality and would serve as a warning to the addressee that the speaker's information might not be as well founded as would normally be expected. So *all I know* in (45) and *they say* in (46) have a metalingual function, that is, they serve as glosses or comments on the extent to which the speaker is abiding by the conversational maxims.

Remember Pat in Chapter 1 and how she hedged Relation when she said

(47) What's your name by the way

Here *by the way* advises Stephen that what Pat has just said is not as relevant at the stage at which it occurs in the conversation as he is entitled to expect. When she was nine, my daughter went with a friend to see *Arsenic and Old Lace*, the play in which two sweet old ladies poison a string of male visitors. She described afterwards how, at one stage in the play, a character had said he thought it was his last glass of elderberry wine, making it clear by the way she related it that *last* was meant to be ambiguous between 'last that evening' (the speaker's idea) and 'last because he was going to die' (how the audience took it). Then she added

(48) It was dead funny – if you see what I mean

If you see what I mean hedges the maxim of Manner. Having said *It was dead funny*, she realized she had produced a second, unintended pun, this time on *dead*, and so added *if you see what I mean* to advise us of the obscurity of her utterance.

We have seen how conversational maxims can be hedged with metalingual glosses. Speakers can also use metalingual glosses to assure their addressees that the maxims are being scrupulously complied with, as the following examples show:

(49) Smoking damages your health and that's all there is to it (Quantity)

(50) Smoking damages your health for sure (Quality)

(51) The point is that smoking damages your health (Relation)

(52) Put plainly, smoking damages your health (Manner)

One important point about these maxim hedges and intensifiers is that none of them adds truth value to the utterances to which they are attached. Thus examples (45)–(52) are true under just the same circumstances as counterpart sentences without the maxim hedges would be. This confirms that the hedges and intensifiers are more comment on the extent to which the speaker is abiding by the maxims which guide our conversational contributions than a part of what is said or conveyed. It seems then that when we talk, we not only convey messages, but frequently like to tell each other how informative, well founded, relevant and perspicuous these messages are.

Checking understanding (4.4) ──────────────────

1. List at least three hedges and three intensifiers for each conversational maxim.
2. Which parts of the utterance have truth value and which maxims do you think are being hedged or intensified by which phrases in the following answer provided by Sir Humphrey in the television comedy, *Yes Minister*?

(53) Well Minister, if you asked me for a straight answer, then I shall say that, as far as we can see, looking at it by and large, and taking one time with another, in terms of the averages of departments, then, in the final analysis, it is probably true to say that, at the end of the day, in general terms, you would probably find that, not to put too fine a point on it, there probably wasn't very much in it one way or the other, as far as one can see, at this stage.

Summary

Speakers frequently use highly grammaticalized hedges and intensifiers to inform their addressees of the extent to which they are abiding by the maxims. These hedges and intensifiers show that the guiding principles for talk suggested by Grice really do exist and that speakers orient reflexively to these principles as they communicate.

4.1.4 Implicature and entailment

So far we have demonstrated that one kind of meaning, implicature, arises as a result of interactants' mutual knowledge of the conversational maxims. The non-conventional status of this meaning is illustrated by utterances like *It's the taste*, which is non-conventional in the sense that it gives rise to different implicatures in different contexts of use. This is really another way of recognizing that an implicature is the result of an addressee drawing an inductive inference as to the likeliest meaning in the given context. So when someone is trying to sell us something, *It's the taste* will give rise to a quite different implicature from that inferred when we are discussing school dinners.

An inductive inference is a conclusion derived from a set of premises sufficient to justify it for so long as no additional data are added which would cause a different conclusion to be arrived at. Consider the following utterance

(54) We have a child

The obvious inference to draw is that we have one and not more, since the Quantity maxim enjoins us to provide as much information as is required. But if additional information inconsistent with the inference is adduced (such as the existence of a second child), then the original inference is no longer valid. So if I am asked when buying a Family Railcard whether we have a child, I can reasonably say

(55) Yes, we have a child, in fact we have two

But there are no circumstances under which I will ever be able to say

(56) *We have a child, in fact we have none

This tells us that (54) entails at least one child and implies not more than one. Any attempt to deny the entailment, the conventional meaning, of (54) (*at least one*) must always result in a contradiction, since the speaker is simultaneously saying *x and not-x*. An implicature, on the other hand, is an inductive inference drawn by the speaker which will be valid on most occasions, a best guess as to the meaning being conveyed. As such, it may be cancelled if an additional premise inconsistent with the inference is added. Hence the implicature inferred from (54) *no more than one* may be denied, as (55) demonstrates.

Notice also that the direction of the entailment and the implicature cannot be derived algorithmically from example (54), but instead is determined by world knowledge. Hence

(57) Maurice Greene can run 100m in 9.8 seconds [Implicature: not less than 9.8], in fact he can run it in 9.7

is grammatical, whereas

(58) *Maurice Greene can run 100m in 9.8 seconds [Entailment: not more than 9.8], in fact he can run it in 9.9

is not.

Summary

We began with Grice's hypothesis that there are agreed guidelines for talk. We have now been able to show two distinct kinds of meaning, one of which, implicature, arises as a direct consequence of interactants accepting these cooperative strategies. Thus what is conveyed in an utterance will typically consist of what is said or entailed on the one hand and what is implied on the other. This is represented in Figures 4.1, 4.2 and 4.3.

conveyed
    said/entailed
    conversationally implicated   **Figure 4.1**

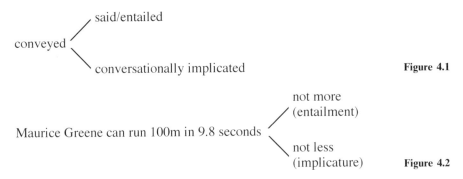

Maurice Greene can run 100m in 9.8 seconds
    not more
    (entailment)
    not less
    (implicature)   **Figure 4.2**

Entailments are conventional or semantic meanings which cannot by definition be cancelled without creating a contradiction; implicatures are inductive inferences which the hearer draws, and may therefore be cancelled:

Maurice Greene can run 100m in 9.8 seconds
    *in fact he can run
    it in 9.9
    in fact he can run
    it in 9.7   **Figure 4.3**

4.1.5 Particularized and generalized conversational implicature

Grice (1967a) drew a distinction between what he termed 'generalized' and what he termed 'particularized' conversational implicature. Generalized conversational implicatures arise irrespective of the context in which they occur. So examples like

(8)   Some people believe in God

and

(10) I've got £100 to last me till the end of the month

always give rise to the same generalized implicatures no matter what the context. And these are clearly implicatures rather than entailments since they can be denied:

(59) Some people believe in God [Implicature: not all], in fact everyone does

(60) I've got £100 to last me until the end of the month [Implicature: not more], in fact I've got 200.

In the case of generalized conversational implicatures such as those that arise in (59) and (60), the issue is not what is the most relevant way to take *some* or *£100* – the same inferences (*not all*; *not more*) will always be drawn whatever the particular context.

However, (8) might also give rise to a whole range of other implicatures which do depend on the context. For example, *you believe in God, you don't believe in God, I believe in God, I don't believe in God, our parents believe in God*, etc. Clearly there are as many implicatures as there are contexts. Similarly, if someone uttered (10), you might draw several different inferences depending on the context – the speaker could imply that she wanted to borrow money from you, or that she could lend you money, or that she was a good money manager, or that she could pay the telephone bill but not the rent, etc.

Because each of these implicatures is context-bound, Grice called them 'particularized'. They are clearly different in kind from the context-free, generalized conversational implicatures associated with words like *some*. Particularized implicatures are inferences that we need to draw if we are to understand how an utterance is relevant in some context. Thus the particularized implicatures that arise in the case of utterances like

(1)   It's the taste

are derived, not from the utterance alone, but from the utterance in context.

The difference between generalized and particularized implicature will turn out to be a very important one for this reason: if all implicatures were particularized, one could reasonably argue that the single maxim of Relation, or Relevance, was sufficient to account for all implicature. The implicature would be what the addressee had to assume to render the utterance maximally relevant in its context. But generalized conversational implicature has little or nothing do with the most relevant understanding of an utterance; it derives entirely from the maxims, typically from the maxims of Quantity and Manner. When a speaker uses the quantifier *some*, it is because they are not in a position to use the quantifier *all*, and are therefore taken to be implying *not all* by the Quantity maxim.

We can now add this further distinction to Figure 4.1 in the previous Summary (see Figure 4.4).

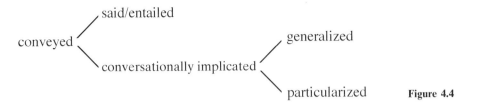

Figure 4.4

4.1.6 Scalar implicature

Gazdar (1979) argues that these kinds of data show that we operate with scales, so that one scale would include *all* and *some* and another *do brilliantly* and *make progress*. Choosing any item on a scale will imply that the items above it (or below it if we're talking about times for running 100m) do not obtain. Other hypothesized scales include <certain ... probable ... possible>, <and ... or> and <must ... may ... might>. This explains why we can resolve the problem of potential ambiguity that arose when I asked my tipster friend at the racecourse

(61) Would you recommend 8 or 9

(meaning horse number 8 or horse number 9). In such a case, *or* might mean *either 8 or 9 but not both* or it might mean *either 8 or 9 or both*. This indeterminacy would be resolved if I added, 'it has to be just one because I haven't enough money left to back both', in which case I would clearly intend *or* to mean *either 8 or 9 but not both*. Similarly, if I added, 'I'm looking for a couple of possible horses for a dual forecast', I would clearly intend *or* to mean *either 8 or 9 or both*. These two meanings can be explained by appealing to the notion of scalar implicature. Because *or* is on a scale below *and*, a speaker selecting *or* would be implying *not and*. Thus *either 8 or 9 or both* is an entailment and *either 8 or 9 but not both* is an implicature. But the implicature is cancelled by adding the sentence about the dual forecast. This account of *or* saves us having to say that there are two different *ors* and that each needs its own dictionary entry. Thus we see how implicature enables us to give a simpler account of the semantic representation of *or*.

It is interesting to listen out for these scales when people talk. I was once at a meeting where I heard a student talked about in the following way:

(62) He wasn't a poor candidate, but he was a weak candidate

It occurred to me that one couldn't have switched these descriptions around to produce

(63) *He wasn't a weak candidate, but he was a poor candidate

although the following dramatic escalation is possible for a more mocking speaker:

(64) He wasn't a weak candidate: he was a poor candidate.

These examples show that when we are talking about candidates, there is a scale that includes <poor ... weak>, with *poor* being a stronger condemnation than *weak*.

These scales also apply to clause structure, so that the use of conjunctions such as *if* and *or* enable us to draw the conclusion that speakers cannot commit themselves to asserting the proposition(s) within the clauses so introduced. Thus

(65) If I've got £100 to last until the end of the month ...

gives rise to the implicature *possibly I have £100 to last until the end of the month /possibly I do not have £100 to last until the end of the month*, although usually the wider context helps the addressee to understand which of the two possibilities is the likelier. Thus when I received information earlier this year about how to get to a conference, I ignored the sentence *If you are staying at the Parliament Hotel, Lord Edward Street is shown on the map* because I had already been told that I would be staying at a different hotel. A colleague was less fortunate. Having forgotten that he had already been allocated a hotel, he assumed that he wouldn't have been informed about the Parliament Hotel unless he had been staying there, and presented himself at midnight after a night on the town, only to find there were no rooms available!

4.1.7 Non-conversational implicature

Our children once chose a tube of toothpaste on the grounds that it had coloured stripes in it. The legend on the tube said

(66) Actually fights decay

I was glad they chose the striped toothpaste because *actually fights decay* is such a perfect example of a conventional, or non-conversational, implicature. The lexical item 'actually' has a literal meaning or entailment – it means *in reality* or *in actuality*. But it also conveys a secondary, implied meaning which is something like *although this is hard to credit*. This is an implicature because it is not part of the entailment of *actually*. It is conventional in the sense that it is closely associated with the particular lexical item. Levinson defines conventional implicatures as 'non-truth-conditional inferences that are *not* derived from superordinate pragmatic principles like the maxims, but are simply attached by convention to particular lexical items or expressions' (1983: 127).

Other examples of conventional implicatures include *but*, *even* and *still*, as in these examples taken from President Clinton's national TV address (18 August 1998) on the Monica Lewinsky affair:

(67) It constituted a critical lapse in judgement and a personal failure on my part for which I am solely and completely responsible. [New paragraph in written version] *But* I told the grand jury today and I say to you now that ...

(Entailment – *and*; conventional implicature – there is a contrast between the two conjoined propositions)

(68) *Even* Presidents have private lives

(Entailment – *in addition/too/as well*; conventional implicature – the proposition to which *even* is attached is at the end of a scale of expectability)

(69) I answered their questions truthfully, including questions about my private life, questions no American citizen would ever want to answer. [New paragraph in written version] *Still*, I must take full responsibility for all my actions

(Entailment – *in the continuing present*; conventional implicature – in spite of what has been said before, there is a further situation to consider in the present).

We can now add conventional implicature to the equation as shown in Figure 4.5.

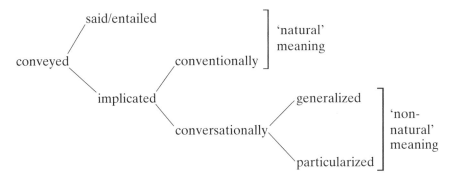

Figure 4.5

Summary – entailment and implicature I have a friend who is a fanatical Manchester City supporter. As Manchester City live very much in the shadow of their more successful neighbours, Manchester United, and had a very bad run of form in the 1990s, he has had to endure a certain amount of ridicule. Imagine he says to me

(70) Some Manchester City supporters are actually sane

we can distinguish the following kinds of meaning.

- Entailment: a number of Manchester City supporters are in reality sane.
- Conventional implicature deriving from *actually*: it's hard to believe what is predicated of *Some Manchester City supporters*.
- Generalized conversational implicature deriving from *some*: *not all Manchester City supporters are sane.*
- Particularized conversational implicature: the possibilities include *I'm sane, I'm not the pitiable idiot you think I am, You should admire my loyalty, Manchester City are a good side despite appearances to the contrary.*

4.1.8 Recognizing implicature

This section will close with a series of exercises containing examples of utterances and written texts which invite the recovery of implicatures. This will enable you to check that you are able to identify the implicatures that arise and the maxims that are hedged and flouted, and the means by which an addressee infers implicated meaning.

Checking understanding (4.5) ————————————————

Conversational implicature as non-conventional In August/September 1992 a WH Smith advertisement featuring various items of stationery appeared on hoardings in Britain. The poster bore the legend:

(71) We don't sell uniforms

This advertisement was followed by a series of 'We don't sell . . .' posters, which included an advertisement shortly before Christmas featuring videos of romantic films bearing the legend:

(72) We don't sell hankies

What are the implicatures in these two advertisements and how do they illustrate the non-conventional nature of conversational implicature?

Checking understanding (4.6) ————————————————

Flouts Which maxim is flouted by each of the following examples? How is the maxim flouted and what is the implicature or effect of the flout in each case?

(73) Am I seeing double (Question put to his friend by a potential customer standing in front of an optician's shop displaying a billboard on which was written *Appointment not always neccessary* [sic])

(74) Standard – sub-standard I call them (Comment made by a friend after lighting a series of disappointing fireworks bearing the *Standard* brand name)

(75) Also available in white (Comment scratched in the dirt on a white car)

(76) Just desserts (Menu heading in a restaurant)

(77) To celebrate a life of note. A coin. (Advertisement for a commemorative coin struck to celebrate Prince Charles's fiftieth birthday)

Checking understanding (4.7) ————————————————

Implicature and stress What is the effect of the stress on *and* in the following advertisement?

(78) Radion removes dirt AND odours

Checking understanding (4.8)

Correcting an implicature What is going on in the following utterance?

(66) That was David Smeaton in, or rather more precisely on, Dartmoor
      (*Today*, BBC Radio 4)

Checking understanding (4.9)

What implicature about the relative quality of the students at the two universities do you infer from

(79) Cambridge don't get the same calibre of students as Durham

and what implicature do you infer about what has been said before from

(80) Can I ask a more serious question

Can you account for what may appear to be rather surprising implicatures?

Checking understanding (4.10)

Implicature and axiology
1. When we see an advertisement for a car that comes in several different models
    at different prices, we expect the price range to go from the lowest to the
    highest (e.g. from £12,999 to £14,999). However, in a recent Skoda advertise-
    ment, this conventional axiology was reversed so that the highest price was
    listed first and the lowest second. What implicature does this convey?

2. Comment on the implicatures that arise in the following cases where the
    conventional axiology is reversed.

(81) England fail to lose (Headline in the *Sun* newspaper after England
      drew a cricket match with South Africa)

(82) Now worse than ever (Advertisement for the *London Dungeon*, a
      museum of horrors)

(83) The value of investments can go down as well as up (Statutory
      warning that accompanies advertisements for financial services in
      UK)

(84) If you're as clever as Alister [our technician], you may be able to do
      it [download a printer file from the internet] for yourself. But if
      you're as clever as me, you'll ask Alister to do it for you

Checking understanding (4.11)

Conventional and conversational implicatures What is conveyed by the
following examples?

(85) It's a humiliation to be sacked even from the Labour Party front bench (Comment by a Conservative member of Parliament on the sacking of a Labour shadow minister [*Today*, BBC Radio 4])

(86) I have not even brought my wife into Horley Town Hall. That's what I think of Horley Town Hall (Leader of Horley Council speaking on BBC Radio 4)

Checking understanding (4.12)

Calculating implicatures Since an implicature is an inference, it must be calculable, in the sense that we can work out the steps that a hearer must follow to arrive at it. I recently stood for election to a faculty post. When the nominations closed, the other candidate telephoned and left a message with our administrator, Sara, which she wrote down as follows (I've changed the name of the candidate): *Hugh Martin called to say he sees you and he are rivals and he is sure the best person will win!* When I read the message, I said to Sara, 'I hope not.' What implicatures can you recover from Hugh's message and my comment, and how are they arrived at?

Checking understanding (4.13)

A series of separate utterances taken from a single television broadcast are given below. They are transcribed so as to show the difference between what was actually said and what the accompanying teletext subtitles shown on screen. Items printed in small capitals represent spoken text absent in the teletext subtitles. What principles does the subtitler use to determine which features of the spoken language to omit from the subtitles?

1. NOW when you eventually married you tried to find them again didn't you?
2. her son and her daughter by her first marriage had BOTH left home
3. BUT sixty years ago the stigma of illegitimacy was strong
4. at the same time it's ALSO frightening
5. but NEVERTHELESS one in which attitudes to illegitimacy
6. I knew I wasn't their flesh and blood SORT OF THING
7. AND OF COURSE we used to get a few swear words IN BETWEEN
8. I remember a family THIS WAS when I was about nine I suppose
9. because she seemed a bit cold towards me I SUPPOSE
10. BECAUSE I MEAN they owned a car and everything
11. and I JUST simply walked down this lane
12. so he JUST took the case off me
13. AND THEN I MUST HAVE passed
14. and you could please yourself COULDN'T YOU SORT OF THING
15. SO did you get on with his mother
16. two or three months ago I SHOULD THINK
17. I just said LIKE

18. and we didn't show it to that extent IF YOU KNOW WHAT I MEAN
19. OH yes YES
20. but I THINK it was when the children started to grow up
21. and the friendship grew from that WHICH WAS LOVELY
22. I grew up for a another six or seven years before it REALLY hit me
23. so I thought WELL if Betty was there
24. WELL IT'S VERY GOOD OF YOU BUT I'm not sure if I want to go on
25. and said WELL I was QUITE sure that's what families were for
26. but ER I rang Gloria in the afternoon
27. we felt as if we'd known each other for a long time ODDLY ENOUGH
28. the WHOLE SORT OF end product REALLY
29. it was nice THOUGH WASN'T IT
30. it's still hard FOR ME to believe that it's happened

The teletext data show how far we have come in this chapter. We began with Grice's hypothesis that there are maxims for the conduct of conversational interaction which can explain how implicit meanings are understood. We have now shown that these maxims enable us to account for the nature of one actually occurring talk type, the teletext subtitle, which systematically eliminates (a) grammaticalized maxim hedges and intensifiers; and (b) lexical items whose entailments can be recovered as implicatures.

4.1.9 Implicature and social meaning

Consider again the following examples from the teletext set of utterances in the last Checking understanding exercise:

(87) her son and her daughter by her first marriage had BOTH left home

(88) at the same time it's ALSO frightening

(89) and I JUST simply walked down this lane

(90) so he JUST took the case off me

(91) it's still hard FOR ME to believe that it's happened

In each of these cases, the item in small capitals is a lexical realization of what is implicated in the lower-case (subtitle) version of the spoken utterance. The speakers are therefore more explicit than the subtitle representations of their utterances. In the subtitles, the meanings that are elaborated in the spoken versions are conveyed implicitly. The issue is whether there is a difference in the social meaning depending on which level of explicitness is chosen. Would hard-of-hearing viewers dependent on subtitles and those listening to the spoken text feel differently about the speakers, or feel that the speakers were in different relationships with each other?

This line of discussion raises the fundamental question of how explicit or how implicit to choose to be when we speak. When I give a lecture, do I say merely 'and' and imply *and then* or do I say 'and then'? My choice must be determined to some degree by my audience – if I am implicit, I convey the notion that we belong to shared world, but at the same time run the risk that the inferences I intend my audience to draw may in fact not be drawn.

Or consider the case of resumptives. I once heard a rather anxious disk jockey on a North Sea ferry say

(92) You have to guess from which country the tune comes from

He was trying to encourage a less than enthusiastic audience to take part in a little bit of the kind of fun and games that most people are reluctant to join in. The usual syntactic explanation for utterances like (92) is that when a constituent moves and leaves a trace, this trace has been filled with a 'resumptive' form (in this case, the second *from*) so as not to disturb the canonical word order. As I listened to the rather tentative plea of the disk jockey, it occurred to me that perhaps resumptives show a kind of pragmatic indeterminacy. He was not sure whether to say

(93) You have to guess from which country the tune comes

(too formal) or

(94) You have to guess which country the tune comes from

(he didn't feel relaxed enough for this). In other words, I drew an inference as to what might be termed 'the social meaning' of his utterance. Since then I have been listening out for resumptives and have been surprised to find how often they seem to have a social meaning. For example, at a university committee meeting I attended, the secretary to the committee, an adminis-trator, was asked to clarify by the academic members how some proposed procedure might work. In the following utterance, her resumptive seemed to me to indicate that she was being tentative to avoid giving the impression of coercing academic members of staff:

(95) We'll need to check out with members of staff the areas in which
        they might be interested in

If she had said the more formal

(96) We'll need to check out with members of staff the areas in which
        they might be interested

this might have conveyed the implicature that it was official policy rather than a suggestion that had still to be agreed. And if she had said

(97) We'll need to check out with members of staff the areas which they
        might be interested in

this might have sounded too familiar and have conveyed the implicature that she was an in-group member who could speak for colleagues rather than a representative of the administrative support system. And after his first match in charge of the England football team, Terry Venables, talking about the importance of making chances, said

(98) ... which I thought we did that.

4.2 Types and tokens

4.2.1 Levels of meaning

So far in this chapter we have distinguished what is said or entailed (what our words mean) from what is implicated (what we mean by our words), and have treated these two categories of sentence meaning and speaker meaning as the superordinate distinction between levels of meaning. In this section, we will see whether we need to discriminate a little more neatly, and whether three levels of meaning might be more appropriate. This will involve looking more closely at the difference between generalized and particularized conversational implicature.

We have already seen how utterances like

(8)   Some people believe in God

give rise to the context-free, generalized Quantity (or Q) inference, that not everyone believes in God, and any number of context-dependent, particularized Relation (or R) inferences, such as that the speaker believes in God, or that the speaker doesn't believe in God, that the addressee believes in God, etc.

A similar phenomenon can be observed with utterances like

(99) I broke a pair of glasses this afternoon

and

(100) I broke a leg when I was sixteen

In (99), the addressee recovers as a Q-inference that the glasses probably belonged to someone other than the speaker as a scalar implicature since the speaker did not say *my glasses*. In (100), the addressee recovers as an R-inference that the speaker probably broke one of their own legs, since breaking someone else's leg is highly improbable.

In his paper 'Three levels of meaning', Levinson (1995) suggests that Q-inferences (and Manner, or M, inferences) are instances of utterance-type meaning, and R-inferences are instances of utterance-token meaning. What does he mean by this?

An utterance-type, as the name suggests, is a predictable type of utterance which has a regular inferred interpretation across a range of contexts. An utterance token is a single instance of an utterance whose one-off inferred interpretation depends upon its context. Thus, utterance-types yield conventional understandings whose meanings, unlike those of utterance-tokens, do not differ according to context. Utterance-type meaning resembles sentence meaning to the extent that it is expectable and thus, in one sense, 'conventional'. But it is unlike sentence meaning in that it is inferred and therefore defeasible (i.e. it can be cancelled) where the context disallows the inference, as in

(57) Maurice Greene can run 100m in 9.8 seconds, in fact he can run it in 9.7

However, because there is a conventional default inference associated with utterance-type meaning, it is unlike utterance-token meaning in that each instance of use does not require an inferential process which takes account of the context in order to determine what is meant by what is said.

As Levinson points out, the property of being to a degree conventional, which utterance-type meaning appears to share with sentence meaning, has made semanticists eager to view it as semantic. And because utterance-type meaning shares with utterance-token meaning the property of being a defeasible inference, pragmaticists too have been eager to claim it for themselves.

Checking understanding (4.14)

1. Earlier in the chapter, we suggested that

(13) I don't drink

invites the implicature that *I don't drink alcohol.* Is this an utterance-type or an utterance-token meaning? In a parallel Cantonese and English text taken from a public information leaflet distributed in Hong Kong, the English version of what one of the speakers says is

(101) I don't drink or smoke

and the Cantonese version (translated is)

(102) do not smoke, do not drink alcohol

Can you comment on the differences?

2. Shortly after the British Government Minister, Peter Mandelson, was forced to resign in a financial scandal, I heard a radio interviewer ask a trade union leader this question:

(103) Well, you've described the leaders of British industry as immoral, so why won't you say something about Peter Mandelson (BBC Radio 5)

Is there an implicature associated with *say something* and, if so, do you think it's an utterance-type or an utterance-token meaning that is recovered?

Levinson argues that utterance-type implicatures result from the insights (usually termed 'heuristics') that inform Grice's two maxims of Quantity and the maxim of Manner. The first Quantity (Q1) maxim – *Make your contribution as informative as is required (for the current purposes of the exchange)*

– is in effect an injunction to say as much as you need to or appropriately can. Thus, as Levinson puts it, 'What is not said is not the case' (1995: 97). Hence saying *some* gives rise to the inference *not all*. The <all ... most ... many ... some ... few ... none> quantifier scale and the <and ... or> logical connective scale, both of which we have discussed earlier, can thus be inferred as two of many such scales. Leech (1983: 91) argues that the Quantity maxim requires the use of the indefinite article when there is insufficient speaker-hearer shared knowledge to refer definitely. When we use *a/some* to refer to not-all the members of a speaker–hearer shared set, it is because we are not able to refer uniquely to all the members of a speaker–hearer shared set with the use of *the*. Hence <the ... a/some> is also a scale.

The Q1 maxim may also account for a well-known gap in the inventory of lexical items which exhibit incorporation of the negative particle. Consider the following:

- natural language can represent the existential quantifier (∃) of formal language (the language of logic) with words such as *a* and its plural form *some*, so that any description containing *a* or *some* refers to a single exemplar case or a number of exemplar cases
- natural language can represent the universal quantifier (∀) of formal language with words such as *all*, so that any description containing *all* refers to all the members of the set described
- natural language can represent the negation of the existential quantifier (~∃) with words such as *none*, so that any description containing *none* asserts that there are no cases (= not some) of what is described
- but natural language cannot represent the negation of the universal quantifier (~∀) with words such as *nall*, to denote not-all cases of what is described.

This phenomenon was first noted by Horn (1972), who attributes the non-lexicalizability of *nall* to the fact that it is a Q1 inference of *some*, i.e. in natural language *not all* is implied by the use of *some*. And since it is already an implicature, it is not lexicalized. The importance of this observation should not be overlooked. What Horn shows is that a conversational maxim – *Make your contribution as informative as is required (for the current purposes of the exchange)* – determines what concepts can be lexicalized. Thus the explanation for this lexical gap is pragmatic. And it turns out that incorporation of the negative particle is impossible in all cases where the meaning already exists as a Q1-inference. Thus:

we find *sometimes* and we find *always*;
we find *never* but we do not find *nalways* since 'not always' is an implicature of *sometimes*;

we find *permitted* and we find *obligatory*;
we find *forbidden* but we do not find *nobligatory* since 'not obligatory' is an implicature of *permitted*;

we find *or* and we find *both*;
we find *nor* but we do not find *noth* since 'not both' is an implicature of *or*.

Grice's second Quantity (Q2) maxim – *Do not make your contribution more informative than is required* – is an injunction to say as little as you can get away with. So that if you can rely on the hearer to resolve the indeterminacy of *child actor* and *child psychiatrist* as Q2 inferences to give 'a child who acts' and 'a psychiatrist who treats children', then you will use the simple, unmarked forms. Indeed, if you use the marked forms *a child who acts* and *a psychiatrist who treats children*, then you will invite an M-inference. Thus you may mean 'a child who acts' by saying *a child actor*, but you will mean something other than 'a child who acts' by actually saying *a child who acts* since there is a default unmarked form already available for conveying this meaning.

Recall the utterance discussed in Chapter 1:

(104) I've just finished a book

In most contexts this utterance-type will imply *finished reading a book*, just as in most (in fact virtually all) contexts *I don't smoke* will imply *don't smoke cigarettes* and *I don't drink* will imply *I don't drink alcohol*. However, there will be exceptional contexts in which (104) will routinely imply *finished writing a book*, just as there may be truly exceptional contexts (perhaps a conversation between two elderly dragons) in which *I don't smoke* will imply *smoke is not coming from me*. Thus these inferences are stereotypical, but will necessarily have exceptions since, as we see, they are not entailments that hold in every context.

Checking understanding (4.15) ────────────────────

1. There is a less than reassuring leaflet displayed in hospital waiting rooms in Britain whose title is

(105) What to do after a death

   Why would

(106) What to do after death

   not be appropriate?

2. Recall

(6)   A: Are you working this afternoon
      B: I'm going back to the office

   Why do you think I understood B's reply to mean that he wasn't going to do any work?

Consider

(107) John went to prison/school/market/church

(108) John went to a prison/school/market/church

and

(109) John went to the prison/school/market/church

Each gives rise to a quite different set of implicatures. Without a determiner, the implicature is that John was a prisoner/a pupil/a shopper/a worshipper, i.e. that he went to do the business typically done. The (107) examples are a typical case of saying as little a possible – the most stereotypical meaning is captured by the least effortful form as a Q2-inference. In the (108) examples, the inference is that John was a visitor and that the prison/school/market/church is not one with which the speaker is familiar. In the (109) examples, the inference is that the prison/school/market/church is one with which the speaker is familiar. These are Q1-inferences resulting from the determiner scale.

Another kind of compact structure is the conjunction reduction we saw in

(101) I don't drink or smoke

Here drinking alcohol and smoking cigarettes are Q2-inferred to be same type activities, an inference which the Cantonese parallel text

(102) do not smoke, do not drink alcohol

does not support. Indeed, *I don't smoke, I don't drink alcohol* would be a marked utterance in English and would invite the addressee to recover an M-inference (see below).

Another notable example of compact structures are conjunction reduced utterances like

(110) They went to the Library and registered for a course

which favours the implicated interpretation that the registration took place in the Library. Similarly,

(111) She took out her key and opened the door

favours the implicated interpretation that she used the key to open the door, and

(112) I forgot my book and couldn't do my assignment

favours the implicated interpretation that not being able to do the assignment was a consequence of forgetting the book. In (110), (111) and (112), the conjunction isn't simply logical, but enables the recovery of the Q2-inferences suggested above. But in

(113) They went to the Library and they registered for a course

the likeliest implicature is that the registration took place somewhere other than in the Library with *and* read as a logical connective. And even in

(114) She took out her key and she opened the door

the sense of temporal sequentiality is perhaps as strong as the Q2-inference that she used the key to open the door. It would be too strong a claim to suggest that only conjunction reduction allows Q2-inferences of this sort since *and* can be more than a logical connective in other cases too, such perhaps as

(115) I forgot my book and I couldn't do my assignment

But certainly conjunction reduction, or saying as little as you can get away with, is a strong pointer to the type of Q2-inference shown in (110)–(112).

Grice's Manner maxim – *Be perspicuous* – is an injunction to avoid marked expressions. Thus non-stereotypical expressions give rise to M-inferences characterizing non-expectable meanings. Earlier, I suggested that the more elaborate utterances and their teletext reduced counterparts perhaps had different social meanings. Although probably accurate as far as it went, we can now see this was probably an inadequate suggestion. Consider

(87)   her son and her daughter by her first marriage had BOTH left home

and

(91)   it's still hard FOR ME to believe that it's happened

These more prolix utterances may well invite M-inferences triggered by *both* in (87) and *for me* in (91). Yet in the teletext versions, *both* and *for me* are recovered as Q2 inferences.

Checking understanding (4.16)

1. I once heard the following 'joke' in an after-dinner speech:

(116) My father said it was time I went out and found a husband, so I
      went out and found Jane's

   Can you explain how this joke works?

2. What implicatures can you find in the following examples and from which
    maxims do they derive:

(117) It's good and loud

(118) It's good and it's loud

(119) It's good AND it's loud

Summary

Q2-inferences are unlike Q1- and M-inferences in that they provide general, expectable interpretations which reflect the conventional ways in which groups of speakers resolve the indeterminacy of minimalist utterances and expressions. As Levinson notes, Q1- and M-inferences are metalinguistic –

Q1-inferences make implicit reference to other, non-present members of a set, and M-inferences make implicit reference to other, unmarked but non-present expressions. Taken together, utterance-type meaning constitutes one of three levels of meaning alongside entailment and utterance-token meaning.

4.2.2 Historical pragmatics

Adjectives and the adverbs derived from nouns often exhibit semantic bleaching (i.e. loss of meaning) in the process of acquiring a new function. Thus, as we saw in the previous chapter, we have: *substance* → *substantial* → *substantially*. Similarly, the development of modal auxiliaries from full verbs in English involved both semantic as well as syntactic change. And once they were restricted to auxiliary function, these modals too gradually developed an epistemic meaning to reflect speaker belief or attitude (as in *she may be coming*) alongside their original deontic one (as in *The law states that children may not buy cigarettes*). Each of these functions is also restricted by syntactic co-occurrence constraints (e.g., deontic meaning does not allow progressive aspect).

From a pragmatic perspective, there is something suggestive about these historical changes – they seem to follow a pattern in which purely semantic items come to have a pragmatic function, including representing speaker attitude. Indeed, the use of a syntactic structure such as a matrix sentence which, as the highest sentence, we would expect to convey propositional meaning is sometimes used to convey propositional attitude with a function that mimics that of a sentence adverb. In (120), both the matrix sentence and the lower sentence have to be true for the sentence as a whole to be true, i.e. the matrix sentence contributes truth value:

(120) It is a truth universally acknowledged, that a married man in
       possession of a good fortune must be in want of a son and heir
       (opening sentence of Emma Tenant's novel *Pemberley*)

By contrast, *It's true that* in (121) reflects the commitment of the speaker to the quality of the proposition contained in the following part of the utterance and does not contribute truth value to the utterance as a whole:

(121) It's true that men want to be fathers

In fact, many pseudo-matrix sentences, such as *I think* and *they say*, hedge speaker commitment to maxims in this way. The question we need to investigate is how forms used to convey propositional meaning come to have a pragmatic function.

Work is only now beginning in the field known as 'historical pragmatics' whose purpose is to show the role of pragmatics in the process of language change. Thus Traugott (1989, 1995) has studied a number of discourse particles and shown how their contemporary meanings and function are instances of a process of gradual 'subjectification'. By this, she means that certain lexical items gradually come to be used to reflect speaker perspective with a discourse marking function. In the case of *in fact*, for example, Traugott traces the appearance of the noun *fact* in the sixteenth century and its occurrence with the preposition *in* in phrases like *in fact and experience* in the seventeenth century. She shows how *in fact* began to be used in the eighteenth century to express an epistemic attitude, i.e. to reflect speaker belief. Soon thereafter, it acquired an adversative function as in *x, but in fact y*, where the speaker advances *y* as a right way of viewing things over the earlier stated *x*. In the nineteenth century a further, not necessarily epistemic, additive function appears in which *in fact* is used metalinguistically as a discourse particle to promote a preferred proposition, as in 'in most (in fact virtually all) contexts', which you read a few pages back, or in the second sentence of this chapter, 'By itself, *It's the taste* means very little – in fact, we are not even told what the taste is or what it does.' Thus, a lexical item, the noun *fact*, acquires first an epistemic function when it occurs in the preposition phrase *in fact*, thus enabling a speaker to express a propositional attitude, and then acquires a further metalinguistic function, allowing a speaker to promote a preferred proposition over a preceding formulation.

In a plenary address at the 1998 IPrA (International Pragmatics Association) conference, Traugott appealed to inference and the three levels of meaning discussed in the previous section as a way of accounting for semantic change. Taking *so/as long as* as an example, she argued that the original temporal meaning first invited one-off inferences, so that as early as Old English *as long as* sometimes has utterance-token conditionality associated with temporal duration. In Early Modern English, the use of *as long as* to introduce non-temporal propositions to do with cognition becomes more frequent. These utterance-token uses favour interpreting *as long as* conditionally. Through a process of preferred use, perhaps motivated by subjectification, these utterance-token uses gradually acquire a conventional status and the conditional meaning becomes a Q2 utterance-type inference. In the final stage, which we find first in the nineteenth century, the conditional meaning of *as long as* is no longer an inference but a new semantic meaning. Time reference is no longer required and adverb promotion within the sentence it introduces is allowed (in contradistinction to the temporal use). This new meaning allows a subjective conceptualization in the clause that *as soon as* introduces which is not possible in the original temporal meaning. If you know German, you can probably trace out this same process for *wenn* (= when), which first began to appear with a conditional meaning in Old High German (Lockwood, 1968).

Historical pragmatics is a very recent area of study. But you can bet your bottom dollar that it is set to grow very rapidly. It's likely that obvious candidates for historical pragmatic analysis, such as the particles we have been dealing with in this chapter, *even*, *still*, *just*, *actually*, and many others that we haven't, like *surely* and *indeed*, will soon be added to by a wide range of other phenomena where pragmatic principles determine the process of grammaticalization.

Summary

The process of grammaticalization in which lexical items acquire new functions is especially obvious in the case of discourse particles like *in fact*, *even* and *indeed*. These new functions are inseparable from the semanticization process in which items acquire new or second meanings. Utterance-type inferences, and specifically Q2- and M-inferences, are likely to contribute to this process. This is because Q2-inferences enrich, and M-inferences, being derived from marked expressions or utterance tokens, invite consolidation as unmarked interpretations.

Conclusion

Some years ago I met a philosopher whose PhD supervisor had been Paul Grice. I couldn't resist asking him if it was true, as I had read, that Grice had a very untidy office. 'Not really,' he said, and indicating a large window went on to describe how Grice had only enough books in his office to fill the space occupied by the window. From the way the story was told, it was obvious that the speaker had expected Grice to have more books in his office. 'But,' the philosopher added in a significant manner, 'he had read them all.' We both laughed at the implicature.

I thought of that same implicature a year or two later, when I was in the office of a professor who was telling me that you could always judge an academic by his library. As I surveyed the rows and rows of books that looked as though they had been disturbed by nothing more intrusive than a duster, it was obvious that the person I was talking to had little in common with Paul Grice.

I cannot resist sharing one more Grice story with you. Not long after Grice died, my father and I were having lunch in the Oxford college were Grice had been an undergraduate (and where Austin and Urmson had worked on speech acts and Searle had been a postgraduate). It occurred to me that my father must have been a contemporary of Grice. Our conversation went like this:

(122) PETER: Were you here with Grice
     FATHER: \<Looks quizzical>
     PETER: Were you here with Paul Grice
     FATHER: \<Wrinkling his brow in an effort of concentration> Y-e-e-e-s \<And then remembering all too clearly> He always struck me as rather a studious type

The implicature was unmistakable – in the view of one of his contemporaries at least, Grice had not allocated his time at university as judiciously as he might have done!

Raising pragmatic awareness: implicit meaning (Grice)

1. This exercise works best with a partner or in a small group. Consider the way in which the likely interpretation of each of the utterances in List A would be altered by the insertion of each of the maxim hedges in List B.
   List A: I don't know, Do you know the way, She didn't say anything, It's a good idea, Tomorrow's Saturday
   List B: well, anyway, honestly, actually
   Make up your own List A and List B in such a way as to provide better examples than these.

2. Working individually, cut four pictures out of a magazine and choose a different comment to attach to each. Each comment should flout a different maxim. Share your pictures and comments with friends or in your tutorial group.

3. Next time you attend a tutorial in a subject other than linguistics, take a sheet of paper and divide it down the middle. On the left-hand side record what is said in a short conversation between the tutor and a student and on the right-hand side what is meant. Decide what implicatures arise and why. Bring this to your linguistics tutorial to share with colleagues.

4. Work with two friends. Each of you should spend a few days listening out for different conventional implicatures such as *actually*, *even* and *but* in conversations. Agree a time to meet up and share your findings.

5. Work with a television or radio interview. Copy down several utterances that contain maxim hedges. Bring them to your next tutorial and write them on the board without the hedges. Your colleagues should try to guess the original hedges. (Acknowledgement: this is Andrew Caink's idea.)

6 Choose a simple comic strip story and white out all the speech in the bubbles. Give it to the other members of your tutorial group and ask them to fill in the bubbles with maxim hedges only.

7. This exercise works best in a small group. Each member of the group takes one of the day's newspapers and identifies all the headlines which violate the Manner maxim. When you share your findings, try to arrange the violations on a cline from the most to the least extreme violation.

8. Each member of your tutorial group brings an utterance to the tutorial which they dictate. As each person dictates their utterance, everyone else writes down an imagined utterance spoken by the previous speaker which causes the dictated utterance to have an implicature. For example, you dictate *The scissors are in the drawer* and I imagine the previous speaker might have said, *Look at this new tie Roger's given me*. When the dictation is over, share the results. (Acknowledgement: this beautiful idea was thought up by Roger Maylor.)

Further reading

Primary texts: Grice, H.P. (1967a); Levinson, S.C. (1995).
Textbooks: Levinson, S.C. (1983: 97–166); Thomas, J. (1995: 55–86); Yule, G. (1996: 35–46).

5 Implicit meaning: Sperber and Wilson's Relevance Theory

'And as to the meaning, it's what you please.'
(*Ballad*, 1862, C.S. Calverley)

Keywords relevance, implicature, explicature, inference, higher level explicature, propositional form, indeterminacy, propositional attitude, procedural and conceptual encoding, salience

5.1 Determining relevance

In the previous chapter, we examined Grice's argument that contributions to talk are guided by the four maxims of Quantity, Quality, Relation and Manner. These maxims are mutually known to speakers and hearers. Thus, hearers are able to infer meanings as a result of the extent to which speakers' utterances appear to satisfy their expectations with respect to informativeness (Quantity), well-foundedness (Quality), relevance (Relation) and clarity (Manner). What is conveyed, therefore, consists of what is *said* (entailments) and what is *implied* (implicatures).

In this chapter, we will examine the argument set out in Sperber and Wilson's major book, *Relevance: communication and cognition* (second edition, 1995), that a single principle of relevance is sufficient to explain the process of utterance understanding. As we shall see, Sperber and Wilson are not satisfied with the probabilistic nature of Gricean implicature. They want a theory which goes beyond the probabilistic and enables addressees to be sure that they have recovered the most relevant of a potentially infinite set of inferences.

5.1.1 Explicature and implicature: three examples

The first example: recall the traffic sign

(1)   Angel parking

which we discussed in Chapter 1. I asked whether passing motorists were being advised that an angel was parking, or that there was a parking place for angels. I might equally have asked whether motorists were being advised that they could park their angels. But in fact you and I know that motorists are being advised that there is a parking place ahead for the vehicles of those who want to visit the sculpture known as the 'Angel of the North'. What's noticeable is that even elaborating the syntactic relation of *Angel parking* requires inferences which demand a great deal of real-world knowledge about angels and what road signs are for. This Q2-like inference results in what Sperber and Wilson call an **explicature**. An explicature is an enrichment of an original utterance, such as *Angel parking*, to a fully elaborated propositional form.

Conclusion: in order to understand what was meant by displaying this road sign, passing motorists needed to recover an explicature.

Here is the second example. When I took up a new post in 1994, the course leader of one of the courses I was to teach left a file in my pigeon-hole containing papers relevant to the course. A note was attached to this file with four written instructions. The third instruction was

(2)   Please attend course planning and examiners' meetings in future

My first reaction was one of panic – Oh no, I thought, I've missed some meeting I was supposed to attend. But as I reflected more carefully, it seemed to me that if I had missed a meeting, the message I'd received would be a rather unfriendly way of communicating such information to a new member of staff and uncharacteristic of the course leader, who seemed to be a very kind person.

What I was worrying about was determining the attitude of the writer of the message – her use of *please* told me that I was being instructed, but was she reprimanding me or was she telling me that a new responsibility had come my way? What I was uncertain of was the speech act description for her utterance. The inference I needed to make would yield what Sperber and Wilson call a **higher level explicature** which would reveal the propositional attitude of the speaker to her utterance.

Conclusion: in order to understand what Alice meant by her message, I needed to recover the appropriate higher level explicature.

The third example is as follows. If someone said to you

(3)   Have you seen my book

you would need to take a lot of context into account in order to determine what the speaker meant by their utterance. If the speaker was your room-mate and you had a habit of borrowing her property without permission, she might be accusing you of taking her book and the utterance might be taken as a demand for its return. But if your tutor said it to you as she handed back an essay, you might take it to mean that if you had read the book she had written you would have written a better essay. These inferences, *I want my book back* or *If you want to pass the exam you'd better read my book*, are **implicatures**. Unlike an explicature, an implicature, because it is entirely inferentially derived, has a logical form different from that of the original utterance.

Conclusion: In order to understand what someone means to convey when they say *Have you seen my book*, we need to recover an implicature.

Of course, in all three of these instances of written and spoken communication, there are explicatures, higher level explicatures and implicatures to be recovered. However, the most salient meanings are an explicature in (1), a higher level explicature in (2), and an implicature in (3). All are recovered as inferences. To put it another way, these inferred meanings are the most relevant ways of understanding what the originators of these messages meant by what they said (or wrote).

Checking understanding (5.1)

1. Recovering the higher level explicature in (2) was made more difficult because, as a new member of staff, I didn't know enough about the institution to enable me to recover even the explicatures. What problems do you think I faced in trying to recover these explicatures?
2. What explicatures and higher level explicatures would you first need to recover from (3) in order to recover the implicatures *I want my book back* (spoken by your room-mate) and *If you want to pass the exam you'd better read my book* (spoken by your tutor)?

5.1.2 Indeterminacy: the motivation for enrichment

Explicature, the inference or series of inferences that enrich the under-determined form produced by the speaker to a full propositional form are motivated by the indeterminacy of language. This indeterminacy is a consequence of the economy of expression which characterizes natural language – by saying *x* I may mean any one of '*A* which is more than *x*', '*B* which is more than *x*', '*C* which is more than *x*', etc. Thus determining even the sense of single items like *book* (physical object, contents, etc.) or *seen* (know the location of, have read, etc.) is far from straightforward. It requires an inferential process which provides an enriched interpretation consistent with the context of the utterance and the speaker's encyclopaedic knowledge. And as we have seen, not only single items, but even apparently straightforward syntactic relations such as that between a possessive determiner and a noun, as in the phrase *my book*, represent a wide variety of semantic relations that have to be inferred on each occasion of use. Previously, we had thought of the 'semantic' element of language as straightforward, but we owe to Sperber and Wilson the insight that, when language is used for communication, pragmatic inferences are required to determine even apparently invariant elements of meaning such as the sense of a lexical item.

Thus the title of a recently published cookery book

(4)   How to eat

is presumably to be explicated as something like *How to eat well*. The original title is enriched by the addition of the conceptual constituent *well*. And

(5)   SOCIOLOGY
       PAPER ONLY

as written on the waste-bin beside the photocopier at the end of our corridor, is to be understood as conveying the meaning that the waste-bin is the property of the Sociology Department and that only paper which has been used and is to be recycled should be put in it. In this case, several conceptual constituents have been added, as has the description of a real-world object, the waste-bin, which was not included in the original written message. And the traffic sign on our university campus that reads

(6)   Car park
       Psychology

is to be explicated along the lines of *This road leads to a car park and to the Psychology Department*. In this case, one of the processes of enrichment involves concept formation around the metonymic use of *Psychology*. (The use is metonymic because it represents only a part of the concept, the *Psychology* of *Psychology Department*, that the speaker intends to convey.) And the label of the package I saw in a supermarket (and then couldn't resist buying as a language souvenir)

(7)   No frills
       Men's disposal briefs

is to be explicated along the lines of *This package contains disposable briefs to be worn by men and which are sold as an item in the 'no frills' range of basic goods*. And the following 'neckbill' on a bottle of Portuguese wine

(8)   Buy 4 750ml bottles and get a short break for two in Portugal for the
       price of one!

is to be explicated so as to make it clear that the short break is not being offered for the price of a single bottle of wine.

As you can see, I've illustrated the point that explicature is necessary with examples where indeterminacy and economy of expression are so evident as to create potential ambiguity. But indeterminacy is present everywhere in language. Thus a Gricean account of what is meant by saying

(9)   Even Presidents have private lives

would identify a conventional implicature associated with *even*, but be principally concerned with determining the implicature. Relevance Theory will also account for the implicature, but not before explicating *Presidents* (Presidents of countries, and particularly this President of the United States of America), *have* (engage in) and *private lives* (extra-marital relationships). In Clinton's utterance, enriching the single term *Presidents* involves the addition of a conceptual constituent (*of countries*) and conceptualizing an exemplar case in the form of a referential description. Notice that in another context, this same utterance could equally easily be explicated along the lines of *Presidents of multinational companies live away from the public gaze.*

Summary

Sperber and Wilson replace Grice's notion of implicature (a non-conventional meaning recovered as an inductive inference) with a two-stage process in which the addressee recovers first an explicature – an inference or series of inferences which enrich the under-determined form of the utterance to a full propositional form, and then an implicature – an inference which provides the addressee with the most relevant interpretation of the utterance. Explicatures preserve and elaborate the propositional form of the original utterance; implicatures are new logical forms. Speech acts are treated as attitudes to propositions rather than as actions, and so speech act descriptions are higher level explicatures.

Checking understanding (5.2) ───────────────────

1. What makes explicatures possible is encyclopaedic knowledge and awareness of context. What knowledge would you need to take into account in order to explicate the following instances of language use so as to infer the meanings presumably intended by their authors.

(10) Avoidance of smoking and alcohol in moderation are also important factors in living a healthy lifestyle (From a University health and safety document)
(11) 'Mad sheep' fears prompt slaughter (Headline in *The Times*, 6 June 1997)
(12) SHAREHOLDERS? COMMISSION? NOT ON YOUR LIFE! (Advertisement for the Equitable Life Assurance Society)

2. How would you modify what I wrote in the last paragraph of the answer to Checking understanding exercise (4.13) (see page 253) in the light of Sperber and Wilson's notion of explicature?

5.1.3 The essential principles of Relevance Theory

In this section, I'm going to list and briefly explain a number of the key principles of Relevance Theory. These are numbered for the sake of clarity.

1. Every utterance comes with a guarantee of its own particular relevance. Thus to understand an utterance is to prove its relevance. Determining relevance (and not only the relevance of utterances) is our constant aim. As Sperber

and Wilson say, 'An individual's particular cognitive goal at a given moment is always an instance of a more general goal: maximising the relevance of the information processed' (1995: 49).

2. Because addressees cannot prove the relevance of the utterances they hear without taking context into account, 'the speaker must make some assumptions about the hearer's cognitive abilities and contextual resources, which will necessarily be reflected in the way she communicates, and in particular in what she chooses to make explicit or what she chooses to leave implicit' (Sperber and Wilson, 1995: 218).

3. However apparently grammaticalized linguistic structure may be, utterances are, as we have seen, radically under-determined. So a single syntactic relation may represent a very wide range of logical and semantic relations. Even the determination of sense requires an inferential process.

4. Once the propositional form of an utterance has been fully elaborated, the utterance may be regarded as a premise, which, taken together with other, non-linguistic premises available to the hearer as contextual resources, enable him to deduce the relevant understanding. Thus in the case of

(3)   Have you seen my book

the time referred to, the referents indicated by *you* and *my*, the sense of *book* and *seen*, the semantico-syntactic relation encoded in *my book* and the speech act status of the utterance all require explicating. This explicated utterance and the hearer's encyclopaedic entries triggered by it (such, perhaps, as whether she wears the speaker's clothes without asking permission, or has written a poor essay) enable an implicature to be recovered as a deductive inference. By that we mean that the implicature is a **logical** conclusion and that therefore no other conclusion can be reached from the premises.

Note also that deductive inferences are still defeasible in conversation. This is because we cannot guarantee that the premises recovered by the addressee are those the speaker wishes to (continue to) entertain. So that if *Even Presidents have private lives* was taken to imply *I'm good at my job*, Clinton could still continue 'Please don't think that I'm good at my job because I'm not.'

5. The most accessible interpretation is the most relevant. This is an important notion because it enables us to discriminate in a principled way, i.e. by taking into account the degree of processing effort, between the various inferences which, time allowing, we might recover. Hence there is a trade-off between relevance and processing effort: 'An assumption is relevant to an individual to the extent that the positive cognitive effects achieved when it is optimally processed are large' (Sperber and Wilson, 1995: 265). ('Positive cognitive effects' are changes in beliefs resulting from new information being added.) Thus the greater the effect of an utterance, the more relevant it is. Similarly, the effects need to be economically achieved: 'An assumption is relevant to an individual to the extent that the effort

required to achieve these positive cognitive effects is small' (Sperber and Wilson, 1995: 266). This means that the harder we have to try to understand something, the less relevant it is. This principle reflects a psychological reality with which we are all familiar, that of not being able to get the point, or at least not being able to get the point in the time available. Grice's Cooperative Principle lacks this psychological dimension.

6. Context is not treated as given common ground, but rather as a set of more or less accessible items of information which are stored in short-term and encyclopaedic memories or manifest in the physical environment:

> people hope that the assumption being processed is relevant (or else they would not bother to process it at all), and they try to select a context which will justify that hope: a context which will maximize relevance. In verbal comprehension in particular, it is relevance which is treated as given and context which is treated as a variable. (Sperber and Wilson, 1995: 142)

In Chapter 1, I said that one of the things you would have to make up your mind about as you studied pragmatics was whether the context determines the way we use language or whether the way we use language determines the context. Here's one way of resolving an issue which we will return to in our discussion of conversation in Chapters 8, 9 and 10.

Let's see how the six principles outlined above apply to a particular instance of communication by reconsidering Alice's instruction

(2) Please attend course planning and examiners' meetings in future

I took her message as relevant and set out to prove its relevance (1). But Alice had over-estimated my contextual resources (2, 3): as a new member of staff I had trouble even recovering the explicatures. One way of resolving *in future* would lead me to recover the implicature that I had missed a meeting in the past and that this message was a reprimand (4). However, try as I may, even six years of processing effort later, I still haven't recovered the single accessible interpretation which satisfies my quest to establish the relevance of Alice's message (5). I know that the relevance of the message is guaranteed, but the contexts were just too variable (6) for me to prove its relevance.

Checking understanding (5.3)

In order to demonstrate how the most relevant interpretation is recovered, explain how the six principles of Relevance Theory outlined above might apply to

(13) She's taken ten years off my life

5.1.4 Procedural encoding

We owe to Blakemore, and particularly her 1987 book *Semantic constraints on relevance*, the crucial distinction between procedural and conceptual encoding. Procedural encodings are processing instructions to be applied to conceptual encodings. Their effect is to make easier the recovery of the most relevant interpretation by constraining (i.e. limiting) the search for the contexts required to prove the relevance of the utterance. Procedural encodings include sentence adverbs like *fortunately* and *clearly*, which help the addressee to recover the propositional attitude of the speaker; disjuncts like *anyway* and *after all* and discourse particles like *so* and *therefore*, which constrain the search for a relevant interpretation by showing how the propositions to which they are attached relate to other propositions in the discourse; adverbial particles like *even* and *only* which speakers attach to propositions to constrain their interpretation; and conjunctions like *but*, one of whose typical functions is to constrain an assumption warranted by the proposition that preceded it. This distinction between conceptual encoding (for example, *Presidents have private lives* in *Even Presidents have private lives*) and procedural encoding (for example, *even* in *Even Presidents . . .*) is the distinction between what Wilson and Sperber call, 'information about the representations to be manipulated, and information about how to manipulate them' (1993: 2).

This second, procedural or computational, type of encoding (i.e. information about how to manipulate representations) constrains the interpretation of conceptual meaning by limiting the available ground in relation to which it is to be interpreted. Let's look at some examples.

Recall that at the end of the last chapter, I said that the philosopher and I had both laughed at the implicature recovered from

(14) But he had read them all

Merely saying *he had read them all* suggests to me that it is worth the processing effort of trying to determine how the philosopher's utterance is relevant, even though I might come to the conclusion that the entailment is actually the salient meaning the speaker intends to convey. However, his use of *but* makes me reconsider the first part of what he had said and make the assumption that academics do not read their books, an assumption that doesn't hold of Grice. The point is that the instruction to manipulate the representation in a particular way, which *but* provides, makes (14) easier to understand, i.e. to find relevant, than the bald utterance *he had read them all*.

In our discussion of

(9)   Even Presidents have private lives

in earlier chapters, we skated over the role of *even*, merely noting that it would be considered a conventional implicature in the Gricean account. However, we can now see that its function is procedural. If it's true that *Presidents have private lives* then it's equally true that *Even Presidents have private lives*. Like most procedural encodings, *even* adds no truth value to the proposition to which it's attached. Rather, *even* advises us that the concept that Presidents have private lives is at, or near, the end of a scale of expectability and helps us to understand how the proposition encoded could be relevant. So if we infer that Clinton is claiming that he can do a good job despite his extra-marital relationship, it is because *even* makes this inference much easier to recover.

Consider again Alice's message which I failed to understand:

(2)   Please attend course planning and examiners' meetings in future

Imagine that instead, Alice had written

(15) So please attend course planning and examiners' meetings in future

Straightaway I know that (15) follows from what has gone before. And what has gone before? I've been told that I'm to take over responsibility for a course and a file of relevant papers has been left in my pigeonhole. I have not been told that I missed a meeting. Thus (15) is a consequence, not of a missed meeting, but of a new responsibility. And I'm now to understand that attending course planning and examiners' meetings is part of this new responsibility. In fact, what is wrong with Alice's message is not just that she over-estimates my contextual resources but the consequence of this over-estimate is that she fails to provide a procedural instruction sufficient to enable me to determine the context that would make the message relevant.

Checking understanding (5.4)

A year or two ago I was sitting by myself in a restaurant in Florence eaves-dropping on the conversation at the next table, which was occupied by two married couples, one American and one British. They had obviously been asked to share the table. At one stage in their conversation, the British woman said

(16) We're only about thirty miles from London

By an extraordinary coincidence, the very next evening in a different restaurant I was eavesdropping on another conversation – this time involving two British couples, when I overheard one of the women say

(17) We're about thirty miles from Birmingham

Can you say how *only* helps you to determine the relevance of (16).

5.1.5 *Salience and inference*

At the beginning of this chapter we noticed that sometimes the most salient interpretation will be an explicature, sometimes a higher level explicature and sometimes an implicature. And I suppose that the most salient interpretation of the sentence you have just read (but not perhaps of this one) is its entailment. This realization suggests that we need to research what determines whether the most salient assumption will be an explicature derived by inferential development of the propositional form of the utterance to a full propositional form, or an implicature derived by inference alone.

The following exchange illustrates some of the difficulties in deciding the most salient meaning. It occurred when the owner of the second restaurant in Florence, the one where the couple from Birmingham were dining, was kind enough to approach my table and engage me in conversation. He asked me if I knew Florence well. Our conversation proceeded as follows:

(18)   PETER: I was last here seventeen years ago
       RESTAURANT OWNER: You were young then
       PETER: Younger

Is the most salient meaning of my first utterance for the restaurant owner the explicated proposition that I had not visited Florence during the 17 years preceding the time of utterance? Or is it an implicature such as *I remember it as a good time*?

Under certain circumstances (which we won't go into here), his utterance, *you were young then*, might contrast with the apparent present reality. If it was intended as such a contrast, and particularly if he was responding to an implicature such as *The speaker remembers it as a good time*, the restaurant owner might intend his utterance to imply that I was romantic then – or even naïve, with the implicated conclusion that *Florence is not such a good place as you thought when you were younger*. This interpretation treats my first utterance as an implicit compliment to Florence and hence, indirectly, to the restaurant owner too. His response is intended as a modest demur.

Alternatively, *you were young then* might imply that I am still young enough for it to be possible to assert that I was young 17 years ago, and I am being complimented on my youthfulness. In this case, the restaurant owner probably takes the explicated entailment of my first utterance, that I haven't visited Florence during the previous 17 years, as the most salient meaning.

And what is the most salient meaning of his utterance for me? Is it the implicature that I am now old? If so, *younger*, might be explicated to yield *the speaker was even younger seventeen years ago than the speaker is at the time of speaking*. My utterance is then to be taken as a denial that I am now old and I imply that I am still young. Notice that in disagreeing with the restaurant owner, I try to minimize our disagreement by using the comparative form (*younger*) of the term he had used to describe me.

Or is the most salient meaning of the restaurant owner's utterance the entailment that I was young then, which I contradict politely by asserting that I was younger than I am now, thereby implying that I was not in fact truly young even then? In which case, there is a further implicated conclusion: that his implicature that my youth led me to take a too-romantic view of Florence is ill-founded – I hold a realistic rather than a romantic view.

Or do I recognize his contribution as a compliment, and like him when offered a compliment, demur modestly by implying that I wasn't young then?

In this case, the speech act description recovered as a higher level explicature is the most salient meaning for me.

In this short, and necessarily complex, account of the possible ways in which the two parties understand each other's contributions to the three-utterance exchange, we see how salient meanings may be entailments, explicatures and implicatures. It is difficult to determine which were in fact the salient meanings in this exchange as we approach it as analysts after the event, although no doubt it was entirely clear at the time to the participants themselves. Superficially, the exchange seems simple – three turns consisting of only twelve words in total. But as we have seen, determining how the contributions are intended to be relevant by the speakers and at which inferential levels they are taken as most relevant by the addressees is far from straightforward. The most salient meaning, whether an explicature or an implicature, is the meaning to which we respond in conversation.

5.2 Relevance Theory and degrees of understanding

Earlier in the chapter, I suggested that Relevance Theory was able to account for the understanding failures which occur when the processing load is too great for relevant assumptions to be recovered or when the addressee lacks sufficient contextual resources to infer the explicatures and implicatures which prove the relevance of the utterance. Relevance Theory is to be preferred over other accounts of utterance understanding to the extent that it recognizes and can account for the fact that not all utterances are successfully understood, and that a particular utterance may be understood in different ways and to different degrees by different hearers.

Accordingly, in this section of the chapter, we are going to study parts of a text which posed real understanding problems for a group of non-native members of the culture who were asked to work though it. I'll first describe the experiment I set up, and then ask you to identify the reasons why the text posed understanding problems for this particular group. The idea is that relevance theoretic principles can be invoked to account for their understanding difficulties.

The understanding test consisted of an extended joke-telling routine from the television programme, *The Two Ronnies*, in which one of the presenters, Ronnie Corbett, sits in a chair and tells the studio audience a joke. The sequence lasts for just over three minutes and contains a series of intermediate jokes as the joke-teller builds up to the main joke. According to Sacks, jokes exhibit 'supposed supposable unknownness to recipients' (i.e. the audience should not have heard the joke before) (1974: 341) and constitute an 'understanding test' (1974: 346). A joke is an understanding test in the sense that there is some supposed audience who would not pass it (although if the test were failed by the real audience, the joke would lose its point). Jokes therefore confirm in-group solidarity by virtue of the expectation that they will not be understood by out-group members.

The group I selected to listen to Ronnie Corbett's joke consisted of non-native-speaker university teachers of English from a single culture with near-native speaker competence in English but limited experience of the British culture of which the joke-teller is a native member. They could tell where the comic effects occurred because the studio audience indicated this with laughter whose intensity varied with the intensity of the effect. The informant group was left to work alone for an hour with a tape of the joke-telling sequence and 20 questions designed to determine the kinds of understanding difficulties encountered.

5.2.1 Implicature and explicature

'We will call an explicitly communicated assumption an explicature. Any assumption communicated, but not explicitly so, is implicitly communicated: it is an implicature' (Sperber and Wilson, 1995: 182). Because explicatures are an intermediate level of understanding between what is said and the implicatures that are entirely inferred, the model provides for the possibility of a failure to understand on a graded scale at three levels – entailment, explicature, implicature.

Checking understanding (5.5) ——————————————

Consider the following fragment from the joke-telling routine:

(19) tonight's story was actually handed down to me by my dear old grandfather (pause) the other night as he was clearing out our attic

The informant group were at a loss to know why the studio audience laughed after *attic*. Can you explain what they failed to understand at this point?

5.2.2 Implicated premises and implicated conclusions

'We will distinguish between two kinds of implicatures: implicated premises and implicated conclusions' (Sperber and Wilson, 1995: 195). Sperber and Wilson show that deriving an implicature from an explicature is sometimes a two-step process which requires a first implicature, or implicated premise, before the consequent implicature, or implicated conclusion, can be inferred. Here then is a further level at which an implied meaning might fail to be recovered. So a hearer might recover both implicated premise and implicated conclusion, or implicated premise only, or neither.

Checking understanding (5.6) ——————————————

In considering the following fragment, the informant group was asked to decide whether the joke-teller was a successful entertainer or not. They concluded that he was:

(20)   it was a scrapbook really of all the ecstatic rave reviews of my past performances (pause) I let go of it at one point and it nearly floated out the window

Can you explain why the group members recovered an implicature which they were not intended to recover?

5.2.3 Speaker judgement and hearer resources

'The speaker must make some assumptions about the hearer's cognitive abilities and contextual resources, which will necessarily be reflected in the way she communicates, and in particular in what she chooses to make explicit or what she chooses to leave implicit' (Sperber and Wilson, 1995: 281). And 'A speaker who intends an utterance to be interpreted in a particular way must also expect the hearer to be able to supply a context which allows that interpretation to be recovered' (Sperber and Wilson, 1995: 16). Of course, these are not new ideas, but they have not been so clearly stated before and they remind us that if the speaker over-estimates the hearer's resources, then intended implicit meanings may not be recovered.

Checking understanding (5.7)

The informant group were asked to explain why the studio audience laughed when they heard

(21)   on with the joke which concerns these two Rugby players who were both spending the summer holidays at Scarborough (pause) for a bet

Why do you think they were not able to do this?

5.2.4 Recovering meanings and processing opportunity

'The organization of the individual's encyclopedic memory, and the mental activity in which he is engaged, limit the class of potential contexts from which an actual context can be chosen at any given time' (Sperber and Wilson, 1995: 138). This reminds us that pressure of time, complexity of structure, etc. limit our ability to recover contexts and that explicatures and implicatures may fail to be inferred for these reasons.

Checking understanding (5.8)

At one stage, the joke-teller says

(22)   I was watching the late-night film you know about Ivan the Terrible and his wife Blodwen the Extremely Disappointed

Can you suggest a reason for the informant group's failure to understand why the studio audience found this funny?

5.2.5 Accessibility

The most accessible interpretation is the most relevant since 'A phenomenon is relevant to an individual to the extent that the effort required to process it optimally is small' (Sperber and Wilson, 1995: 153). Of course, there are degrees of accessibility, and the means chosen to convey meanings may have different accessibility properties for different addressees.

Checking understanding (5.9) ————————————————

1. Talking about a tooth that had been giving him problems, the joke-teller says

(23) It was still plaguing me this morning at rehearsals so I thought it's no use I'll have to have it out so I went along to the BBC emergency dental service they have no appointment necessary you just go up to one of the scene boys and tell them to get a move on and that's the end of it

   Why do you think the informant group failed to get the joke?
2. Why do you think the group had problems teasing out exactly what was implied in the following part of the joke:

(24) she's just come over to learn the language and she's doing very well (pause) this morning she said to me I hope you'll be forgiving me my extremely bad language but I'm afraid my grandmaster needs touching up

5.2.6 Garden-path utterances

Relevance Theory predicts that in garden-path utterances a hearer will not escape being led up the garden path and encouraged to infer an inappropriate meaning since 'The first hypothesis consistent with the principle of relevance [is] the best' and 'The principle of relevance does not normally warrant the selection of more than one interpretation for a single ostensible stimulus' (Sperber and Wilson, 1995: 168, 167). If the speaker does not intend the hearer to recognize that they have recovered a garden-path meaning, at least at first pass, the principle of relevance should, and does, lead an addressee to recover an inappropriate implicature even if led to it deliberately by the speaker.

Jokes frequently allow 'more than one interpretation for a single ostensible stimulus'. Indeed it is often necessary for there to be more than one interpretation. The following joke, for example, is about a man who is thrown off a fairground big wheel. His friend rushes up to him in horror, and the joke ends in the following way:

(25) Terry he said Terry he said are you hurt (pause) the friend lifts himself on one elbow and said well of course I'm hurt he said I went round three times and you never waved once

The joke turns precisely on the interpretation of *hurt* to mean 'physically hurt' when the friend asks *are you hurt* and to mean 'emotionally hurt' in Terry's reply. Thus the audience must understand *hurt* differently from the way Terry takes it for the joke to work. We are led up the garden path to the extent that we recover an explicature for *hurt* that turns out not to be the operative one.

Checking understanding (5.10)

This is how the joke-teller talks about his *au pair* girl:

(26) she's been doing a bit of work for us this weekend at home (pause) and (pause) no she's just come over it's true she's just come over to learn the language

Because the informant group did not get led up the garden path, they couldn't understand what they were supposed to laugh at at each pause and at *she's just come over to learn the language*. Why were they not led up the garden path though?

Summary

Relevance Theory postulates a trade-off between processing effort and determining the relevance of an utterance. Like many advertisements and newspaper headlines (see Chapter 4), joke-telling routines also constitute an understanding test in which the processing effort is very great but worth engaging in because the understanding is correspondingly more rewarding. However, the processing overload that jokes may impose is easily demonstrated when the audience consists of non-native speakers or cultural out-group members who lack the necessary contextual or linguistic resources. Relevance Theory can predict this lack of understanding and supply an explanatory account of it.

5.3 Why implicature?

When we discussed deixis in Chapter 2, we suggested that it was useful to have a small number of lexical items whose reference was determined in the contexts in which they occurred. When we look at explicature, we see a similar principle at work, this time at the propositional level. Think how uneconomical language would be if there had to be a different grammatical structure for each of the logical meanings encoded even in simple possessive structures like *my mother's son, my mother's mother, my mother's friend, my mother's car, my mother's cooking, my mother's politics, my mother's foot*, etc. Like deixis, explicature and especially implicature allow us to make use of context in the interpretation of what is said to us, and thus makes possible an immensely more economical language than we would otherwise need. It's obvious that without inference, virtually every utterance would need to be formally unique – not a very practical proposition!

Implicature is like deixis in another way too – because it allows us to communicate meanings as inferences rather than entailments, it is particularly attuned to face-to-face communication. Being defeasible, inferences are by nature more tentative than entailments. In fact, we often expect that our addressees will not concur with the inferences we calculate they will recover from our talk. If you study business negotiation closely, you will often notice that entailments are preferred for less controversial and implicatures for more controversial suggestions.

But implicatures also make possible the very opposite of tentative talk – because an implicature assumes that speaker and hearer can access a meaning which is conveyed but not stated, it reinforces solidarity between them. When my children's friends are in our house, I often notice that implicatures pass between members of our family that my children's friends do not recover. We use implicature as a confirmation of our solidarity and common knowledge.

The availability of implicature as a means of conveying meaning also means that we can let context do more of the work for us. Thus, there will be occasions on which we favour explicit encoding of meaning, others on which we convey meaning implicitly, and yet others on which we allow context 'to speak for itself'. For example, if my wife and I take the car somewhere, we don't usually need to discuss who'll drive, who'll sit where, which of our work-places we'll go to first, etc. We let context speak for itself. However, if we offer a lift to someone whose habits we know less well, we negotiate where they want to go to, whether it would be all right if we dropped so-and-so off first, whether they'd mind sitting in the back, etc. Similarly, my wife and I need far fewer words to advise each other on whether a particular clothes purchase would be wise than I would think appropriate were I to accompany you on a shopping trip for the first time. So if I say to my wife that something she is trying on looks like the one Maja has, only she will recover the implicature, and the shop assistant will be in the dark as to whether or not I am recommending a purchase.

It seems probable that it's not only individuals who vary in the degree to which they favour explicit encoding, implicit encoding or letting context do the work. Whole cultures also divide into what Hall (1976) has called 'high context' (where the context does more of the work) and 'low context' (where the relationships between people frequently need to be negotiated linguistically). We already had a tiny, relatively trivial glimpse of this possibility in the previous chapter when we compared a sentence in the Cantonese and English versions of a parallel text and saw how the English version required *alcohol* to be recovered as an explicature whereas in the Cantonese version *alcohol* was explicitly stated. Single examples like this mean little when taken alone, of course, but I think you could reasonably argue that different types of cultural organization favour different default systems for conveying meanings. For example, we might hypothesize that:

- societies in which individualism is a positive value will favour implicature because the understanding is recovered by the message receiver rather than explicitly stated by the message originator
- societies where no clear distinction is made between in-group and out-group members will need to take into account a more pluralistic audience in communication situations, and will thus allow for the more individualized understandings that implicatures, as context-dependent inferences, permit
- societies that are orderly and have strong in-group identity will favour explicatures in which inferences preserve and elaborate the underlying logical forms of utterances. Although inferred, the recovered meanings are more conventional than meanings that are recovered as implicatures, where a new logical form is inferred
- implicatures are more frequent in low context culture discourse. This is because the default setting for human behaviour is high context which, in its prototypical manifestation, exhibits the phenomenon of no talk. But because relatively little can be taken for granted in low context cultures, speakers frequently use implicature to test the ground in the negotiation of meaning. This is possible because inferred meanings, unlike entailed propositions, are not truth correspondent.

Of course, these are mere hypotheses and would be regarded by many as controversial. However, in a study of Chinese and English business correspondence in Hong Kong (Grundy, 1998), I was able to show that more explicit encoding has a more directive force and suggests that decision-making is concentrated in relatively few hands rather than being more broadly shared. Thus each type of cultural organization favours a particular communication style. Or, put the other way round, the way in which we make meanings salient is one of the ways in which we create the cultures to which we belong.

5.3.1 The relative strengths of Gricean and relevance theoretic accounts of language understanding

Which of the two accounts of utterance understanding examined in this and the previous chapter is to be preferred?

Gricean Generalized Conversational Implicature (GCI), particularly as developed by Gazdar (scalar implicatures) and Levinson (utterance-type meaning), shows a regularity across uses of language which is based on heuristics such as 'say as much as you need to or appropriately can', 'say as little as you can get away with', and 'avoid marked expressions'. The generalized nature of utterance-type meaning is absent in the relevance theoretic account which implies an individual case treatment in which forms are enriched to provide explicatures. This is not to say that the argument for an individual case treatment isn't strong – after all, the same form is not always enriched to the same explicature.

Levinson's neo-Gricean development of GCIs can also be shown to have explanatory power in accounting for the historical development of one kind of polysemy. (Polysemy is the property a lexical item may have of having more than one meaning.) The process begins with one-off utterance-token interpretations which gradually become conventionalized as an utterance-type interpretation, and finally code a new meaning. This process has been shown to account for the development of many discourse particles and conjunctions. It probably also accounts for the process by which creative metaphors appear, and then become conventionalized over time as conceptual metaphors, and finally take on new coded meanings.

On the other hand, the relevance theoretic account provides a psychologically plausible model of utterance understanding involving a trade-off between processing effort and the recovery of relevant assumptions in contexts that license them. Relevance Theory is also able to show the function of procedural encoding as an instruction to operate on conceptual encoding in order to assist relevant understanding. In addition, the theory provides a psychological generalization across the process of utterance understanding which predicts ease and difficulty of interpretation.

Raising pragmatic awareness: implicit meaning (Sperber and Wilson)

1. This exercise works best in a small group. Each person should think up a sentence. Write up all the sentences in random order on the board. Try to see how each sentence could be relevant in the context provided by the previous sentences. As you do this, think about the problems anyone would have in working out the connections for themselves and what contextual resources are required. Try inserting additional sentences to reduce the processing effort required of the reader.
2. In your tutorial group, choose any of the keywords at the beginning of this chapter and write an entry for your chosen word for a dictionary of pragmatics. Compare your proposed entry with those of colleagues.
3. Record a short conversation between friends before your next tutorial. Choose three or four utterances and ask your colleagues to help you decide on the enrichment necessary to provide full propositional forms for them.
4. Working with the data collected in (3), try to identify utterances where the next speaker takes (a) the explicature (b) the higher level explicature and (c) the implicature as the most salient meaning.
5. Listen out for utterances whose relevance you could only determine with difficulty, or maybe couldn't determine at all. Report them to your tutorial group and explain why you think they were problematical for you.

Further reading

Primary texts: Sperber, D. and Wilson, D. (1995); Carston, R. (1988); Wilson, D. and Sperber, D. (1993).
Textbook: Blakemore, D. (1992).

6 Presupposition

'He that hath knowledge spareth his words.'
(*Proverbs* 17:27)

Keywords background assumption, pragmatic presupposition, semantic presupposition, presupposition trigger, factive, defeasibility, negation, metalinguistic negation, projection problem

The two previous chapters were about the way an addressee comes to conclusions after hearing an utterance as to the meaning the speaker intends to convey. This chapter, in contrast, is about the existing knowledge common to speaker and hearer that the speaker does not therefore need to assert. This presupposed knowledge is then taken together with the propositions asserted in the utterance and the addressee's knowledge of the world as the basis on which an inference is drawn as to the implied meaning, or implicature, that the utterance conveys.

Thus in an utterance like

(1)   I enjoyed working with Anne when she was setting assignments

I presuppose that there is such a person as Anne and that she set assignments, and assert that it was at that time that I enjoyed working with her. These entailments may be contrasted with other meanings, i.e. implicatures, that I might be thought to be conveying. For example, if you heard me say (1), you might think that I was implying that I didn't especially enjoy working with Anne when she wasn't setting assignments. But this is only an inference and may or may not be a meaning that I was intending to convey.

In fact, temporal clauses introduced by *when*, such as the one above, typically give rise to presuppositions. By contrast, as we saw in Chapter 4, real conditionals introduced by *if* give rise to implicatures. Thus

(2)   If we're setting assignments

causes a hearer to infer that maybe we're setting assignments/maybe we're not setting assignments. This is why we tend to prefer fire-warning notices in lifts that say

(3)   If there is a fire, do not use the lift

to ones that say

(4)   When there is a fire, do not use the lift.

Notice also that there is a scale from clearly presuppositional at one end via possibly presuppositional possibly not presuppositional to clearly non-presuppositional at the other:

> When there is a fire – presupposition triggering
> In the event of fire – ? presupposition triggering
> In case of fire – ? non-presupposition triggering
> If there is a fire – non-presupposition triggering

Another way of looking at presuppositions is to think of them as ways of expressing shared or non-controversial knowledge. The person to whom I was speaking when I uttered (1) knew, or was prepared to accept as non-controversial, that Anne was setting assignments. In this respect, presupposition can be compared to and contrasted with the use of deictics. In both cases, the speaker intends to refer or denote. But whereas in the case of deixis it is necessary to identify a *demonstratum* in relation to the indexical ground in order to effect reference, in the case of presupposition the hearer is content to take the existence of the referent on trust.

The rest of this chapter is divided into three sections. In the first section, we will expand the set of presupposition triggering phenomena beyond the two examples of proper names such as *Anne* and temporal conjunctions such as *when* discussed so far. In the second section, we will see that our first explanation of these phenomena as more semantic than pragmatic needs some qualification. And in the third section, we will look at what happens when a lawyer introduces presuppositions into her courtroom cross-examination of a hostile witness.

6.1 Presuppositions as shared assumptions

6.1.1 The principle of economy

When someone speaks to us, we typically make all sorts of assumptions about the background to their utterance which we presume to be mutually known before the utterance ever occurred. I once came across a book whose title was

(5)   Tell Madonna I'm at lunch

Imagine for a moment that someone actually said this. There wouldn't be much point in saying *Tell Madonna I'm at lunch* unless the speaker was expecting a visit from Madonna, knew that the addressee was going to be in when she arrived, expected Madonna to appear in the near future, and assumed that the addressee knew what she looked like and was willing to pass the message on to her. Unless these conditions are met, there is something wrong with saying (5) – which perhaps explains why you and I have probably never said it to any of our friends. Thus when someone says *Tell Madonna I'm at lunch*, they presuppose that the addressee is going to be in when Madonna arrives, that Madonna is likely to appear soon, and that the addressee knows who she is and will pass the message on. We can call these kinds of background assumptions pragmatic presuppositions because they are clearly non-linguistic in nature. In fact, they are the felicity conditions that would need to obtain for it to be appropriate to say (5).

It is very convenient that we can rely on presupposition, otherwise we would have to speak in a much more elaborate way. Instead of (5), we would have to say something like this: 'I know you'll be in and I'm expecting Madonna soon and since I know that you know what she looks like and I know that you are willing to pass on the message that I am at lunch, please tell her that I'm at lunch.'

Checking understanding (6.1) ——————————————

What is pragmatically presupposed in each of the following?

(6) Can I have a twenty pence coin in the change please

(7) Thank you for not smoking

6.1.2 Shared assumptions: definite descriptions, iteratives, questions

The pragmatic presuppositions discussed above are related to the context in which (5) is uttered. There is a further presupposition which is not related to the context of utterance, namely that there is such a person as 'Madonna'. In fact, whenever a proper name like *Madonna* or a definite description like *the image Madonna projects* is used, the existence of some referent that matches the description is presupposed. We will call this kind of presupposition a semantic presupposition because it seems not to be context (i.e. pragmatically) determined and thus to be a conventional way of understanding triggered by use of a definite description.

There is a sense in which both the pragmatic and the semantic presuppositions associated with

(5) Tell Madonna I'm at lunch

precede the addressee's working out the likely implicature that the person who left the message is anxious to avoid her. This is even clearer when we remember that *Tell Madonna I'm at lunch* is actually the title of a book: because the pragmatic presuppositions or conditions on uttering the sentence do not obtain, the reader recovers the implicature that the author pretends to be important enough (or, if male, sufficiently resilient to Madonna's charms) to be able to get along quite well without spending time with her.

So far we have seen that semantic presuppositions arise when a definite description occurs. And even when the pragmatic presuppositions associated with (5) do not go through (e.g., when the expression is used as the title of a book rather than as a felicitous utterance), the semantic presupposition that there is such a person as Madonna does.

Other structures that give rise to presuppositions include iteratives such as

(8)   Can I ask another question

which presupposes that the speaker or one or more other earlier speakers had already asked at least one question before; and *wh*-questions such as

(9)   Who said to tell Madonna that he was at lunch?

which presupposes that someone said to tell Madonna that he was at lunch; and embedded *wh*-questions such as

(10)   I wonder what you are thinking about

which presupposes that the addressee is thinking about something.

Checking understanding (6.2)

1. Identify the semantic presuppositions in the following first lines of Shakespeare plays.

(11)   In delivering my son from me, I bury a second husband (*All's Well That Ends Well*)

(12)   Come here my varlet, I'll unarm again (*Troilus and Cressida*)

(13)   When shall we three meet again, in thunder, lightning, or in rain? (*Macbeth*)

(14)   Who keeps the gate here? ho! (*Henry IV, Part II*)

(15)   Who's there (*Hamlet*)

(16)   I wonder how the king escaped our hands (*Henry VI, Part III*)

(17)   If music be the food of love, play on (*Twelfth Night*)

2. Identify the entailment(s), semantic presupposition(s), pragmatic presupposition(s) and implicature(s) in

(18)   Joanna's made another of her telephone calls

6.1.3 More shared assumptions

Other phenomena that trigger presuppositions include change-of-state predicates such as *begin, continue, stop* and *play on* (as in 17). The following change-of-state examples also contain temporal clauses/phrases introduced by *after* and *before*:

(19) I began jogging after a visit to the doctor

presupposes (a) that I did not jog before and (b) that a visit was made to the doctor,

(20) I continued jogging after my son became a faster runner than me

presupposes (a) that I was jogging before and (b) that my son became a faster runner than me, and

(21) I stopped jogging after a visit to the doctor

presupposes (a) that I used to jog before and (b) that a visit was made to the doctor.

   Presuppositions are also triggered by implicative verbs such as *remember, forget, manage* and *happen*, so that

(22) The then Prime Minister didn't remember/forgot to keep a record of her instructions at the time arms were exported to Iraq

presupposes that she should have kept a record.

(23) Her successor managed to win the election that followed

presupposes that winning the election was not easy. And

(24) A similar thing happened to an American President who exported arms to Iran

presupposes that what occurred was a matter of chance.

   You might want to argue that (22)–(24) are really examples of conventional implicature. If you did, you would be in the good company of Karttunen and Peters, who argue that if there is 'a rule of the language that associates a presupposition with a morpheme or grammatical construction' (1979: 11), then the supposed presupposition is a conventional implicature. In fact, all the presuppositional phenomena considered so far in this chapter, apart from the pragmatic presuppositions in (5)–(7), constitute strong *prima facie* evidence for the view that presuppositions are conventionally associated with morphemes and grammatical constructions.

Checking understanding (6.3) ————————————————

What presuppositions can you identify in this example?

(25) My friend didn't bother to open a bank account until she started to earn money

6.1.4 Shared assumptions and subordination

In Checking understanding (6.3), you will have identified the proposition contained in the temporal clauses, *she started to earn money*, as a presupposition. As in (19)–(21), the temporal clause provides a background against which some event such as taking up, continuing or abandoning jogging, or in the case of (25) opening a bank account, is highlighted. In fact, Talmy (1978) suggests that main sentence assertions and embedded temporal sentence presuppositions are a linguistic realization of the figure/ground *gestalt* first mentioned in Chapter 2. Thus in an example like

(26) Since you started this book, you must have paused several times for thought

I take it for granted that you started this book and against this background I make an assertion. If you respond to my claim, it'll be the figure (*you must have paused for thought*) that I expect you to comment on, not the background (*since you started this book*). Similarly, if you say

(27) When I started this book, I thought I'd never finish it

you would take a reply such as *I knew you would* to relate to the figure (*I thought I'd never finish it*) and not to the ground (*when I started this book*).

The link between presupposition and subordination extends beyond temporal clauses. It is a moot point whether propositions that are so subordinated as to have become appositional are still being asserted or whether they are the raw material of, or have actually become, presuppositions. So you will have to decide for yourself whether the non-restrictive relatives *who were clever* and *who were cleverer still* in the following example are asserted or presupposed:

(28) The Greeks, who were clever, invented geometry; the Arabs, who were cleverer still, invented algebra.

Notice that restrictive relatives never give rise to presuppositions, so that in (29) *who were clever* and *who were dim* restrict the class of Greek described and contribute to the truth-value of the sentence:

(29) While the Greeks who were clever were inventing geometry, the Greeks who were dim were visiting the oracle

And the embedded sentences in clefts are also presupposed, so that in

(30) It was the Scots who invented whisky

there is a presupposition that *someone invented whisky*.

In Chapter 4 and again at the beginning of this chapter we saw how real conditionals give rise to the implicature that the proposition contained within the conditional may or may not come about. Unlike real conditionals, counterfactual conditionals *presuppose* that affirmative propositions contained in the *if*-clause did not occur and negative propositions contained in the *if*-clause did occur. Hence

(31) If you had sent me a Christmas card last year, I would have sent you
      one this year

presupposes that you did not send me a Christmas card last year, and

(32) If you hadn't sent me a Christmas card last year, I would still have
      sent you one this year

presupposes that you did send me a Christmas card last year.

Another spectacular example of the relationship between subordination and presupposition was described by Kiparsky and Kiparsky, who detailed the properties of what they termed 'factive' predicates (1971). Kiparsky and Kiparsky show that a fact-S, like *the fact that Pat wanted to talk to Stephen*, will be presupposed in the highly restricted set of structures in which they may appear either as the subject or the complement of a factive predicate. Thus all the following examples (in which the factive predicates are italicized) presuppose that Pat wanted to talk to Stephen:

(33) The fact that Pat wanted to talk to Stephen *is odd*
      The fact of Pat's wanting/having wanted to talk to Stephen *is significant*
      That Pat wanted to talk to Stephen *is exciting*
      Pat's wanting/having wanted to talk to Stephen *matters* to me
      It*'s tragic* that Pat wants to talk to Stephen
      His friends *regret* the fact that Pat wanted to talk to Stephen
      Her friends *weren't aware of* Pat's wanting/having wanted to talk to
      Stephen

Thus *is odd*, *is significant*, *is exciting*, *matters*, *is tragic*, *regret* and *be aware* are all factive predicates. Apart from the extraposed *It's tragic that Pat wants to talk to Stephen*, none of these structures is possible with non-factive predicates like *seem*, *believe* and *turn out*, whose subjects or complements are not presupposed. (You can demonstrate this for yourself by trying *seem*, *believe* and *turn out* in place of the factive predicates in the examples above.) On the other hand, these non-factive predicates have their own set of structures which are ungrammatical for factives.

Checking understanding (6.4)

How many presuppositions can you identify in the following example and which morphemes or structures appear to trigger them?

(34) One of the former Prime Ministers, who was removed from office by
      her colleagues, regrets that she stopped taking notes when allowing
      exports to Iraq

6.1.5 Focus and presupposition

We have already seen that *wh*-questions give rise to presuppositions, so that

(35) Why did Sue give Oxfam a donation

presupposes that Sue gave Oxfam a donation and asks for a reason. A non-
wh- question like

(36) Did Sue give Oxfam a donation

does not trigger any presuppositions (except those that arise independently
of the question, i.e. that *Sue* and *Oxfam* exist). But (36) does invite an
addressee to respond in such a way as to treat at least some part of the
question as presupposed. Figure 6.1 shows how different proportions of
possible answers to (36) are divided between presupposition (to the left) and
focused, or 'new', information (to the right).

Presupposition	*Focus*
She gave them	£100
She gave them	her old clothes
She gave	something to save the children
She	was out

Figure 6.1

So if someone is in a pet shop and asks

(37) Do you have any dogs going cheap

the reply

(38) No, they're all expensive

treats their having dogs as presupposed and asserts that they are expensive
(*No* denies that they are cheap); the reply

(39) No, we only have cats

treats their having stock as presupposed and asserts that their stock consists
of cats (*No* denies that they have [cheap] dogs); the reply

(40) No, they all go bow-wow

treats their having dogs as presupposed and asserts that they go bow-wow
(*No* denies that they go 'cheep', the sound associated with birds); and the
reply

(41) No, our birds go cheep

treats their having stock (dogs) as presupposed and asserts that the stock
which goes 'cheep' are birds (*No* denies that their dogs go 'cheap' or perhaps
'cheep').

6.1.6 Stress and presupposition

I once saw the first line of *Twelfth Night*

(17) If music be the food of love, play on

spoken with a very strong stress on *If*. This had the effect of turning the real conditional (implicature: maybe music is the food of love, maybe music is not the food of love) into a counterfactual conditional with the accompanying presupposition that music is not the food of love and the consequent implicature that the music being played at the time was not particularly tuneful.

The relationship of contrastive stress and presupposition is discussed by Lakoff (1971: 333), who points out that

(42) John called Mary a Republican, and then SHE insulted HIM

presupposes that calling someone a Republican is an insult.

These examples are important because they show the speaker making decisions about meaning at the level of phonetic realization, and are truly pragmatic in the sense that the meaning conveyed is independent of the meaning of the lexical items themselves. Thus

(43) John called Mary a Republican, and then SHE praised HIM

presupposes that to call someone a Republican is to praise them.

6.1.7 Negation and presupposition

It is generally agreed that presuppositions 'survive' negation so that if you negate

(22) The then Prime Minister didn't remember/forgot to keep a record of her instructions at the time arms were exported to Iraq

(23) Her successor managed to win the election that followed

and

(24) A similar thing happened to an American President who exported arms to Iran

the same presuppositions arise. Thus

(44) The then Prime Minister remembered/didn't forget to keep a record of her instructions at the time arms were exported to Iraq

still presupposes that she should have kept a record, but now asserts that she did, so the presupposition survives and the truth value of the assertion is reversed;

(45) Her successor didn't manage to win the election that followed

still presupposes that winning the election was not easy, but now asserts that he did not win it, so again the presupposition survives and the truth value of the assertion is reversed.

(46) A similar thing happened to an American President who exported arms to Iran

is more problematical because we do not usually find this use of *happen* negated. Nevertheless, if say

(47) It didn't happen to the American President who exported arms to Iran

we assume that, had it happened, it would have been a matter of chance. If you look again at (26)–(31), you'll see that their presuppositions all survive negation too.

The standard definition of semantic presupposition is often considered to be its ability to survive negation, so that a presupposition is a proposition that is true if the sentence in which it occurs is true and is also true if the sentence in which it occurs is false. So if I harbour murderous thoughts towards my neighbour who plays loud music and say either that this is a matter of regret or that it is not a matter a regret, and whether in either case I actually regret or do not regret my feelings, that I harbour murderous thoughts is always presupposed:

(48) I (do not) regret that I want to murder my neighbour.

Treating the proposition that *I regret x* as A and the proposition that *I want to murder my neighbour* as B, this may be schematized as in Figure 6.2.

A is true A is not true not – A is true not – A is not true	B is true

Figure 6.2

Summary

We have described the assumptions that are taken for granted as the background to utterances as of two kinds, those that are necessary for the utterance to be appropriate or felicitous – such as assuming that your addressee knows the identity of a person to whom you are instructing them to pass a message, and those that seem to be triggered by morphemes or grammatical constructions. Among the second category, we counted iteratives and noticed how *another* (8), (18), (28), *a second husband* (11), *again* (12), (13), and *former* (34) act as presupposition triggers. The resulting presuppositions, because they are a linguistic phenomenon, are 'conventional' and, like conventional implicatures, not cancellable.

6.2 Presuppositions as pragmatically conditioned

The first section of this chapter treated presupposition as semantic because it was argued that presupposed assumptions are triggered by lexical or structural items. This reflects Strawson's (1950) view of presupposition as an entailment that survives negation and is truth-conditional. This approach to presupposition was refined by Karttunen and Peters (1979), who argued that presupposition is conventional to the extent that it survives negation but pragmatic to the extent that it is non-truth-conditional.

In the second section of this chapter we will be considering whether all presuppositions should be treated as pragmatic in the much wider sense in which the 'pragmatic' presuppositions of

(5)   Tell Madonna I'm at lunch

are non-linguistic background assumptions required to render the utterances appropriate. Indeed, we will be exploring what I meant when I suggested at the beginning of the chapter that another way of looking at presuppositions is to think of them as ways of expressing shared or non-controversial knowledge.

We will do this by arguing that it is not enough for there to be 'a rule of the language that associates a presupposition with a morpheme or grammatical construction' for a presupposition to occur. Something more is required. Seuren puts it well when he says

> The defining feature of presuppositions seems to be the fact that a sentence B_A (i.e. B presupposing A) is fit for use only in a discourse that already contains the information carried by A. A discourse or, more properly, a discourse domain is seen as a cognitive 'working space' for the interpretation of new incoming utterances. The information carried by each new utterance is added to the information already stored in the discourse domain. The technical term for this specific form of 'adding' information to a given discourse domain is *incrementation* ... What counts here is that a sentence B_A is considered unusable in a discourse not allowing for the incrementation of A. (1998: 439–40)

Seuren's point will be clearer if we go back to the first example in the chapter and I tell you a bit about the discourse context in which the utterance

(1)   I enjoyed working with Anne when she was setting assignments

actually occurred. Anne and I were each teaching one of two parallel classes. Somehow, she ended up setting one fewer assignment than she was meant to. Of course, you can guess what happened – the students complained that the two classes weren't being treated equally. But because this occurred in Hong Kong, it was Anne's class who complained that they'd been deprived of one of their assignments rather than mine that complained that they had had one too many! At the end of the meeting with our course leader that followed, I couldn't resist saying

(1)   I enjoyed working with Anne when she was setting assignments

Although technically what I said still presupposes that Anne set assignments (and indeed she did set one or two), what I meant by saying (1) was that she sometimes didn't. It's not therefore the presupposition that Anne set assignments that I want to convey in this particular discourse context, rather it's the implicature that she wasn't so good to work with when she didn't set them. Thus *when she was setting assignments* serves the pragmatic purpose of conveying that Anne didn't always set them, rather than the presupposition that she set assignments.

One frequently cited example that seems problematic for the semantic analysis of presupposition is the apparently inconsistent effect when the verb *die* occurs in temporal clauses. Consider

(49) He suffered a series of illnesses before he was persuaded to make a will

which presupposes that he made a will. However,

(50) He died before he made a will

does not. Clearly what we know about the world, that when you die that's it, would not be consistent with assuming that later he made a will. In other words, this suggests that the presupposition of (49) is a meaning we recover as a result of bringing together a linguistic form (a temporal clause) and an understanding of the world (that you can, and perhaps should, make a will after a series of illnesses). The pragmatic nature of this inference is confirmed by the fact that *he died before* does not necessarily pre-empt a presupposition, as (51) and (52) show:

(51) He suffered a lot of pain before he reached the hospital

(52) He died before he reached the hospital

Both these sentences presuppose that the person referred to reached hospital.

Another problematical area for temporal clauses is the case of forward-looking examples. There is a parallel with *if* here: backward-looking conditionals are counterfactual and give rise to a presupposition of non-existence in respect of the situation described in the *if*-clause; but forward-looking conditionals give rise to implicatures of possible existence in respect of the situation described in the *if*-clause. What about temporal clauses? In Chapter 4 we noticed that *wenn* in German has both a temporal and a conditional meaning. In English too *when* sometimes has a conditional meaning. When (?if) I say

(53) When you get the chance, you should come to Durham

do I presuppose that you will get the chance? Or when (?if) I say

(54) Come to Durham wherever it suits you

do I presuppose that it ever will suit you?

6.2.1 Gerunds and temporal clauses

The gerund's status as a vehicle for conveying factivity is also doubtful. Is the proposition that *she ate her cake* presupposed in the following examples:

(55) She left before she ate her cake

(56) She left before eating her cake

In (55) and (56) both the she-ate-her-cake and the she-did-not-eat-her-cake readings are possible, although the she-did-not-eat-her-cake reading is favoured.

The acceptability of the negative polarity items *any* and *at all* in (57) and (58)

(57) She left before she ate any of her cake at all

(58) She left before eating any of her cake at all

also supports the she-did-not-eat-her-cake reading. This is because, as negative polarity items, *any* and *at all* only occur within the scope of a negative. Once again, these examples suggest that the presupposition supposedly associated with temporal clauses is in fact a matter of pragmatics and depends upon both the triggering structure and knowledge of the world.

6.2.2 Factives

And if you don't believe that I'm as hard as I appeared to be when I wrote about my attitudes to my neighbour at the end of the first part of this chapter, you might say about me

(59) Perhaps he regrets wanting to murder his neighbour

In this case, it's a moot point whether it's presupposed that the person referred to (i.e. me) wants to murder his neighbour. It depends on whether you think that I really do want to murder my neighbour and might now be regretting it (i.e. the scope of *perhaps* is limited to the *regret* sentence) or whether you think that I might be both wanting to murder my neighbour and regretting having this urge (i.e. the scope of *perhaps* extends over both the *regret* and the *want* sentences). Presumably a hearer would appeal to non-linguistic knowledge to determine whether or not to allow the presupposition. Nor is it contradictory to say things like

(60) Although he hasn't taken his driving test yet, he's already regretting failing it

In the real world, factive predicates are often not accepted as such in everyday speech. When he was Archbishop of Canterbury, I once heard Robert Runcie say on television

(61) I contest the fact that the church is more divided

Although this may sound contradictory, we all know what he meant. This is a particularly interesting example because *contest* exhibits the syntactic behaviour of a factive predicate in allowing the following structures.

(62) The fact that Pat wanted to talk to Stephen is contested/contestable
      The fact of Pat's wanting/having wanted to talk to Stephen is
      contested/contestable
      That Pat wanted to talk to Stephen is contested/contestable
      Pat's wanting/having wanted to talk to Stephen is
      contested/contestable
      I contest that Pat wants to talk to Stephen
      His friends contest the fact that Pat wanted to talk to Stephen
      Her friends weren't contesting Pat's wanting/having wanted to talk to
      Stephen

Yet semantically this 'factive' predicate casts doubt on whether the fact-S sentence is a fact at all. Thus although Kiparsky and Kiparsky (1971) suggest two syntactic frames, one for assumed knowledge and one for non-assumable knowledge, we see that pragmatic knowledge also needs to be taken into account.

6.2.3 Definite descriptions

In the days when Marxist ideology was in favour in some places, visitors to Britain from Socialist countries often found it hard to accept that when they talked about *the bourgeois society*, their British friends had no idea what they were talking about. Although the existence of a referent is presupposed by the use of the definite description, the referent was unidentifiable to most people who had no familiarity with Marxist ideology. There is a clear distinction between *the bourgeois society*, where the referent is not yet known to some addressees and cannot be located, and the definite description in *Mind the table*, where the referent may not be known to the addressee but the utterance is taken as an instruction to locate it (Hawkins, 1978: 113).

6.2.4 Change-of-state verbs

If a speaker were to say

(63) At least we won't have to give up sex

they would typically be taken to be presupposing that they were having sex (and implying that they enjoyed it). Yet I heard (63) in a radio interview with a Catholic priest who was contemplating unwelcome changes that he foresaw in the future and seeing this one silver lining on the cloud. Clearly our knowledge of the world tells us that the expectable presupposition does not go through in this case – in fact the humour derives precisely from the fact that the utterance has a different pragmatic effect on this occasion from the one it would usually have.

Summary

The section you have just read shows how context and linguistic form interact to cause us not to identify the potential presuppositions that in most contexts are typically triggered by the linguistic forms in question. We therefore see that it is safer to argue that the recovery of presuppositions is pragmatically conditioned, even in the case of temporal clauses, gerunds, factives, definite descriptions and change-of-state verbs.

Checking understanding (6.5)

Can you think up your own examples of temporal clauses, factives, definite descriptions and change-of-state verbs which do not give rise to the presuppositions we might typically expect to find associated with them? As you do this, it may help you to remember that:

*   temporal clauses are introduced by conjunctions such as *after*, *before*, *when* and *while*
*   Kiparsky and Kiparsky's (1971) list of factive predicates includes *grasp* (in the cognitive sense), *realize, take into account, bear in mind, ignore, make clear, mind, care (about)*
*   definite descriptions are determined by the definite article, possessives, the demonstratives *this/these* and *that/those*
*   change-of-state verbs include *carry on, continue, cease, commence, begin, start, stop, leave off, go on.*

6.2.5 *Presupposition and speaker choice*

More generally, it is notable that there is a good deal of speaker choice in the area of presupposition. For example, speakers commonly decide whether to give lexical realization to what might otherwise be presupposed. We saw a similar phenomenon in Chapter 4 where the teletext subtitler decided to delete the lexical realization from utterances where the same meaning could in theory be recovered as an explicature. I heard a good example of this on the radio when what might have been presupposed was given lexical realization by the speaker who chose to say

(64) They returned to the place they had left

Being an iterative, *return* (or, perhaps, the *re* of *return*) is typically held to give rise to the presupposition that those referred to in (64) had been in 'the place they had left' before.

   Another area of speaker choice occurs in the case of *some* – which usually gives rise to the presupposition of existence, and *any* – which does not. The presupposition-neutral status of *any* accounts for our inconsistent reaction to the road sign

(65) Sorry for any delay

posted at the end of roadworks in Britain. When we have not been held up, we think how courteous it is of the Ministry of Transport to apologize, especially when an apology is unnecessary. But when we have been held up, we find the road sign infuriating precisely because it does not presuppose that there has been the delay which we have just experienced. Under these circumstances

(66) Sorry for the delay

might be more appropriate, but this sign is only very occasionally posted, presumably because it would be inappropriate to situations in which no delay had occurred and in which no referent for the definite description *the delay* could therefore be identified.

Thus McCawley observes that 'sentences with *any* do not commit the speaker to the proposition that the domain of the quantifier is not empty, whereas sentences with *every* and *all* do' (1981: 112). In saying this, he is claiming that, unlike *every* and *all*, the use of *any* does not presuppose that there are at least some examples of the description quantified by *any*. Thus (67) and (68) each presupposes that at least some ministers have a secret life, but (69) does not:

(67) Every minister who has a secret life risks reading about themself in the newspapers

(68) All ministers who have secret lives risk reading about themselves in the newspapers

(69) Any minister who has a secret life risks reading about themself in the newspapers.

Every, *all* and *any*, along with *each*, are natural language analogues of the universal quantifier ($\forall$) of formal logic. *A/an* and *some* are natural language analogues of the existential quantifier ($\exists$) of formal logic. It seems hard to account for the fact that *any* does not presuppose the existence of examples of the description it quantifies and *some* does, especially when *some* is so frequently a suppleted form replaced by *any*. It is notable that in first and second language acquisition, this is felt to be unexpected too, so that both small children acquiring English as a first language and second language learners frequently produce utterances like

(70) I've locked the door so someone doesn't get in

Such utterances are entirely logical if you take the view that only an idiot would lock a door if there was no presupposition that someone might get in. Examples like (70) show that presupposition is a matter of speaker choice rather than a formal requirement.

One noticeable difference in the use of *some* and *any* occurs in the department I work in, where my four American colleagues frequently privilege *some* over *any* in situations where my British preference would be for *any*. So when our American Professor asked for information to take with him to a meeting recently, adding by way of explanation

(71) in case I have to say something to somebody

I inferred (wrongly as it turned out) that he had someone in mind for a telling off. Maybe the association of a presupposition of existence with the use of *some* depends as much on the speaker as on the linguistic form.

6.2.6 Defeasibility

As we saw in Chapter 4, 'defeasible' is the term pragmaticists use to mean that a proposition can be cancelled. If presuppositions are conventional semantic meanings, they will not be defeasible since, by definition, no entailment can be denied or cancelled without giving rise to a contradiction. Indeed, we have already seen that the standard definition of semantic presupposition is that it is an entailment that survives the negation of the containing sentence.

But is it always true that presuppositions are not defeasible? Another category of predicate held to give rise to presuppositions are verbs of judging. So

(72) I criticized Bill for mumbling

presupposes that Bill mumbled and asserts that mumbling is a bad thing; and

(73) I accused Bill of mumbling

presupposes that mumbling is a bad thing and asserts that Bill did it. So according to the standard definition

(74) I didn't criticize Bill for mumbling

also presupposes that Bill mumbled; and

(75) I didn't accuse Bill of mumbling

also presupposes that mumbling is a bad thing.
  So far, so good.
  Yet I can reasonably say

(76) I didn't criticize Bill for mumbling – not that he did anyway

which can hardly presuppose that Bill mumbled; and

(77) I didn't accuse Bill of mumbling – not that mumbling's (such) a bad thing

which can hardly presuppose that mumbling is a bad thing. Both these examples appear to cancel presuppositions.
  And not only can the expected presuppositions fail to go through, they can also be suspended, which again would be impossible in the case of a conventional semantic meaning. So

(78) I didn't criticize Bill for mumbling – if that's what he was doing

causes the presupposition that Bill mumbled to be suspended; and

(79) I didn't accuse Bill of mumbling – if mumbling's to be condemned

causes the presupposition that mumbling is a bad thing to be suspended.

Earlier in this part of the chapter we saw how a potential presupposition fails to arise if the discourse context does not license it. In this sub-section, we have seen how co-text can cause a potential presupposition to be denied or suspended. Something therefore has to give: either presuppositions are not entailments or their denial is more apparent than real.

Checking understanding (6.6) ——————————————

Consider the following examples from the first part of this chapter and in each case add text which either negates or suspends the presupposition:

(10) I wonder what you are thinking about

(15) Who's there?

(19) I began jogging after a visit to the doctor

(23) Her successor managed to win the election that followed

(30) It was the Scots who invented whisky

(31) If you had sent me a Christmas card last year, I would have sent you one this year

6.2.7 The status of presupposition cancelling negation

The status of 'presupposition cancelling negation' has been and still is contentious. Essentially the issue is this: a negative particle can be used and the presupposition survive it, as in

(80) Her successor didn't manage to win the election that followed (assertion: her successor did not win; presupposition: winning was difficult)

or in

(48) I (do not) regret that I want to murder my neighbour (assertions: I regret/do not regret *x*; presupposition: I want to murder my neighbour)

But is this the same kind of use of the negative particle as in

(76) I didn't criticize Bill for mumbling – not that he did anyway

which prevents the potential presupposition that Bill mumbled from arising?

A way out of this difficulty is to argue that the negative particle has two different functions, logical negation, i.e. mapping one value on to another by means of introducing or eliminating the negative particle, and metalinguistic negation (Horn, 1985). Metalinguistic negation is a device for objecting to some aspect of an utterance on any grounds except its conventional meaning. Thus in

(81) It wasn't the Scots who invented whisky, it was the Irish

the negative particle is used metalinguistically to object to the choice of *the Scots*.

Burton-Roberts (1989: 235–8) argues that metalinguistic negation operates on the mention of a proposition rather than truth-functionally on the proposition itself. Thus the speaker of an utterance like

(76) I didn't criticize Bill for mumbling – not that he did anyway

is objecting to the term 'mumble' rather than denying the truth of a presupposed proposition. Distinguishing in this way between objecting to the mention of an item and denying the truth of a presupposed proposition might seem like splitting hairs, but it has the important consequence that it allows a theory of semantic presupposition to be maintained.

Checking understanding (6.7)

Horn defines metalinguistic negation as 'a device for objecting to a previous utterance on any grounds whatsoever, including the conventional or conversational implicata it potentially induces, its morphology, its style or register, or its phonetic realization' (1989: 363). Identify the potential presuppositions that are being objected to metalinguistically in the suggested answers for Checking understanding (6.6). Which of the suggested answers exhibit metalinguistic negation?

6.2.8 The projection problem

Another issue which has consumed a great deal of energy is the 'projection problem'.

Given that there are three classes of expression with different abilities to create presuppositions

• those that are presupposition creating such as factives

(48) I (do not) regret that I want to murder my neighbour

• those that are not presupposition creating, including non-factives such as

(82) I believe my neighbour is going deaf

• and those that sometimes are and sometimes are not, such as

(83) I don't know that my wife fancies the milkman

which sometimes seems to presuppose that my wife fancies the milkman and sometimes does not.

And given that examples like (48) may be embedded under predicates that do not create presuppositions, or only sometimes allow them, as in

(84) I believe he regrets wanting to murder his neighbour

and

(85) I don't know that he regrets wanting to murder his neighbour

how do you determine whether the resulting sentences allow the presuppositions associated with the embedded sentences?

In practice, determining whether (84) and (85) allow the presupposition that the person referred to wants to murder his neighbour seems to be a matter of speaker belief based on encyclopaedic knowledge of the world and expectations about the role of the utterance in its discourse context.

Checking understanding (6.8)

Structures like *regret* (+S) that allow presuppositions are called 'holes', structures like *believe* (+S) that do not trigger presuppositions are called 'plugs', and structures like *don't know* (+S) that sometimes allow and sometimes do not allow presuppositions are called 'filters'. Which of the italicized structures in the following examples of courtroom data are holes, plugs and filters and what presuppositions do the holes and filters actually or potentially trigger?

(86) Your lawyer *urged* that you be given a suspended sentence on humanitarian grounds

(87) Do you *remember* your lawyer telling the magistrate that you had married a Hong Kong resident

(88) Were you married to Mr So *at the time* you appeared in the magistrate's court

(89) Did you *tell* your lawyer you came here in order to take care of your husband's 92-year-old mother

Summary

In the first section of this chapter we saw how semantic presuppositions were triggered by morphemes, lexical items or structures and appeared to pass an independent test of their status, the ability to survive negation. In the second section, we have studied a number of cases where the expected presupposition does not arise because it would be inconsistent with the discourse context or with the addressee's beliefs about the world. Thus the discourse context and the addressee's encyclopedic knowledge determine whether a presupposition triggering structure or lexical item actually triggers a presupposition. Semantic presuppositions are pragmatically licensed by their discourse context and their occurrence depends upon the speaker and hearer achieving a degree of intersubjectivity.

6.3 Presupposition in the real world

Earlier in this chapter we considered examples such as

(26) Since you started this book, you must have paused several times for thought

I suggested that if you responded to this claim it would be the figure (*you must have paused for thought*) that I would expect you to comment on, and not the background (*since you started this book*). But imagine a situation in which someone says to you

(88) Were you married to Mr So at the time you appeared in the magistrate's court

and the background assumption that you appeared in court has no basis in fact. How would you respond to the question asked, bearing in mind that whether you answer yes or no to it, you seem to accept the background presupposition that you appeared in the magistrate's court? Put another way, before you respond to the question, you need to reject the embedded presupposition that is not consistent with the previous spoken or implicitly understood discourse/real-world facts.

   In this section, we will look at what happens when a speaker tries to introduce presuppositions into a discourse that does not contain the information carried by these same presuppositions. The discourse in question is a court record collected in Hong Kong as part of the *International Corpus of English*. We have already seen some of these data in (86)–(89). Here is the full context in which these utterances occurred as part of the cross-examination by a defence council, Mrs Panesar, of a prosecution witness, Mrs Wong. The data are set out in the left-hand column and my commentary on them is set out in the right-hand column.

(90) PANESAR: Madam Wong, during the plea and mitigation, your lawyer urged that you be given a suspended sentence on humanitarian grounds, and those grounds were that you had been in Hong Kong just 10 days. Is that right?

Mrs Panesar sets out a situation and then by means of the higher level predicate 'is . . . right' asks if it is true.

WONG: I don't know.

PANESAR: Do you remember your lawyer telling the magistrate that you had married a Hong Kong resident in China earlier that year in 1991?

As we saw in Checking understanding (6.7), *remember* is a filter and might be taken to presuppose the complement sentence, 'your lawyer . . . in 1991', that follows.

WONG: This is not true. My previous marriage, it was a man in China.

Mrs Wong does not answer the question 'Do you remember . . .' but denies the validity of the presupposition that she married a Hong Kong resident.

COURT: It's not true that you told your lawyer that?

The judge ('Court') intervenes to clarify whether Mrs Wong had ever given her lawyer the information which Mrs Panesar's question presupposes.

WONG: I did not say that to my lawyer.

PANESAR: Was your lawyer making up things?

COURT: No, she can't answer that.

PANESAR: Were you married to Mr So at the time you appeared in the magistrates court?

WONG: We were then cohabiting.

The presupposition that Mrs Wong appeared in the magistrate's court goes unchallenged, presumably because it is consistent with what is known in the discourse context.

PANESAR: But you weren't married to him. Is that right?

Again Mrs Panesar advances a proposition and then by means of the higher level predicate 'is . . . right' asks if it is true.

WONG: Not yet – I mean the marriage was not yet registered.

PANESAR: And you had only met Mr So here in Hong Kong a few months before?

WONG: Yes.

PANESAR: Did you tell your lawyer you came here in order to take care of your husband's 92-year-old mother?

As we saw in Checking understanding (6.7), *tell* is a filter and might be taken to presuppose the complement sentence, 'you came here . . . 92-year-old mother', that follows.

WONG: I did not say that to my lawyer. In fact what I said to him was my present husband was introduced

This is a rape case in which Mrs Wong alleges that her former landlord, Mr Lau, to me by some friend and I was aware that he had a mother of that age. In fact I did not see my husband before I came to Hong Kong.

raped her after she left her accommodation to move in with Mr So, whom she subsequently married. It's important for Mrs Wong's case that she should not be portrayed as having had a relationship with Mr Lau (as Mrs Panesar will seek to establish later) between first knowing Mr So and marrying him. Mrs Wong denies the presupposition that she came to Hong Kong to take care of her husband's mother since she did not know her husband-to-be at the time.

COURT: You are talking about Mr So?

WONG: Yes, So.

PANESAR: Did you say to your lawyer you came to Hong Kong to take care of your elderly mother-in-law?

WONG: No, I said nothing of that sort.

Again, on some readings this question might be taken to presuppose (a) that Mrs Wong had a mother-in-law and (b) that she came to Hong Kong to take care of her.

Presuppositions embedded in questions put to witnesses are particularly damaging in courtrooms because the witness is supposed to answer the question asked. In answering the question, the witness necessary implies acceptance of the presupposition it contains. Despite the difficulty of denying presuppositions embedded in questions, notice how skilfully Mrs Wong deals with Mrs Panesar's presuppositions in her answer

(91) I did not say that to my lawyer. In fact what I said to him was my present husband was introduced to me by some friend and I was aware that he had a mother of that age. In fact I did not see my husband before I came to Hong Kong.

The illocutionary force indicating device 'In fact' is used together with the presupposing pseudo-cleft 'what I said to him' and the factive predicate 'was aware' to indicate just exactly what Mrs Wong can agree to in Mrs Panesar's question. 'In fact' is then used again in a sentence that denies one of Mrs Panesar's presuppositions and acknowledges through a temporal clause the presupposition that is uncontested, that Mrs Wong came to Hong Kong.

Another notable feature of the use of presuppositions in cross-examinations of this sort is that they typically cause the judge to intervene to protect the witness.

You might like to work on the use of presupposition in the following series of extracts from the cross-examination of Mrs Wong with which this chapter concludes. To help you with this, presuppositional and potentially presuppositional data of particular interest are italicized and, where appropriate, suggestions and comments are made in parentheses.

(92) PANESAR: You have told us in your evidence *that Mr So was introduced by a mutual friend to you*. Is that right? ('Is that right?' questions only whether Mrs Wong did indeed provide such evidence.)
WONG: Yes.
PANESAR: Had you expressed the wish to *this mutual friend that you were seeking to get married and looking for a partner*? (Two presuppositions: 'this mutual friend' and 'that you were ... partner'.)
COURT: Sorry?
PANESAR: Had you expressed the wish *that you were wishing to get married and seeking a partner*?
WONG: Yes.

(93) PANESAR: And *at the time you met Mr So*, did he have his own flat?
WONG: That was a public housing unit.
PANESAR: This place you have told us you rented *where the alleged incident took place on 29 November*, 41B, Hung Fook Street, 3rd floor, of Tokwawan, was that bought or was that rented? (What, if anything, is the effect of 'alleged' with respect to presupposition?)
WONG: It was a rented premises.

(94) PANESAR: Is this right, *when you met the defendant on the 24th and 25th*, did you tell him *this flat had been bought for you by Mr So*?
WONG: I did not say that. (Would the answer *I did not* have been different with respect to the potential presupposition inherent in the question?)
PANESAR: Madam Wong, isn't it right that it was *when you told Mr Lau here, the defendant, Mr So had bought you a flat and the defendant said 'Well, now that you have got a flat, surely you can afford to return my $50,000'*? (Pay special attention to several presuppositions and presupposition triggers: temporal clause introduced by 'when', definite descriptions, complement sentence following 'said', temporal clause introduced by 'now that', 'return'.)
WONG: No, not true. I did not have a flat for my own and I never borrowed such money from the defendant.
PANESAR: What *excuse* did you *give* the defendant for *leaving* him? (Notice the implicatives 'give an excuse' and 'leave'. 'Leave' is also implicative in Cantonese, the language in which Mrs Wong's evidence is given.)
COURT: For leaving him?
PANESAR: For leaving him.

AIKEN: Leaving him when? (Aitken is the prosecution lawyer and Mrs Wong is his principal witness. How does he deal with the implicative nature of 'leave'?)

COURT: Yes, when?

PANESAR: When you *left* the defendant *for* Mr So. (How does 'for' support implicative 'leave'?)

AIKEN: Wait a minute.

COURT: What do you mean by that? She doesn't say, she doesn't admit that she was ever *with* the defendant. (How does 'with' support implicative 'leave'? Notice how 'admit' is a speech act description consistent with the presupposition Mrs Panesar seeks to establish.)

PANESAR: Well, perhaps I can rephrase my question then, my Lord.

PANESAR: What *excuse* did you *give* the defendant *when you left the roof-top hut to go and live with Mr So at the new address*? (As well as the temporal clause, there are the two implicatives 'give an excuse' and 'live with'.)

WONG: *At that time when we were having tea together*, I told the defendant *that I had met a man, I wanted to marry that man*, and I *gave him back* the keys to that hut on the roof-top and requested him to write a note to me and I said I would not stay in that hut *anymore*.

PANESAR: Madam Wong, I suggest *what you said to the defendant* prior to your departure on or around 28 October 1991 was that you were *leaving* him to go and reside with *your brother*.

COURT: Leaving him to go and reside . . .

PANESAR: To go and reside with *her brother, Madam Wong's brother*.

WONG: No, I've got no brother.

PANESAR: Well, you may have no brother but did you *give that reason* to the defendant? (Does Mrs Panesar presuppose that Mrs Wong would have needed to give some reason at least?)

WONG: No, not true. On that day I gave him the keys and I told him, I said 'Look, this is my phone number. You may call me in future if there's anything you want to contact me.'

(95) PANESAR: In fact it is right, is it not, that you, prior to your departure on or about 28 October, were in the habit of complaining constantly as to why *this defendant will not improve his job and his earning capacity*? Is that right?

WONG: It's not of my concern whether he makes more money or not. (Is Mrs Wong's answer addressed to the question or the presupposition it carries?)

PANESAR: I put it to you, Madam Wong, that you *left* the defendant *when his money ran out*.

COURT: Sorry?

PANESAR: You *left* the defendant *when his money ran out*.

WONG: No, not true.

PANESAR: I put it to you that by this stage, Mr So had become a *better catch* for you with more money. (Is 'catch' implicative or not in your opinion? And do comparatives presuppose positives too – i.e. is it presupposed that Mr Lau was a good catch, or not?)

WONG: No, not correct. In fact Mr So, *apart from* giving me the usual money for the housekeeping, he never gave me extra money. (Does 'apart from . . . housekeeping' survive negation, or not?)

COURT: Who? Sorry.

INTERPRETER: Mr So.

COURT: So.

WONG: I like Mr So but not *his money* – I mean not for the sake of money. (Why does Mrs Wong repair 'his money'?)

PANESAR: Madam Wong, I suggest that *everything you did up to leaving the defendant* was for money. (Notice two presupposition triggers: 'everything you did' and 'up to . . .')

INTERPRETER: I beg your pardon?

PANESAR: I suggest that everything you did up to *the leaving of Mr Lau*, the defendant, was for money.

COURT: After leaving the hut?

PANESAR: After leaving the hut.

Raising pragmatic awareness: presupposition

1. Working by yourself, collect a few advertising slogans with interesting pragmatic properties (maxim flouts, implicatures, presuppositions, etc.) and bring these to your tutorial group to discuss.
2. Work with a partner. Choose any lyric with a strong story-line – Beatles songs work particularly well – and agree on three or four lines that you and your partner will work with. Then separate and each draw the scene depicted in the lyric in such a way as to represent all the presuppositions. Come back together to compare drawings and discuss the way you each represented the presuppositions. (Acknowledgement: this idea was thought up by Csilla Szabo.)
3. This exercise works best in a small group. Each person should think up a sentence containing a presupposition and dictate it to the group. As each sentence is dictated, you each write down a product which it could be used to advertise and the reason why it could be used in this way.
4. Working in a small group, choose a short news story from a newspaper and together rewrite it as a feature article making as much use of presupposition as you can.

Further reading

Green, G.M. (1996: 72–86); Levinson, S.C. (1983: 167–225); Seuren, P. (1998: 423–41).

7 Politeness

PHYLLIS: He's a very polite-spoke man aren't you
PETER: It's not what they say at home

> *Keywords* politeness, universal, context, usage, power, distance, etiquette, (dis)agreement, redress, face, face threat, positive face, negative face, imposition, 'folk' view

In their classic book on politeness, which we will be discussing later in this chapter, Brown and Levinson note a growing interest in 'the linguistic expression of social relationships' (1987: 49). Thus in Chapter 3 when we eavesdropped on the quarrelsome couple at breakfast, we appealed to the notion of politeness to account for parts of the data and made the point that politeness strategies can be a way of encoding distance between speakers and their addressees. In this chapter we will be considering the role of politeness phenomena in the language we use to communicate social meaning.

7.1 Politeness phenomena

Politeness principles have been considered to have wide descriptive power in respect of language use (Lakoff, 1972, 1973), to be major determinants of linguistic behaviour (Leech, 1983), and to have universal status (Brown and Levinson, [1978] 1987). Politeness phenomena also extend the notion of indexicality because they show that every utterance is uniquely designed for its audience. Needless to say, not all of these claims have gone unchallenged, but they make good starting points for our study.

Seen as the exercise of language choice to create a context intended to match the addressee's notion of how he or she should be addressed, politeness phenomena are a paradigm example of pragmatic usage. Among the aspects of context that are particularly determinate of language choice in the domain of politeness are the power–distance relationship of the interactants and the extent to which a speaker imposes on or requires something of their addressee. In being 'polite', a speaker is attempting to create an implicated context (the speaker stands in relation x to the addressee in respect of act y) that matches the one assumed by the addressee.

Politeness phenomena are one manifestation of the wider concept of etiquette, or appropriate behaviour. In the next chapter, we will study an extended service encounter involving a travel agent and a customer. At one stage in this encounter, in an act of doubtful etiquette, the customer repairs his utterance and substitutes *I pay you* for *it costs*:

(1)   now if I buy a ticket from you then it costs I I pay you £100

The grounds for criticizing the customer's etiquette are that *it costs* is better adapted to its context (i.e. 'more polite') than *I pay you*. *I pay you* may serve the customer's immediate purpose, being, as we shall see, the shortest route to the required result. But it is not in accordance with expectations for proper conduct. This suggests that there are conventions in linguistic etiquette just as there are in non-linguistic etiquette and that linguistic politeness phenomena are predictable in relation to the contexts in which they occur.

In the last chapter, we noted that presupposition, and pragmatic presupposition in particular, encourages economical communication by allowing shared propositions to be taken for granted without being stated. Politeness phenomena go in the opposite direction, as we saw in the introductory chapter with

(2)   Could I just borrow a tiny bit of paper

which is less economical but more likely to serve the speaker's purpose than

(3)   Give me a sheet of paper

Utterances frequently (although not invariably) exhibit such a trade-off between economy and the speaker's preference for a more elaborate linguistic strategy than is strictly needed to communicate the relevant proposition. Of course, there will be situations when the strategy most likely to enable speakers to satisfy their needs will be to utter (2), and other situations when (3) will be more productive. But it is very often the case that politeness phenomena depart from the principle of maximal economy of utterance – if by maximal economy we mean uttering only the proposition to be conveyed.

7.2 The effects of politeness

Being on the receiving end of politeness affects each of us differently because polite utterances encode the relationship between the speaker and ourselves as addressee. Thus we would expect one person, perhaps someone who happened to be sitting next to us in a lecture and whom we didn't know all that well, to say *Could I just borrow a tiny bit of paper*. And we would expect a different person, perhaps an older brother, to put the request in the more direct way: *Give me a sheet of paper*. If we do not see the relationship between ourselves and the person who addresses us as they do, we will be upset by the strategies they employ, since these strategies imply the nature of our relationship as they see it. This function of language, to imply the most appropriate speaker–addressee relationship, is what I take linguistic politeness to be. Let me illustrate this claim with two examples.

The first is a fax I received from a travel agent in Hong Kong. You need to know the context to understand her message. This is what happened: I telephoned Lam, the travel agent, and asked her to book me a return flight from Hong Kong to London on specified dates. The next morning I received a fax on my number but addressed to a Dr Waters saying that the flights I had asked for had been reserved for me. So I telephoned Lam to say that I was glad about the flights but I wasn't Dr Waters: could she confirm that the seats had been booked in my name? She said she was sorry about muddling me with Dr Waters. In fact the dates she had reserved for me were different from those reserved for Dr Waters. No, I said, the dates were right – it was just the name that was wrong. No, she said, the dates were wrong too. OK, I said, cancel those and book me on the same flights as Dr Waters. As the conversation continued, I began to suspect that Lam didn't actually know who she was speaking to. So I said, 'You do know who I am, don't you?' 'Yes,' she replied, 'you're Mr Guest.' So we had words. Later she sent me another fax which began with the following apology:

(4) URGENT

TO: MR PETER GRUNDY

FROM: LAM

SORRY EVERYTHING THIS MORNING. JACKIE SEND THE WRONG FAX NUMBER TO HER CLIENT DR WATERS & RECEPTION TOLD ME YOU ARE MR GUEST WHO IS ONE OF MY CLIENT & HE BOOK THE SAME THING JUST DIFFERENT DATE. YOUR VOICE SEEMS LIKE HIM. SO OUR COMMUNICATE TOTALLY DIFFERENCE. TERRIBLY SORRY.

Although her English is non-standard. Lam's fax is pragmatically perfect. I wasn't expecting an apology, but when it came, it exactly matched my idea of what an apology in such a situation should be. Because Lam was so good at pragmatics, I didn't desert her for a more efficient travel agent.

Checking understanding (7.1)

Imagine you were Lam. First, try and improve her English. How do the pragmatic effects of the original and improved texts compare? Now try and compose your own message apologizing for the muddle. Can you do it any better than Lam?

The second example involves a visit to the doctor. When I got to the surgery, the following written message was displayed prominently in the waiting room:

(5)   Owing to unforeseen circumstances, one of our Doctors has not been able to attend morning surgery. Consequently, the other partners are running late. We apologize for any inconvenience this may cause you, and assure you that all patients will be seen as quickly as possible.

As the minutes ticked by, I began to get more frustrated. And I began to think about the message and how annoying I found it. What 'unforeseen circumstances', I thought? Why 'our' doctors and why the capital 'D'? Why 'has not' rather than *hasn't*? Any why 'any' inconvenience? And why 'may'? Why not simply *apologize for the inconvenience*, or even *apologize that you're having to wait*? And is 'assure you' really necessary? And what does 'as quickly as possible' really mean? And then I began to imagine a nightmare scenario in which I eventually got to see Dr Moore and he started to talk like his notice.

But when I eventually did get to see him, we had a normal, jokey conversation. What a difference between our relaxed chat and the formal, distance encoding message in the waiting room. So, after I'd seen the doctor, I popped back into the waiting room and wrote down the message to share with you.

Checking understanding (7.2) —————————————————

1. It's difficult to imagine a doctor talking in the register used for the message in the waiting room. If you're like me and feel that the way the message is written is inappropriate, can you rewrite it in a more appropriate way? What sort of person would find the original message appropriate do you think?
2. You can test my claim that the purpose of linguistic politeness is to imply the most appropriate speaker–addressee relationship by ranking the following texts on a scale from the one you would be happiest to receive yourself to the one you would be least happy to receive. You might like to try this with a friend or a colleague in your class: you should each read the four texts and rank them for acceptability, and then share your reasons.

(6)   *Text A* (a letter I received from a colleague in another department)
      Dear Peter,
      Thank you very much for agreeing to register our students on
      Tuesday. I know it must have made a very difficult day even more
      fraught but it was very helpful to me. I appreciate what you did and I
      feel indebted to you.

(7)   *Text B* (a letter from an airline replying to my complaints about poor service)

Dear Mr Grundy,

RE: LHR-BRU-WAW-BRU-LHR 13 and 19 December '93

We acknowledge receipt of your recent letter regarding the above. We were extremely concerned to learn of the problems you encountered, but trust you will appreciate that we are unable to comment before an investigation has been made. As soon as we are in possession of the facts, we will of course contact you further.

In the meantime, we would be grateful if you would kindly accept our most sincere apologies for the inconvenience caused.

(8)   *Text C* (extract from a letter my wife received from an employment agency)

At Alfred Marks, we place a high value on our temporary workers' opinions of the service we provide, and would, therefore, appreciate your comments.

(9)   *Text D* (sign displayed in the bar at the Royal Station Hotel, Newcastle)

Residents wishing to drink after 10.30 p.m. must produce their room key or residents card.

3.   When our water supply is interrupted for repairs, the water company puts a postcard through our letter box the week before. The company keeps revising the text of this postcard. Study the three versions below – the first is the earliest version and the third is the latest. Which do you like the best, what changes can you identify, and why do you think the company keeps changing its text? A good way of doing this task is to work with a partner and study either Texts 1 and 2 or Texts 2 and 3. Then find another team who chose a different pair of texts and discuss your findings.

(10) *Text 1*

INTERRUPTION OF WATER SUPPLY

Please note that your Water Supply will be
turned OFF on
Sunday 11th November 1990
From 4.00 a.m. for up to 7 hours
During this period it would be inadvisable to draw hot water or to use any mechanical appliances connected to the supply. It is essential to ensure that all taps remain shut to avoid the risk of flooding when the supply is restored.
For further advice please telephone 091-2654144

(11) *Text 2*

WATER OFF

Please note that your water supply will be
TURNED OFF
WEDNESDAY 28TH FEB
FROM 9AM TO 1PM

During this time please minimize the use of hot water and ensure
that all taps remain shut to prevent the risk of flooding when the
supply is restored.
We regret any inconvenience this may cause you.
For help and advice contact Customer Services on the telephone
number overleaf.

(12) *Text 3*
ESSENTIAL MAINTENANCE
In order to carry out work to the water mains your
WATER SUPPLY
will be temporarily
TURNED OFF
Friday 9th July
from 10:00hrs to 14:00hrs
We apologize for any inconvenience and we will work as quickly as
possible to restore your supply. During this time you should not use
hot water or any mechanical devices connected to the supply such
as washing machines and dishwashers. Please ensure that all your
taps are turned off so that the water does not run when the supply
is restored. Conventional heating systems may be operated but if you
have a combined central heating/hot water system the hot water
should not be used. Do not use instantaneous water heaters during
the interruption.
For help and advice contact Customer Services on the telephone
number overleaf.

In ranking the texts in the Checking understanding exercises for acceptability, you were making decisions about the way that propositions were
conveyed. For example, in

(7)   We acknowledge receipt of your recent letter regarding the above. We
were extremely concerned to learn of the problems you encountered,
but trust you will appreciate that we are unable to comment before
an investigation has been made. As soon as we are in possession of
the facts, we will of course contact you further.
    In the meantime, we would be grateful if you would kindly accept
our most sincere apologies for the inconvenience caused.

There were a number of givens, typically noun phrases describing presupposed entities: *your recent letter regarding the above, the problems you
encountered, the facts, the meantime, our most sincere apologies, the inconvenience caused.* In ranking this text, you were making decisions about how
these were conveyed (e.g., the writer chose *the facts* rather than *what
happened*) and what was said about each of them (*we would be grateful if
you would kindly accept x*). In particular, you were measuring what was said
and how it was said against your expectations of how the writer should be

addressing you under the circumstances. 'Politeness' is the term we use to describe the extent to which actions, including the way things are said, match addressees' perceptions of how they should be performed.

This supremely pragmatic definition presupposes that every instance of communicated language exhibits politeness. In fact, the pervasiveness of politeness is such that we hardly notice it. Yet questions like

(13) Do you wear glasses

rather than

(14) Do you need glasses

or

(15) Do you have to wear glasses

show the speaker's concern for their addressee's self-esteem. Similarly, I overheard one student say to another in the corridor

(16) Are there any toilets around

Not

(17) Where's the toilet

or

(18) I need the toilet.

What the student actually said, (16), and what she might have said, (17) and (18), each has a slightly different politeness status. (17) and (18) would be appropriate in other situations with different discourse participants – and probably in these situations (16) wouldn't be appropriate.

In the following sections, I'm going to comment on a small number of utterances which will give some idea of the nature of the ways in which politeness is manifested and the kinds of purposes 'polite' speakers have in mind. Let's begin with the exchange between Phyllis, our tea-lady, and myself that occurs at the beginning of this chapter.

7.2.1 Dealing with compliments

One afternoon at work I was pouring myself a cup of tea in the kitchen when our tea-lady, Phyllis, said to someone else in the kitchen but about me

(19) He's a very polite-spoke man aren't you

to which I replied

(20) It's not what they say at home

Of particular interest in this exchange are Phyllis's switch to me as addressee (*aren't you*), and my choice of *it's* in my response. Phyllis was talking about me to a third party in my presence, and therefore politeness required that I should be included in the conversation. Phyllis does this with the tag *aren't you*, which, strictly speaking, renders her utterance ungrammatical. Since her utterance was a compliment, I felt obliged out of modesty to demur in some way, and chose *It's not what they say at home*. This kind of demur is a standard politeness strategy comparable to the kind of thing I feel I have to say when you come to my house and you feel you have to say

(21) What a lovely room.

I then reply, equally untruthfully,

(22) We've often thought of moving actually

What is interesting about my response to Phyllis's utterance is the choice of *it's* rather than *that's*. I could have said

(23) That's not what they say at home

The cleft structure of both (20) and (23) give rise to the presupposition that they do say something else at home. But *that* would have been taken to refer to the proposition that the person described is a very polite-spoke man and I would have implied that they say something different at home, thus implicitly contradicting Phyllis's opinion. But in saying *it*, I merely imply that at home they don't say what she says, and thus convey that she is kinder than my family. And at the same time I satisfy the requirements of modesty. This example illustrates the pervasive nature of politeness: even the choice between seemingly semantically empty categories such as anaphoric *it* and *that* is politeness driven.

One last point about this exchange: notice that I reacted to Phyllis's compliment by demurring rather than thanking her. Holmes (1995: 125) suggests that men tend to see compliments as threatening and women to see them as a means of expressing rapport or solidarity. So if I had been a woman, my contribution might well have exhibited its politeness status in a different way.

7.2.2 Unequal encounters

When I wrote the first edition of this book, our department had just acquired the last word in new photocopiers. It worked brilliantly but took some understanding. In its first week in our corridor, I happened to be passing when the Dean was using it. It seemed to me that politeness required that the Dean be acknowledged and that some reference to the new machine would be appropriate. This was our exchange:

(24) PETER: It's brilliant this machine isn't it
      DEAN: Yes it has a mind of its own
      PETER: That's also true

Taking a positive view of the world with an utterance like *It's brilliant this machine* is a generally recognized way of conveying respect to the addressee, and attaching the tag, *isn't it*, allows for the possibility of a second point of view. The Dean, who was finding the complexities of the machine more apparent than its brilliance, did indeed have a second point of view. Although superficially agreeing with me at the level of literal meaning, and signalling this with the overt agreement marker *Yes*, his *it has a mind of its own* implies something rather different: that he did not think it was so brilliant, presumably because he could not get it to do what he wanted it to do. *That's also true* confirms this implicature and continues the fiction that we are in agreement, matching the Dean's *Yes* with my *also*. So although I represent the machine as brilliant and he has another opinion, our politeness strategies minimize our disagreement. I am able to agree with the Dean (and hopefully curry a little favour), and the Dean too has an easier life if unity prevails.

One last point about this exchange: notice how I assumed that, as the less important person, I should speak first when I met the Dean in the corridor. Gu (1990) says that an inferior always speaks first in an encounter in China. Do you think there is a politeness norm in this area in the culture of which you are a native member?

7.2.3 The preference for agreement

One notable feature of (24), as pointed out above, is that both the Dean and I were keen to avoid disagreeing although in fact we had different opinions. This turns out to be a strong motivation in 'polite' exchanges. Consider the following exchange, which occurred in a pub on a hot summer evening when the cooling system for the beer had failed and an engineer had been called to repair it. The time is ten past eight, and the barman is talking to a customer:

(25) BARMAN: It [the beer] should be cool by half past
      CUSTOMER: What ten
      BARMAN: It should be cool by then

Notice how, in his second turn, the barman resists the temptation to correct the customer and say *No eight*, but instead maintains the customer's witticism in a way that avoids contradicting him.

Or consider the following question put to me by a Central American academic at a conference after we had just listened to a lecture given by a well-known but rather showy academic from the USA whom I will call 'Charles Bloggs':

(26) I don't know if I can ask you this question. It is very difficult, but, well, I will ask, did you think as an Englishman that Charles Bloggs was just a little bit vulgar?

How am I to answer? I'm torn between agreeing with the questioner – a preferred strategy but one which necessitates being bitchy, and taking the dispreferred option of disagreeing with the questioner. Notice how she makes it easy for me to agree with her *as an Englishman* and by minimizing the degree of Bloggs's vulgarity.

Checking understanding (7.3) ──────────────────

Discuss what was said in two different bookshops when I approached an assistant holding the first edition of a well-known textbook and asked if they had the second edition in stock.

(27) PETER: Have you got the second edition of this – it doesn't seem to be on the shelves
DILLONS (after consulting the computer): No it's not in stock. We can order it for you

(28) PETER: Have you got the second edition of this – it doesn't seem to be on the shelves
WATERSTONES (after consulting the computer): No we did have it but it's sold out.

7.2.4 Minimizing face loss

If you listen carefully, you'll notice how frequently speakers try to avoid disagreement (as in the case of the barman) or coming out with overtly disappointing utterances (as in the case of the bookshops which didn't have the book in stock). We frequently offer those we talk to something they have not asked for by way of redress rather than tell them we cannot satisfy their need. In this way, we minimize their loss of face. Thus when I couldn't see any bacon buns in the sandwich shop where I sometimes buy one at lunchtime, the exchange went like this:

(29) PETER: Are there any bacon buns
ASSISTANT: Only sausage

Here the offer itself as well as the implicit apology (*only*) have politeness status.

It may seem surprising when you first think about it, but politeness very often occurs where there is a difficulty of some kind. I once went to the garage in a tearing rage when the repair attempt on my car the day before had proved entirely ineffective. All the way there I was rehearsing how I was going to tear a strip off the service manager. When I got to the garage, there were two customers in front of me, each of whom did to the service manager exactly what I had been planning to do. When my turn came, he looked up at me with big sad eyes and, running the back of his hand across his forehead, said

(30) I need a cup of tea after that

I felt so sorry for him that my complaint collapsed into

(31) You'll need a cup of coffee after me

and we both had a good laugh. I expressed my displeasure but, by making a joke of it, in a way that minimized the extent to which he was going to lose face.

Checking understanding (7.4) ——————————————

1. This is an example from Brown and Levinson (1987: 80). Imagine you were on a station platform and two people approached you one after the other. The first said

(32) Got the time, mate?

   and the second said

(33) Excuse me, would you by any chance have the time?

   What assumptions would you make if you were addressed in these two ways and why would you make them?
2. Imagine a parent says to a young child

(34) Just eat it up

   and the child says to the parent

(35) Aren't you going to eat it

   Each intends to get the other to eat their dinner. Why would they use different strategies to achieve the same effect?
3. Imagine you have a five-year-old daughter called Honey with a personality to match her name and you want to spend a morning shopping but without a small child in tow. How would you ask Honey's best friend's mother to look after Honey for the morning? Why not write down your suggested strategy in example (36) before consulting the key.

(36)

   Now imagine you have a five-month-old baby called Howler, also with a personality to match her name. You've been invited to stay with a friend who hates babies so you want to dump Howler on your neighbour overnight. How would you ask your neighbour to look after her? Again, write in your suggested strategy:

(37)

   What are the differences between the way you would make the two requests and what reasons can you suggest for these differences?

7.3 Brown and Levinson's model of politeness strategies

The most fully elaborated work on linguistic politeness is Brown and Levinson's *Universals in language usage: politeness phenomena* (1978), re-issued with a new introduction and revised bibliography as *Politeness: Some universals in language usage* (1987). Working with data gathered from Tamil speakers in southern India, Tzeltal speakers in Mexico and speakers of American and British English, they provide a systematic description of cross-linguistic politeness phenomena which is used to support an explanatory model capable of accounting for any instance of politeness. Their claim is that broadly comparable linguistic strategies are available in each language but that there are local cultural differences in what triggers their use.

Brown and Levinson work with Goffman's notion of 'face', a property that all human beings have and that is broadly comparable to self-esteem. In most encounters, our face is put at risk. Asking someone for a sheet of paper, or telling them they have to wait to see the doctor, or asking them if they have glasses, or complaining about the quality of their work on one's car, or asking them the time, these all threaten the face of the person to whom they are directed. So when we perform such actions, they are typically accompanied with redressive language designed to compensate the threat to face and thus to satisfy the face wants of our interlocutors. So we may ask someone just to 'lend' us 'a tiny bit' of paper, or apologize for the inconvenience caused by having to wait to see the doctor, or treat glasses as a garment, or make a joke of our complaint, or ask the time in a way that either stresses our solidarity with the addressee or acknowledges the trouble we are causing. These are all examples of politeness, the use of redressive language designed to compensate for face-threatening behaviour.

In Brown and Levinson's account, face comes in two varieties, 'positive face' and 'negative face'. Positive face is a person's wish to be well thought of. Its manifestations may include the desire to have what we admire admired by others, the desire to be understood by others, and the desire to be treated as a friend and confidant. Thus a complaint about the quality of someone's work threatens their positive face. Negative face is our wish not to be imposed on by others and to be allowed to go about our business unimpeded with our rights to free and self-determined action intact. Thus telling someone they cannot see the doctor at the time they expected to is a threat to their negative face.

In dealing with each other, our utterances may be oriented to the positive or to the negative face of those we interact with. In

(32) Got the time mate

the kinship claiming *mate* and the informality of elliptical *Got* show that the utterance is oriented to the positive face of the addressee, who is being treated as a friend and an equal. It is therefore an example of 'positive politeness'. But in

(2)   Could I just borrow a tiny bit of paper

the remote *could*, the minimizing *just* and *a tiny bit*, and the euphemistic *borrow* are all oriented to the addressee's negative face and seek to compensate for and play down the imposition and potential loss of face that having to give someone a piece of your own paper involves. It is an example of 'negative politeness'.

Checking understanding (7.5)

1. Which parts of the Central American academic's question (26) are addressed to my positive face and which parts are addressed to my negative face?
2. Recall the train announcement examples in Chapter 2:

(38) The next station is Kowloon Tong. Passengers may change there for MTR trains

(39) The next station is Kowloon Tong. Passengers should change here for KCR trains

(40) The next station is Newcastle. Passengers for Sunderland, Middlesbrough, Carlisle and the Newcastle Metro should change here
Do you think there's a difference in the extent to which the three announcements address positive and negative face?

When we have a face-threatening act to perform, in Brown and Levinson's model there are three superordinate strategies that we have to choose from. They are: do the act on-record, do the act off-record and don't do the act at all. By 'on-record', they mean without attempting to hide what we are doing, and by 'off-record' they mean in such a way as to pretend to hide it. Thus if I were to say

(41) Oh no, I've left my money at home

this would be an off-record way of hinting that you might lend me some. In theory you could ask if I was hinting that you should lend me some money and I could deny that I was and claim that I was merely making an observation – in this sense, I am acting off-record.

Of the three superordinate strategies, the first – perform the face-threatening act on-record – is the most usual. In fact, there are three subordinate on-record strategies, making a total of five available strategies when we have a face-threatening act to perform.

1. Do the act on-record (a) baldly, without redress; (b) with positive politeness redress; (c) with negative politeness redress.
2. Do the act off-record.
3. Don't do the act.

An illustration may help. Let me tell you about a real-world problem I had a few years ago. At the time, we had a neighbour across the road who bought a very old car which he kept parking outside our gate. The car invariably dropped oil all over the road right outside our house. This was not only unsightly but threatened to get walked on to our carpets. What should I have done? I knew that speaking to him about it constituted a face-threatening act, but how should I have done it? I could have done it baldly without redress and said

(42) Don't park your leaky old banger outside our house any more

Or I could have tried positive politeness:

(43) Bill my old mate, I know you want me to admire your new car from my front room, but how about moving it across the road and giving yourself the pleasure?

Or I could have tried negative politeness:

(44) I'm sorry to ask, but could you possibly park your car in front of your own house in future

Or I could have tried an off-record strategy like

(45) Is your car all right outside our house?

Or I could have chickened out, being content to harbour vandalistic fantasies instead.

Eventually, I decided to combine positive and negative strategies to produce a hybrid, and so one Sunday I said

(46) I'm sorry to ask, Bill, but do you want us to have the pleasure of admiring your new car from our front room for ever? It's just that we've nowhere to park when it's outside our house.

Notice that what I said counted as an apology (negative politeness) – *I'm sorry to ask*, followed by the use of his given name (positive politeness), followed by a joke (positive politeness), which included admiration of his 'new' car (positive politeness), minimized by *just* (negative politeness).

In picking one of these five strategies, speakers work with an equation in which any distance differential and any power differential and any imposition are computed:

Social Distance + Power Differential + Degree of Imposition = degree of face threat to be compensated by appropriate linguistic strategy

In Checking understanding (7.4) you worked on politeness strategies which were the result of each of these three factors being particularly strong. When Bill and I talk, there is no power relationship between us since we work in quite different jobs and are more or less the same age. There may be some distance differential depending on how we each see our own and the other's place in the world and the degree of mutual familiarity and solidarity we each feel. But because we are neighbours and chat regularly in the street, we are reasonably close. Thus in dealing with this problem, the most important factor in the equation that adds up to x degrees of face threat is imposition – there is a significant imposition and hence threat to face involved in being told where we should or should not park on a public road, even when the speaker is a neighbour who we know quite well.

Notice also that my strategy in talking to Bill about his car is rationalistic (i.e. I work out what I want to achieve by reasoning) and teleological (i.e. I have an end in mind) and I decide on the means of achieving it – saying (46).

The most important point about Brown and Levinson's five strategies is that they are ranked from *Do the act on record baldly*, which has no linguistically encoded compensation, through a sequence of escalating politeness strategies to *Don't do the act*, where the face threat is too great to be compensated by any language formula so that the most appropriate politeness strategy is not to do the act. A speaker will only choose a highly ranked strategy where the face threat is felt to be high since being 'too polite' implies that one is asking a lot of someone. My problem with Bill's car is a simple one, either it's just too face-threatening to try and tell someone where to park, so I won't try, or, because he is a neighbour and a sort of friend, I can make a joke of it (positive politeness) and at the same time apologize for the coercion (negative politeness), as in (46). What would you have done in my position?

Checking understanding (7.6)

1. I stole the following notice from a hotel I was staying in. Read it carefully and decide on the writer's purpose and the politeness strategies intended to achieve this purpose.

(47) Dear Guest,
The items in this room have been provided for your convenience and remain the property of the Room Attendant in charge. Should you be interested to collect any of the guestroom items as souvenirs of your stay at the Petaling Jaya Hilton, you may purchase them from our Executive Business Centre at the Main Lobby.
Thank you.

2. Here's another notice on display in our doctor's waiting room.

(48) Please note
Patients who are required to provide samples for analysis, are reminded that they may only be accepted if they are presented in the appropriate specimen bottle.
These are available on request from reception or the practice nurse.
Samples which are presented in non-sterile containers present a health and safety hazard to our staff and therefore cannot be accepted.

Can you identify examples of the following in this notice and say what their effects are?

- agentless passives
- deference strategies
- impersonal statements of general rules
- institutional first person plural pronoun
- reason/explanation

Why do you think doctors communicate with their patients like this?

3. Make a list of several different ways of telling someone to stop talking so loudly. Then try and match each of them to Brown and Levinson's five superordinate politeness strategies.

7.3.1 Non-canonical politeness phenomena

One typical source of humour in television sit-coms is the use of politeness strategies that are not the result of expected computations of Power, Distance and Imposition. Very occasionally this happens in real life. I remember a wonderful occasion in my first teaching job when the Headmaster and I took a group of 25 boys camping. This was a very rare event for the Headmaster, who was perhaps trying to relive his own youth and whose memories of camping dated mainly from the Second World War. To the great amusement of the boys, he began by setting a working party to digging a latrine (of which he was destined to be the sole user). Another working party was sent scavenging for timber to make a camp-fire. A third group assisted in the preparation of the evening meal, a monster stew into which the Headmaster threw everything he could lay his hands on, including, towards the end of the preparation period, several rather earthy potatoes that he couldn't be bothered to peel.

When the meal was eventually served, there was an apprehensive circle of boys with enamel plates swimming in doubtful stew watching to see what the Headmaster would do. The Headmaster served himself last, by which time all the cutlery had been taken. 'Have any of you chaps seen a fork?' he asked, whereupon a cheeky 13-year-old chimed in with

(49) I'd try a spade if I were you sir

I can't say that the Headmaster smiled. The humour resulted from the very great power differential which was being ignored in the positive-face oriented joke, and the implicit ridiculing of hours of painstaking cooking which threatened the Headmaster's negative face. Laughter, on this occasion and frequently in sitcoms, is one way of marking the incongruous politeness status of an utterance.

Checking understanding (7.7) ─────────────────────

In (49) the speaker used a positive politeness strategy, joking, in a situation which did not allow positive politeness. Brown and Levinson (1987: 102, 131) give a list of positive and negative politeness strategies:

Positive politeness	Negative politeness
Notice/attend to hearer's wants	Be conventionally indirect
Exaggerate interest/approval	Question, hedge
Intensify interest	Be pessimistic
Use in-group identity markers	Minimize imposition
Seek agreement	Give deference
Avoid disagreement	Apologize
Presuppose/assert common ground	Impersonalize
Joke	State the imposition as a general
Assert knowledge of hearer's wants	rule
Offer, promise	Nominalize
Be optimistic	Go on record as incurring a debt
Include speaker and hearer in the activity	
Give (or ask for) reasons	
Assume/assert reciprocity	
Give gifts to hearer (goods, sympathy, etc.)	

This list probably isn't exhaustive. You can also challenge Brown and Levinson's categorization of particular strategies as positive or negative if you wish.

1. Recall two or three occasions when the politeness behaviour you observed was particularly striking and try to work out why this was, referring where appropriate to strategies listed by Brown and Levinson.
2. Return to the four texts (6)–(9) that you listed in order of appropriacy In Checking understanding (7.2). Can you identify any of Brown and Levinson's politeness strategies in them and say how the politeness strategies contributed to your ranking?

7.3.2 The universal character of politeness

In the answer to Checking understanding (7.4), I made the point that over-classes tend to favour distance encoding negative politeness strategies and under-classes tend to favour solidarity encoding positive politeness strategies. This may be schematized as shown in Figure 7.1.

Powerful speakers	Powerful speakers
negative politeness	negative politeness
↓	↑
↓	↑
↓	↑
positive politeness	positive politeness

Figure 7.1

We also stated at the very beginning of the chapter that Brown and Levinson believe that politeness phenomena are universal. If this is right, we should be able to extrapolate the intra-societal politeness behaviour we noted in over- and under-class communication to whole societies. Thus in hierarchical societies with strong class distinctions, the over-classes will see to it that the under-classes employ more negative politeness strategies when addressing their 'elders and betters' as a way of encoding and thus maintaining the distance between socially stratified groups who acquire face status through birth. More egalitarian societies, on the other hand, will employ positive politeness strategies as a way of encoding and thus confirming a less territorial view of face. In such societies face is said to be 'ascribed' on merit rather than 'acquired' by birth.

With this in mind we turn to one challenging line of criticism of Brown and Levinson's model, that the politeness usage they describe is not universal. Thus Matsumoto (1988) argues that in Japanese the structures associated with negative politeness strategies in Brown and Levinson's model do not have a negative politeness function but instead constitute a social register. Gu (1990) argues that the model is unsuited to Chinese usage in which politeness phenomena still reflect to some degree the etymology of the word for politeness, one of whose constituent morphemes (*li*) denotes social order. Like Matsumoto's and Gu's, most other criticisms of the Brown and Levinson model on these grounds post-date the 1987 re-issue of their book.

Of course, we would not expect identical computations of appropriate politeness formulae across cultures any more than we would across varying situations in a single culture. Just as we employ different strategies to get different people to do things for us, so asking for assistance when, for example, your car breaks down will impose to different degrees in different societies (Nwoye, 1992). It is important therefore to separate culturally variable estimates of power, distance and imposition, which we would expect to occur, from the strategies and linguistic manifestations of strategies which a universal account of politeness would need to capture.

Much of Matsumoto's criticism centres on the way that deference is manifested in Japanese honorifics. She claims, in my opinion rightly, that Brown and Levinson's formulation does not account for such data. But her perspective raises the issue, not of whether politeness phenomena are universal, but rather of whether Brown and Levinson are right to treat deference as a politeness strategy. As she says, 'It is far from clear that deference can be equated with the speaker's respecting an individual's right to non-imposition' (1988: 409). In fact, we probably need to distinguish two uses of deference:

- the situation where it is given expectably and unexceptionally as an automatic acknowledgement of relative social status; in this case the use of honorifics reinforces an existing culture and is not a chosen politeness strategy at all
- the situation where it is given expectably but exceptionally in a particular situation as a redressive strategy.

In the first situation, the speaker is attempting to produce a context-reflecting utterance acceptable to the addressee as addressee, and in the second to produce a context-creating utterance acceptable to the addressee in the situation shared by speaker and addressee. The problem of course is in distinguishing between situations where speakers have little or no option in their choice of *tu/vous* type alternatives and situations where they do, and can thus use honorifics as politeness markers to invoke a new context. Perhaps an illustration will help.

I once took part in a debate with a Conservative Member of Parliament many years my senior in which I probably said some hard things about his speech. After the debate I bought a round of drinks. When it came to asking him what he would like, this is how the exchange went:

(50) PETER: And for you sir
      MP: Oh so it's sir now is it

Mine was clearly a politeness strategy that misfired as I tried to create a context to match my addressee's perception of how he should be addressed. Matsumoto (1988) gives examples of four ways that you might ask someone in Japan if they were going to have lunch, each displaying deference at an appropriate level. One could hardly imagine a Japanese professor addressed with the elaborate deference that professors customarily receive in Japan challenging the speaker in the way that the Member of Parliament challenged me:

(51) Oh so it's o-yuuhan mesiagari-masu now is it (Oh so it's honorific-
      dinner eat (subject honorific)-polite now is it)

This shows that we need to distinguish between language which is reflective of presumptive context (the Japanese professor) and genuine politeness phenomena which are used to bring a context into being (the Member of Parliament situation in which the context I tried to bring into being was rejected).

In fact, objectors to Brown and Levinson's account frequently cite exotic sounding examples of apparent deference which are claimed as evidence that some notion of social order or societal interdependence rather than positive and negative face underlies politeness. A typical example is provided by Gu (1990) who cites the etymology of *bai* (to prostrate oneself at the foot of another) as in *baidu* (to read) as evidence that knowing one's place underlies Chinese politeness. Without being a native member of Chinese society it is very difficult to say anything definitive about this claim, but I rather doubt it. To me it would be like claiming that the Greek word *polis*, meaning *city*, from which 'politeness' is derived somehow determines the principles of politeness in the societies whose word for politeness is derived from a common ancestor. Or take the case of a request to pass the salt, as in

(52) Can you pass the salt

This request is frequently represented by

(53) Can you give me the salt

in non-native speaker English, often because this is a literal translation from the mother tongue. Surely this does not mean that deference is a motivating principle in the mother culture politeness systems of such speakers. What I am suggesting is that the prostrating-oneself element of *baidu* is as conventional and inert as a politeness strategy as the notion that a salt-giver is a powerful person being invited to dispense a valued commodity to others of inferior status. And in fact the untenability of this putative account is confirmed by the pragmatic acceptability of (53) amongst equals such as family members or close friends who know each other well.

Whether Brown and Levinson have proposed a model that is universal is always open to discussion; but what is really important about their work is their observation that politeness is not equally distributed. As they say: 'It is not as if there were some basic modicum of politeness owed by each to all' (1987: 5). Rather what is owed depends upon the calculation of what is expected in each social and situational context that arises.

7.3.3 Redefining the folk term

Much of our thinking about politeness is bedevilled by the fact that 'politeness' is a folk term. In Britain 'politeness' is typically used to describe negative politeness, which is presumed to be 'a good thing'. A typical folk view of politeness is implied in Phyllis's use of *very polite-spoke* in the exchange with which this chapter begins. I guess a strong connotation of *very polite-spoke* is standard or RP speech and that such a folk view of politeness as the speech style of the over-classes is strongly indicative of value for the speaker. Thus the value-neutral way in which 'politeness' is used as a term of pragmatic description applicable to all communicative instances of language use is easily confused with the quite different, but widely held, ideological attitude to politeness in society at large. This is why, in our earlier discussion, I deliberately highlighted the importance of *it's* in the exchange between Phyllis and myself and ignored the folk view implied by the use of *very polite-spoke*. From a pragmaticist's point of view, as we said earlier, 'politeness' is the term we use to describe the relationship between how something is said to an addressee and that addressee's judgement as to how it should be said. According to this definition, a theory of politeness is potentially capable of accounting for pragmatic uses of language, but will always be liable to being confused with a prescriptive approach to linguistic etiquette. Indeed, Gu's description of address modes in Chinese (1990: 250) in which non-familial addressees are styled *grandpa* or *aunt* as a mark of respect seem to me to be essentially descriptions of prescriptions rather than descriptions of context-creating politeness phenomena.

7.3.4 Politeness as merely redressive?

In this chapter, I have been saying that all instances of language in use have politeness status. This contrasts with the view of politeness as no more than a bolt-on redressive element which is typically found in interactional but not in transactional discourse:

> Conversational behaviour that is consistent with the requirements of transactional discourse will thus be characterized by close observance of the Cooperative Principle. Interactional discourse, by contrast, has as its primary goal the establishment and maintenance of social relationships (Kasper, 1990: 205)

As Kasper goes on to point out, this is to claim that observing maxims of Quality and Manner will have priority over satisfying face-wants in transactional discourse while the opposite will obtain in interactional discourse. In my opinion, this claim misses the point that face-wants are satisfied precisely by giving priority to veracity and clarity in certain situations, including in transactional discourse such as you find in a book like this. Thus in casual conversation it is preferred to begin with a safe topic such as the weather. But this is not the case when talking on the telephone where time costs money. Both strategies are adapted to their contexts, including in particular to addressees' expectations of how talk should be directed to them in such contexts. For this reason, an adequately formulated theory of linguistic politeness which can account for the extent to which the things we say match our addressees' perceptions of how they should be said would be a strong candidate theory of pragmatic usage.

Raising pragmatic awareness: politeness

1. Working individually, eavesdrop on two or three conversations and write down what people say when they smile. Try to identify the politeness status of what is said. Share your findings with friends or other members of your tutorial group. Finally, invent a further eavesdropping task with a politeness dimension for members of your tutorial group to try.
2. Devise and carry out a simple rapid anonymous sampling experiment such as mine in the two bookshops described in Checking understanding (7.3). Report your findings to you colleagues in your next tutorial.
3. Cut out of a colour magazine a picture which shows two people who are clearly together. Write down five or six different ways in which one of the people might:
   (a)   invite the other out
   (b)   ask the other the time
   (c)   accuse the other of telling a lie
   (d)   tell the other he/she smells.
   Bring your picture and possible utterances to the tutorial and ask your colleagues to decide which way of expressing the proposition would be most appropriate for the people concerned.
4. This exercise works best in a small group. Pick a nation and decide how that nation is stereotypically seen. Then try to associate this stereotype with typical politeness strategies. If you can get this exercise to work, do the same thing with an intra-cultural group such as the young or the old within your own culture or with some

ethnically or gender-constituted group. If possible, follow this up by careful observation of a representative of the group you were stereotyping to see whether your
stereotype is at all reflected in your subject. To what extent is stereotyping one
person's view of another person's pragmatics? (Acknowledgement: this is Kelly
Glover's idea.)

5. Listen out for the way people reflect their own status in talk. Make a careful note of
what you hear and report it to your next tutorial group.

Further reading

Brown, P. and Levinson, S.C. (1978/1987) (especially the 1987 introduction), key
passages are also reprinted in Jaworski, A. and Coupland, N. (1999: 321–35); Foley,
W.A. (1997: 270–5) (for a very clear perspective on Brown and Levinson's model);
Leech, G.N. (1983: 79–84); Matsumoto, Y. (1988, 1989); *Journal of Pragmatics*, Vol.
14, No. 2 (special issue on politeness, including papers by Gu and Kasper); *Journal
of Pragmatics*, Vol. 21, No. 5 (special issue on politeness across cultures).

8 Speech events

'Suit the action to the word, the word to the action'
(*Hamlet* III.ii.17)

Keywords speech event, speech act, utterance, context, expectation, indirect speech act, strategy, genre, activity type, conversation, goal, E-language, I-language

---

In this chapter we show how speech acts play a role in the wider context of sequences of utterances and actions that, taken together, follow an expectable pattern and constitute a recognizable routine. As we shall see, speech event theory extends the notion of intentionality that underlies speech act theory by showing how every utterance has a role in a larger goal-directed language 'game' or activity.

8.1 The role of utterances in speech events

In Chapter 3 we saw how sentence types such as interrogatives are frequently used to do things other than ask questions. In fact, the list of interrogatives below, which we have already met in earlier chapters, are exactly of this kind. As you read each of them again, try to recall the context in which it occurred and consider its function in this wider speech event context.

(1)   What's your name by the way

(2)   Do you usually have this sort

(3)   Are we all here

(4)   Right, shall we begin

(5) May I speak English

(6) What's your name again

(7) Is it tea or coffee

(8) Would you like tea or coffee

(9) How are you doing

(10) Are you here Peter

(11) Have you got a plastic bag

(12) Could I just borrow a tiny bit of paper

(13) Why do farmers have long ears and bald heads

(14) Shall I pick you up at eight

(15) Do you sell postage stamps

(16) Do you know about our offer on oil

What is important about all these indirect speech acts is that they play a recognizable role in a larger context. So (13), for example, is recognizable as the first turn in a joke inviting the standard response *I don't know*. (16) is recognizable as an offer to tell, inviting the standard response, *no*, with a fall-rise intonation contour. In the case of (3), spoken by a senior colleague when a meeting was due to start, we saw that the most appropriate response was non-verbal – indeed to provide an answer such as *No, we're not* would be accurate but useless. All that one can safely say about these utterances is that since they are open propositions, each invites some sort of response. But the functions of the utterances and the nature of the responses depend on their roles in the speech events of which they are a part. They are expectable just to the extent that they have roles in recognizable routines.

This is not to deny the possibility of routines taking unexpectable directions, as happened on the occasion when I responded in a dispreferred way to (16) (p. 60), or when the resident in the old people's home responded in an unexpected way to the Lord Mayor's question *Do you know who I am* (p. 55), or when Mr Logic responded in his absurd but 'logical' way to the expectable response to his utterance, *Do you sell postage stamps* (p. 56). But even when speech events take unexpected directions, the participants in them still act in a goal-directed way. For example, the utterance *what's it for* usually occurs when someone sees an object or instrument whose function they do not know. In the following exchange it has a different function:

(17) A: What is it
     B: A kittle
     A: A kittle?
     B: Yes a kittle
     A: What's it for

You have probably already guessed that *What's it for* is a strategy aimed at getting B to provide sufficient information for A to understand *a kittle*. Since B is a non-native speaker of English describing a picture to her English teacher, A's question constitutes a novel strategy which both satisfies a pedagogic purpose and duly brings about a problem-resolving response. The whole sequence goes like this:

(18) A: What is it
      B: A kittle
      A: A kittle?
      B: Yes a kittle
      A: What's it for
      B: It's for boil water
      A: Oh a kettle

Anybody listening to this exchange would be able to 'type' the speech event as an encounter involving a native and a non-native speaker, and would define *what's it for* in terms of its function in the speech event, which is to enable A to determine what B is describing.

8.1.1 Genres

Another way of making the point just made would be to say that speech events are genres. This is clearest when we look at the properties of a recognized genre such as a recipe. Consider this example.

(19)

Scampi Provençale

Method

1. Fry the onion and garlic gently in the butter or margarine until cooked but not browned.
2. Add tomatoes, wine, seasoning, sugar and parsley, stir well and simmer gently for 10 minutes.
3. Drain the scampi well, add to the sauce and continue simmering for about 5 minutes, or until they are just heated through.
4. Serve with crusty French bread, or boiled rice.

Ingredients

1 onion, chopped
1 clove of garlic, chopped
25g (1oz) butter or margarine
1 375g (15oz) tin tomatoes, drained
4 15ml (table) spoons dry white wine
seasoning
pinch sugar
1 15ml (table) spoon parsley, chopped
200g (8oz) frozen scampi, thawed

Serves 4

This text is recognizable as a recipe in form and style. Indeed, the form is partly defined by the style, so that the verbs under *Method* are finite (*fry*, *add*) and under *Ingredients* non-finite (*chopped*, *drained*). The noun phrases have determiners under *Method* but not under *Ingredients*. The *Method* column has preposition phrases (*in the butter*) and post-predicate modification (*stir well, simmer gently*) while the *Ingredients* column has neither preposition phrases nor predicate modifiers. Thus the *Methods* column exhibits cohesion, but the *Ingredients* column is just a list which does not even exhibit concord (*4 15ml (table) spoons*). There is also a characteristic way of reading this text. If you try it yourself, you'll see that you get as far as *the* in *Fry the onion* in the *Method* column before going to *Ingredients* column to answer the question 'What onion?' which you'll have asked yourself. Thus the first three words in the left-hand column are read first and then the entire right-hand column is read next before the reader returns to the left-hand column. When this process is accomplished you have passed the understanding test and can cook *Scampi Provençale*, a description which is neither English by grammar (a noun + modifier combination) nor by lexis.

Recipes are a unique genre whose formal and stylistic properties are what makes them recipes. Notice also that recipes closely parallel the set of instructions for making sentences – the *Method* is like a set of phrase structure rules and the *Ingredients* are like a lexicon. Because a recipe is a stable written genre, it is relatively easy to describe. The unique character of most speech events is harder to demonstrate, partly because they are spoken rather than written. Speech events are genres whose properties are sets of predictably deployed speech acts.

8.1.2 The formal properties of speech events

In his paper on the structure of speech events, Levinson argues that 'activity type' is a better term than 'speech event' because 'speech event' implies that all the acts which constitute it are acts of speaking. Levinson defines an activity type as 'any culturally recognized activity, whether or not that activity is co-extensive with a period of speech or indeed whether any talk takes place in it at all' (1979: 368). A telephone conversation is an activity co-extensive with a period of speech, whereas a 100m sprint would not be expected to contain talk. In determining the function of any utterance, 'we depend both on the meaning of the words which serve to differentiate the utterances, and on the possible roles which utterances can play within such a game' (Levinson, 1979: 367). This suggests that to understand properly the structure of an activity type or speech event is to account for the roles of the speech acts that make it up. This was especially clear to me on one occasion when I was in a motorway restaurant and the person on the next table was using his mobile phone. This is what I overheard:

(20) A: OK well I'd better go Mum
      B:
      A: No she's already done that
      B:
      A: OK bye-bye

I was struck by *OK well I'd better go Mum*. What made it feel strange was precisely that the speaker was literally going to go, i.e. to leave his present location. Usually, when we say *I'd better go* as part of the closing sequence of a telephone conversation, we aren't actually 'going' anywhere.

Checking understanding (8.1)

1. What expectable routines can you identify in A's contributions to the telephone exchange above?
2. What do you think B's contributions were?

Levinson defines activity types as

> goal defined, socially constituted, bounded, events with constraints on the participants, setting and so on, but above all on the kinds of allowable contributions. Paradigm examples would be teaching, a job interview, a jural interrogation, a football game, a task in a workshop, a dinner party and so on.   (1979: 368)

Utterances have force 'by virtue of the expectations governing the activity' (1979: 372). Thus the same lexical item, *Pass*, makes activity-specific contributions to the television general knowledge contest, *Mastermind* (as we saw in Chapter 3), a game of bridge and a game of football.

8.1.3 The style of a speech event

The goal-directed nature of speech events reflects the intentionality of language use. So the goal of television chat-show interview, for example, might be to get the guest to talk freely and entertainingly in a number of topic areas (career, future plans, etc.) to three kinds of audience (interviewer, studio audience, overhearing home audience). This is a simplification but one that enables us to consider the strategies that might enable this goal to be achieved. Since 'the various levels of organization within an activity cohere and can be seen to derive as rational means from overall ends' (Levinson, 1979: 390), it ought to be possible to specify the style by which the overall ends of a speech event such as a chat-show interview are achieved.

Working with data drawn from a television chat-show, I am going to show how the language used is constrained by the goals and setting of the activity type and can best be explained (perhaps only be explained) as constitutive of the event.

Consider the following interrogative structure used by a chat-show host to Sir Edmund Hillary:

(21) I wonder its er you are one of the sort of great adventuring figures of of this century and one wonders er you know where that all starts

> from and stems from did you have the er any sort of sense of destiny
> as a as a child

The final interrogative structure contains a repaired false start, *the er any*; a hesitation, *er*; a hedge, *sort of*; and a redundant repetition, *as a as a*. Thus in (22), only the items in Roman script represent the propositional content of the question put; the other items have a hedging function:

(22) did you have *the er* any *sort of* sense of destiny as a *as a* child

The other parts of this turn show the same property:

(23) you are one of the *sort of* great adventuring figures of *of* this century

(24) *I wonder it's er* you are one of . . .

(25) one wonders *er you know* where that all . . .

Thus exaggerated statements such as *you are one of the great adventuring figures of this century* are moderated by repairs and redundancies, and by hedges and hesitations. Given the inherently threatening nature of the interview format of chat-shows which clashes with the goal of promoting free and entertaining talk, guests have to be put at their ease. This is accomplished by overstating their achievements. But these Quality-flouting overstatements have to be mitigated by hedges and other devices, or they run the risk of being 'over the top' or even seeming ironical.

Checking understanding (8.2) ──────────────────

Identify the repairs and reformulations, redundancies and repetitions, hedges, and hesitations in the following questions put by the chat-show host to Sir Edmund Hillary.

(26) How determined were you er yourself to be the the er first man to to climb Everest

(27) Was there er er a physical or specialist advantage that you had er yourself in in enabling you to to to climb Everest I mean were you a better climber than anybody else or were you physically stronger or what

───

Example (27) also illustrates the way that the inherent threat of questions is mitigated. The interviewee appears to be asked to choose between two answer options, physical advantage or better technique. This question is put twice. The hedge, *I mean*, before the second formulation indicates that the interviewer doubts the clarity of the first formulation. But the second formulation ends with *or what*, an open invitation to give any answer at all. In this way, the force of the question is mitigated since any answer is a good answer. And the implied compliment that the interviewee is both physically stronger and has superior technique can now be modestly denied without providing a dispreferred answer. The way questions were asked in (21) and (26) displayed similar mitigating techniques. In (21) the interviewer speculates on the impossibility of providing an answer to the question (shown by *I wonder, one wonders*) and in (26) the question presupposes that the interviewee was *determined* but leaves him the option of indicating the degree of his determination.

A chat-show host must ask questions. But asking questions constitutes a face threat which is liable to frustrate the goal of the activity. Therefore it is characteristic of this speech event that the interviewer employs a range of techniques to mitigate their force.

Checking understanding (8.3) ────────────────────

A number of other questions asked by the host in this chat-show are listed below. Show how each is designed to mitigate the inherent threat of the speech act.

(28) you also of course you you played a er a um a extraordinary episode in your career er if I remember arightly was it you rescued er did you not er er um um a masterpiece an Italian masterpiece

(29) do you agree with that do you

(30) but once you saw it and once it was there what you I mean you had to conquer it had you

(31) finally I'd like to ask you its er er a daft question I know but I've always wanted to ask this of somebody who's obviously displayed great courage and you had to have that at least to climb Everest what frightens you

The limited space available does not permit an exhaustive account of the goal-directed strategies employed in activity types. Instead, I am going to cite just four examples of data which show a range of the goal-directed strategies employed by this chat-show host.

Strategy   Do not pursue/do not allow another speaker to pursue controversial topics:

(32) HILLARY: it's impossible for us to stop the change
INTERVIEWER: yes
HILLARY: and I deplore this
INTERVIEWER: yes
HILLARY: but what can one do about it
INTERVIEWER: yes conversely of course I mean I'd like to ask all three of you this too

Strategy Respond encouragingly by exaggerating interest or displaying polite incredulity:

(33) INTERVIEWER: I mean what is it that you having had close contact
with these people um have gained from THEM from
HILLARY: knowledge
INTERVIEWER: knowledge
HILLARY: self-knowledge
INTERVIEWER: really

Strategy Compliment off-record by understatement:

(34) INTERVIEWER: you say once said of yourself you had a rather nice
phrase

Strategy Use concessives when referring to face-threatening situations to imply that they are untypical:

(35) INTERVIEWER: what made you though when you were a child feel
insecure

Summary

We have shown how speech acts play a role in the speech events that contain them and how each particular utterance has distinct, goal-directed properties. Thus an utterance like *what's it for* is prototypically used to request information about the function of an object, but, as we saw, there will be occasions when the same utterance has a less prototypical function. Thus *what's it for* has different illocutionary forces in different contexts and hence different speech acts are performed. But at the same time, the illocutionary force of *what's it for* transforms the context in some way so that the request for information and the attempt to understand the unintelligible utterance are both contexts created to some degree by the same speech act. This returns us to a consideration of the relation of context and language: is the language of the chat-show prescribed by the external context (the context-as-given view) or is the context created by the particular assemblage of linguistic values displayed in the chat-show? Language use therefore has a predictable quality which can be accounted for as the stylistic realization of the structure of a speech event.

8.2 Conversations as speech events

In the next chapter we will study conversational methods from a Conversation Analytic (CA) perspective. We will discover that these methods include turn-taking and the preference for particular types of contribution in particular talk situations. Most conversations, or talk events, also exhibit 'procedural consequentiality'. That's to say, each contribution to a talk exchange is purposeful and contributes relevantly to an outcome – it helps to bring about consequence.

In this second part of the chapter, we are going to examine a talk exchange involving a customer and a travel agent from a speech event perspective. As we shall see, the customer has a goal, to discover whether it would be cheaper to fly to Edinburgh or to take the train. You might think this goal would be readily achieved, but as it turns out, the customer, an educated 35-year-old male, employs a very wide range of strategies in an attempt to achieve the outcome he desires. The travel agent is a 25-year-old female. This is how the exchange between them begins.

(36) CUSTOMER: can you help me I have to go to Edinburgh (.) somebody told me it was cheaper to go by plane than by train (.) is that right
TRAVEL AGENT: (1.5) well we're not British Rail agents so I don't know the difference
CUSTOMER: oh I see

Below I draw your attention to a number of issues raised by this short opening exchange and pose a number of questions for you to consider.

1. Who should speak first? And what is the effect of the customer seizing the initiative in this way?
2. The customer's opening turn is four units long with brief pauses approximately equivalent to the time it takes to say one syllable [indicated by (.)] between the second and third and the third and fourth units. This is a comparatively long and rather unusual turn in the sense that it contains four units. What do you think its effect on the travel agent might be?
3. The customer says *I have to go to Edinburgh*. He does not have to give a reason for asking for information, although as we saw in the last chapter, giving a reason is a politeness strategy. But by their very nature, politeness strategies imply that there is something to redress, like troubling someone else for information. Do you think giving a reason for asking for information in this situation is a good strategy or not?
4. If it is appropriate for the customer to give a reason for asking for information, what advantages or disadvantages would there be in using a different formula, such as *I'm going to Edinburgh, I want to go to Edinburgh, I must go to Edinburgh*? Unlike *must*, in most varieties of British (but not American) English, *I have to* conventionally implicates that this decision was made for the customer by someone else. What conversational implicatures are triggered by *I have to*: Does the customer imply that he is an important person? Does he imply that it is not his fault that he is troubling the travel agent by making this inquiry? If the latter, does *have to* count as a kind of apology?
5. The customer is careful to be impersonal: he says *somebody told me* rather than *I was told* and *is that right* rather than *is he right*. Do you agree that by doing this he makes it easier for the travel agent to reply

that the information is wrong without suggesting that the customer, or someone known to him, is mistaken? Again, this is a politeness strategy.

6. What do you make of the customer's use of two past tenses *someone told me it was* rather than past + present *someone told me it's* or two present tenses *I've heard it's*? Would you agree that this seems to be a politeness strategy, with the information being represented as historical rather than contemporary, and therefore easier for the travel agent to contradict without giving offence?

7. Notice the customer's choice of *right* rather than *true*. Again, the customer will lose less face if this information turns out to be false and the travel agent has to contradict it.

8. Taken altogether, this opening is marked by politeness strategies. These have the effect of making it easier for the travel agent to contradict the customer, but at the same time they place a distance between the customer and the travel agent. For example, we don't talk to our close friends or family in this way (unless we're Mr Logic). Perhaps these strategies are the customer's way of saying that he is male, middle-class, educated, a customer, and someone who expects to be served. Do you think he would have done better to have been more familiar, to have gone to the opposite extreme, leant across the counter, taken the travel agent by the neck and said 'Give us a kiss, love – is it cheaper to go to Edinburgh on the train or the plane?'

9. Can you account for the long pause before the travel agent begins to speak? Is this because she is overwhelmed, or because she is deciding whether or how to disappoint the customer?

10. *Well* often signals that a dispreferred or unexpected conversational contribution is upcoming. It is therefore in a sense conciliatory and counts as a kind of apology. The travel agent's response also contains two propositions *we're not British Rail agents* and *I don't know the difference*. Which of these do you consider answers the customer's question better and responds more appropriately to his request for assistance? Which, if either, is syntactically or pragmatically subordinate? What do you learn about her position from her use of the institutional *we* in one proposition and *I* in the other? What effect is the institutional *we* intended to have on the customer? Given the illocutionary force, a refusal to comply with the customer's request for information, can you think of other utterances that would have conveyed this meaning equally successfully?

11. *Oh* is an expletive used to express surprise. *I see* implies that the preceding utterance is unsatisfactory, perhaps by flouting Quantity. Do you think this kind of indirectness is the customer's best strategy at this stage? What does his turn achieve?

12. In his opening, the customer pragmatically presupposes that the travel agent has and is willing to supply information. The travel agent

responds in such a way as to challenge this presupposition. We might expect the rest of this interaction to be about finding a formula that enables both the customer and the travel agent to save face. Or we might expect it to proceed in such a way as to enable one or the other of them to come out of the encounter with what they want at the expense of the other. Based on what you have seen so far, which of these outcomes would you put your money on?

Looked at strategically, the exchange so far has gone something like this:

CUSTOMER: request for information (reason given)
TRAVEL AGENT: refusal to supply information (reason given)
CUSTOMER: indication that this is not a sufficient response

Can you guess what the travel agent does next?

What the travel agent actually produces next is not information but an offer to provide information:

(37) TA: I can tell you what it is to go to Edinburgh

This offer is expressed in such a way that the customer must suggest the extent of the information he thinks it would be reasonable or expectable for the travel agent to provide. Note also that the travel agent's use of *can* rather than *'ll* forces the customer's next contribution. This comes in two parts, with the second part supplied after a one second pause in which the travel agent was offered but declined to take the turn, thus obliging the customer to spell out the extent of the information the travel agent is expected to give:

(38) C: yes (1.0) by plane

The travel agent then confirms her agreement to the terms of the offer

(39) TA: by plane

and by breaking off forces the customer to take the turn again. The customer uses this to confirm that the terms are agreed, whereupon the travel agent reaches for the timetable. After a pause of nearly two seconds, the customer 'types' the sequence by expressing gratitude:

(40) C: yeh (1.7) thanks very much

Thus the whole opening sequence of the encounter goes like this:

(41) C: can you help me I have to go to Edinburgh (.) somebody told me
         it was cheaper to go by plane than by train (.) is that right
     TA: (1.5) well we're not British Rail agents so I don't know the
         difference
     C: oh I see
     TA: I can tell you what it is to go to Edinburgh
     C: yes (1.0) by plane
     TA: by plane
     C: yeh (1.7) thanks very much

We might expect the travel agent to use her next few turns to tell her customer the cost of flying to Edinburgh. But what will happen after that? And do you still put your money on the outcome you predicted before?

It takes the travel agent 13 seconds, while she studies the timetable, before she takes her turn. The next four turns are

(42) TA: (13.0) well there's a shuttle service (0.4) um (.) £60 one way (2.5)
          er (2.3) when do you want to go
     C: I want to go at the weekend
     TA: (0.3) what weekend=
     C: =next weekend

The customer opts to give the lexical realization *I want to go* rather than allow it to be presupposed. Is this a way of refusing to allow the travel agent to construct part of his turn for him? And if so, what does it convey? The customer's *at the weekend* is a deictic which would usually be taken to refer to the weekend following the time of utterance. But the travel agent does not process it in this way; she appears to reprimand the customer's failure to name a specific weekend by her choice of the potentially metalingual *what* (which questions the notion of weekend) rather than the preferred *which* (which would presuppose a set of weekends to choose from). The customer indicates his displeasure by the speed of his response (indicated in the transcription by the two 'equals' [=] symbols), which consists of a deictic elaboration of his original turn, *next weekend*.

But in fact they are at cross-purposes, as the continuing sequence will show. For the travel agent, weekends are a list of dates in the timetable with different prices written beside them, so that her conception of weekend is not deictic at all. For the customer, weekends are deictically stacked up ahead of the time of utterance. Thus from the travel agent's perspective *what weekend* is perfectly logical and refers to a timetable entry. But the customer has failed to reconstruct this perspective. So how do the customer and the travel agent stand now that the customer has mistakenly supposed that the travel agent has reprimanded him in refusing his deictic and has reprimanded her in return? His reprimand will seem unmotivated to the travel agent just as the customer felt he had received an unmotivated reprimand before.

Is your money still on the same outcome?

The entire encounter is printed below. As you will see as you read it through, there is a third speaker, the manager, a 45-year-old male. He first speaks at line 26 but remains at the back of the shop busying himself over a pile of papers until l.84–5, when he comes up to the counter. In the transcription, the beginning and end of each overlapping utterance is marked by deep brackets, inaudible contributions are marked by square brackets enclosing empty spaces, and pauses indicated in tenths of a second in brackets. Very short pauses are indicated by a stop in brackets, roughly equivalent to a pause of one-syllable length.

(43) C: can you help me I have to go to Edinburgh (.) somebody told 1
      me it was cheaper to go by plane than by train (.) is that 2
      right 3
TA: (1.5) well we're not British Rail agents so I don't know 4
      the difference 5
C: oh I see 6
TA: I can tell you what it is to go to Edinburgh 7
C: yes (1.0) by plane 8
TA: by plane 9
C: yeh (1.7) thanks very much 10
TA: (13.0) well there's a shuttle service (0.4) um (.) £60 one 11
      way (2.5) er (2.3) when do you want to go 12
C: I want to go at the weekend 13
TA: (0.3) what weekend= 14
C: =next weekend (3.5) how does that work you just turn up for 15
      the shuttle service 16
TA: (0.8) that might be cheaper then (1.8) that's 50 17
C: 50 18
TA: that's a saver (0.7) bᵤrit it's a standby 19
C: a stᵣandby ⌉ 20
TA: ᴸyou haᴶve to book it in advance but um (.) 21
C: are you guaranteed a seat 22
TA: (8.0) I don't think you are 23
C: so you buy a ticket beᵣfore butᵓ 24
TA: ᴸRon   ᴶ with the shuttle saver 25
M: (0.8) yeh 26
TA: um (.) are they guaranteed seats 27
M: (3.5) er 28
TA: this is a new one that Marie's just added in here (1.7) oh 29
      hang ⌈ on see   ⌉ 30
M: ⌊ British Airwaysᴶ 31
TA: see see stop press [   ] 32
M: (0.3) British Airways 33
TA: yeah 34
M: er yeah the flight's a standby guarantee (..) yeah you you 35
      turn up and you've got to er (1.0) if they can't get on one 36
      flight they'll put you on the next any of the next two 37
C: (0.2) and hᵣand   ⌉ 38
TA: ᴸ[   ]ᴶ 39
C: [   ] how often do they go 40
M: every two hours 41
C: every two hours (1.6) so you could wait four hours 42
TA: (1.0) yeh 43
C: um hum (2.0) and that's £50 one way 44
TA: yes 45
C: (0.8) and have you got a timetable for 46

TA: not to give out no (0.7) I can tell you the times but I   47
don't   48
C: ye-es could you tell me how often they go Saturdays and   49
coming back on Sundays   50
TA: (13.0) all right (0.3) Saturdays you're going out   51
C: yeh   52
TA: (1.0) yeh   53
C: yeh   54
TA: 7.40 9.40 11.40 13.40   55
C: (0.6) 7.40 11.40   56
TA: (0.5) 7.40   57
C: 9.40   58
TA: every two hours   59
C: every two hours on on on 40 minutes   60
TA: till (.) 19.40   61
C: yes (1.3) good   62
TA: and coming back they er (3.4) er (0.4) you're coming back   63
Sunday aren't you   64
C: Sunday please   65
TA: (2.8) 9.40 11.40   66
C: ah ha (.) so it's 40 either way and it starts at 7.40 on   67
Saturday from London and 9.40 from Edinburgh on Sunday (.)   68
until what time on Sunday night   69
TA: same time 19.40   70
C: 19.40 (.) now what happens if you turn up for the 19.40   71
flight and they get you on any of the next two does that   72
mean Monday (1.5) or do they guarantee to do something   73
about it on Sunday night   74
TA: (2.0) I don't know (.) Ron what happens if he wants the last   75
flight (3.7) will they do it like that or don't they allow   76
that   77
M: (1.0) what's that   78
TA: what happens if he wants the last fl⌈ight⌉   79
C: ⌊if I⌋ want to come back   80
on the ⌈last flight on the Sunday night⌉   82
TA: ⌊ ⌈   ⌉ they don't put   ⌋ on an extra plane   82
do they ⌊ [   ]   ⌋   83
M: (1.4) well theoretically if it's full they're supposed to   84
put a back-up plane on   85
C: um hum   86
M: in theory (2.1) whether or not it works in practice I don't   87
know   88
C: (3.0) now if I buy a ticket from you then it costs I I pay   89
you £100 ⌈ (.) n⌉   90
M: ⌊yes ⌋   91
C: then I go there and (0.6) n I'm in their   92
hands   93

M:	that's right sir yes	94
C:	do you know what the rail return (.) weekend return to	95
	Edinburgh is by any chance	96
TA:	we're not British Rail ⌈agents⌉	97
C:	⌊you're⌋ not a ⌈gents I see⌉	98
M:	⌊but I'll ⌋ give you	99
	a rough idea	100
C:	ah ha thank you very much	101
M:	(12.0) £68.60	102
C:	68.60 (0.6) good thank you very much (.) I ⌈thin ⌉	103
M:	⌊that's⌋ from	104
	London sir	105
C:	that's from London (.) either way I've got to get myself (.)	106
M:	yeh	107
C:	to the right ⌈place⌉	108
M:	⌊yes ⌋	109
C:	yeh I'll think about it	110
M:	yeh	111
C:	thanks very much that's very helpful (.) bye-bye	112

Seen as a whole, the exchange enables us to reconstruct a wider social context. Because the travel agent is not a British Rail agent, the young female member of staff with low-status office-fronting responsibilities has been trained not to provide information about rail travel. Such privileged information can only be given by the manager at his own discretion. The customer does not know this when he walks into the shop. But through his persistence, he reinforces the existing social structure in which real business is done by males of higher status over the head of the low-status female employee whose job it is to prevent such business from needing to be done. Thus each of the three interactants replicates a recognizable routine and creates once again the society that was waiting to be re-made.

Thinking back to the initial politeness strategies of the customer, we see how this outcome was scripted when he began the encounter by establishing his status through distancing himself from the travel agent. When the distance between the customer and the travel agent is great enough and the information sought precious enough, the manager is called in. This situation is recognizable to us all and re-made many times in everyday life, as the stereotype of the secretary who guards the manager's door reminds us.

Within this overview in which the distal social structure outside the interaction and re-made in it has been sketched in, there are a number of notable features of the exchange that are worth commenting on.

- Line 102: The customer does get the information he was seeking. It takes him just over four minutes to obtain the information that it takes the travel agent thirteen seconds and the manager twelve seconds to find.
- Lines 25–34, 75–83: It is notable how difficult it is for the travel agent to

engage the manager's attention. At l.25 and l.27 and at l.75 and l.79, she raises her pitch, a strategy identified by Loveday as a typical subservience feature of female speech. In fact, it takes her two turns on each occasion to gain what passes for the manager's full attention. On the first occasion when his assistance is sought, he declines to approach the place where the negotiation is being conducted and remains a voice-throw away at the back of the shop.

- Lines 62, 67, 101, 103: The customer's two metapragmatic *ah-ha*'s and two metapragmatic *good*'s acknowledge that he has secured something of value – at l.67, that he has understood an utterance that he had had problems with; at l.101, that he has been promised the information he was seeking and had been denied until that point.

- Line 80: The travel agent invites the manager into the conversation as her informant, but the customer sees his chance and quickly manages to redirect the interaction from a customer ↔ assistant exchange to a customer ↔ manager exchange. Is this because he decides that man-to-man or customer-to-manager talk is more likely to secure the outcome he wants? Is it prompted by the travel agent referring to the customer at l.75 and again at l.79 heterogeneously by her use of *he*, as someone excluded from the homogenous group that includes herself and the manager and excludes the customer? The customer achieves this re-direction by taking the manager's turn through starting to speak before the manager responds to the travel agent's question at l.79. Although the travel agent did not have the information sought and for that reason brought the manager into the interaction, she tries to stay in the conversation at l.82 by providing a putative answer to her own question during what has now become the customer's turn. After this failed attempt to contribute to the interaction, she will have one more utterance only, the formulaic *we're not British Rail agents*.

- Line 89: The interaction takes a decisive turn when the customer, after a long pause, indicates with a non-deictic *now* that the encounter is moving to a new phase. The *then* in *if I buy a ticket from you then* implies an agreement, although the customer has still to discover the price of the alternative means of travel. The repair which replaces *it costs* with *I pay you* personalizes a matter, the exchange of money, which is usually not so directly mentioned, but elicits an overlapping *yes* from the manager followed at l.94 by the defence marker *sir*. This is the moment at which the customer, with suitable politeness strategies, asks for the information he requires, this time by making reference to a felicity condition that can hardly be denied (whether the manager has the requisite knowledge) and expressing his request pessimistically (*by any chance*). The manager saves face with his offer to *give . . . a rough idea*.

- Lines 103–105: As soon as the manager sees that he is not going to make the sale, he provides additional information without prompting, *that's from London*, and repeats the deference marker, *sir*. All of a sudden, the information held by the travel agent has become cheap, in fact free, as the manager attempts to secure a sale that no longer looks likely.

Summary

In this section of the chapter, we have seen how Levinson's categorization of activity types as 'goal defined, socially constituted, bounded, events with constraints on participants, setting and so on, but above all on the kinds of allowable contributions' (1979: 368) can be productively applied to a speech event whose end is achieved through means specific to an event which seems at first glance to have no special institutional status.

8.2.1 Activity types and knowledge of language

The phrase 'knowledge of language' was used in a very particular way by Chomsky in his book of that title (1986). In many places in his work, Chomsky draws a distinction between knowing a language on the one hand and the use of language on the other. In *Knowledge of language*, he draws a distinction between the external manifestation of language and the internal knowledge underlying our ability to use it. He describes how generative linguistics shifted the focus in language study 'from the study of language regarded as an externalized object to the study of the system of knowledge attained and internally represented in the mind/brain' (1986: 24). In *Knowledge of language*, the external manifestation of language is termed E-language and the internal representation, I-language. Chomsky argues that what we know about language as revealed in our ability to discriminate the grammars of sentences like

(44) they left room empty

and

(45) they left the room angry

is the proper study of linguistics, and the way we choose to deploy language pragmatically is not part of that knowledge. There is a general consensus that knowledge of language (the domain of syntactic theorists) and knowledge of the rules of use (the domain of pragmaticists) are different knowledge domains. Thus the study of the grammar of *what's it for* and the study of the use of *what's it for* in a variety of contexts as an utterance with a variety of possible illocutionary forces are different disciplines.

Although this distinction is clear, the narrow view of the study of I-language can only be sustained if one regards as primary data invented sentences like (44) and (45) or idealized examples like (46) and (47) below:

(46) You are one of the great adventuring figures of this century

(47) Did you have any sense of destiny as a child

But when you look at real utterances like

(21) *I wonder its er* you are one of the *sort of* great adventuring figures of *of* this century and one wonders *er you know* where that all starts from and stems from did you have *the er* any sort of sense of destiny as a *as a* child

is it credible to argue that the italicized language whose functions are clearly pragmatic is a-grammatical and somehow outside our knowledge of language? Surely we have strong intuitions as to the syntactic constituents to which the italicized strings are attached. Is this not a reflection of our knowledge of language? Of language which could not be I-language without its E-language function? And ought not a properly thought through representation of our knowledge of language be able to account for all the data of utterances like (21)?

Raising pragmatic awareness: speech events

1. Choose an utterance that you recently overheard and write an entry for it in a dictionary of speech acts. Your entry should discuss its possible role in a variety of speech events. Exchange your work with a partner and discuss each of your entries together.

2. This exercise works best in a small group. Choose a word like *intelligent*, *stupid*, *generous*, *mean*, *young*, *old*, etc. Think of several synonyms for your chosen word and then imagine these synonyms in the following sentence frames: *she's/he's/they're/you're so/completely/100% ...* Discuss the speech events in which each of these utterances would be expectable. (Acknowledgement: this is Kelly Glover's idea.)

3. This exercise works best in a small group. Imagine an activity type setting such as ordering a meal in a restaurant, talking to a tutor, booking a holiday, etc. Then decide on language forms you would expect to find in this speech event – register, lexis, structure, turn taking, etc. (Acknowledgement: this is Kelly Glover's idea.)

4. Recall a recent speech event in which you were a participant and which was ends oriented. Spend a few minutes noting down defining contributions and then share your work with a colleague.

5. Recall a recent speech event in which you were a participant and which was ends oriented. Spend a few minutes noting down the constraints on participants, setting, allowable contributions, etc. and then share your work with a colleague.

Further reading

Hymes, D. (1962); Levinson, S.C. (1979, 1992).

9 Talk

'And like a downward smoke, the slender stream
Along the cliff to fall and pause and fall did seem.'
(Alfred Tennyson *The Lotos-Eaters*)

> *Keywords* talk-in-interaction, conversation, rationalistic and empirical pragmatics, members' method, sequential ordering, turn constructional unit, adjacency pair, latching, transition-relevance place, account, overlap, (dis)preferred contribution, repair, pause, *aizuchi*, formulation, self-formulation, causal explanation, attribution, ethnomethodology, clarification, lapse, folk term, macro/micro contexts, social structure

9.1 Pragmatics and conversation

In the early chapters of this book, the majority of the examples were single utterances or very short exchanges and were used largely to exemplify varieties of pragmatic meaning such as illocutionary force, implicature and presupposition. Rather than exemplify varieties of pragmatic meaning, in this chapter we will continue the examination of talk we began in the last chapter – but in this chapter from a conversation analytic (CA) perspective.

The expectation you hold as you begin this chapter, then, should perhaps be that the varieties of pragmatic meaning you are familiar with will be useful in explaining how meaning is conveyed utterance by utterance, but that these accounts of utterance meaning may be inadequate as accounts of how extended talk works.

One more perspective before we begin our work on conversation: in a paper which appeared in the *Journal of Pragmatics* in 1995, Roman Kopytko drew a distinction between what he called 'rationalistic' and 'empirical' pragmatics. In particular, Kopytko challenges the approach to pragmatics which is theory- rather than data-driven and argues against the means-ends teleology of activity type analysis. He objects to what he sees as the reductionist (i.e. simplifying and generalizing) nature of rationalistic explanations for complex data. And he cites Brown and Levinson's treatment of politeness phenomena as an paradigm example of rationalistic or ends-driven explanation. In fact, you may recall that I used the terms 'rationalistic' and 'teleological' in Chapter 7 when discussing how to stop Bill parking outside our house; and in the last chapter I twice mentioned Levinson's categorization of activity types as 'goal-defined'.

However, it isn't only our treatment of politeness and activity types that Kopytko would challenge. As you think back over the previous chapters of this book, you will see that our approach has been largely rationalistic from the outset – in our work on speech acts and implicature we have for the most part started with a theory and exemplified its principles with examples of observed language use. We have not followed the 'empirical' approach in which data drives our theorizing. This is now set to change. The conversation analytic approach to language understanding is characterized by the search for patterns in talk which reflect its culturally recognizable and therefore expectable nature. Unlike rationalistic pragmatics, empirical pragmatics, and CA in particular, makes no *a priori* assumptions about the data that are studied.

9.2 Members' methods

Consider the opening of what will turn out to be a six-and-a-half-minute conversation involving a university student and the head porter of the college where she lives.

```
(1)   P: hello young lady=
      S: =hiya (1.5) em I was round yesterday I've had some CDs
         nicked (.) ⌈from Yoko⌉
      P:            ⌊so they  ⌋ tell me (.) and I put (1.0) in your
         pigeonhole (.)
      S: right
      P: [you know] (.) a little parcel like that
      S: that's what Magda said ⌈she saw it yeah   ⌉
      P:                         ⌊and it was a little⌋ bit torn mind
         (.) but I put it in ⌈(.)  ⌉ and when Robin phoned me last
      S:                     ⌊well⌋
      P: night (.) I said I remember (.) I can't remember which name
         it was but I knew it was in the first pigeonhole
         ⌈A B⌉ C or D
      S: ⌊yeah⌋
```

```
S: yeah that's what me and Magda had looked ⌈in to see our
P:                                           ⌊that's right
S: mail⌉
P: and ⌋ it was there
```

The conversation begins with an exchange of greetings

(2) P: hello young lady=
     S: =hiya

The first thing to notice is that these two greetings occur sequentially, i.e. one of the two parties greets the other first. If you knew nothing about the organization of talk, you might expect both parties to greet each other simultaneously. But it turns out that overlaps are rare in talk, and even exchanges such as greetings occur as distinct **turn constructional units**, or turns.

Greetings are a special kind of turn known as an **adjacency pair**, adjacent utterances produced by different speakers and ordered so that the first member of the pair, or **first pair part**, requires an appropriate second member, or **second pair part**, of a relevant type to be produced as a response. Typical examples of adjacency pairs are greeting–greeting, invitation–acceptance/refusal, apology–acceptance/rejection (Schegloff and Sacks, 1973). Notice also the transcription convention, the equals signs at the end of one turn and the beginning of the next, which indicate that the two turns are **latched**, i.e. that there is no detectable gap between the end of the first pair part, and the start of the second. Latching isn't a particular property of adjacency pairs – it may occur in this case because the address term 'young lady' isn't part of the greeting and the student is therefore encouraged to complete the adjacency pair rapidly.

After her greeting which completes the adjacency pair, there is a significant 1.5 second pause, before the student cites the motivation for her visit:

(3) S: =hiya (1.5) em I was round yesterday I've had some CDs
        nicked (.) ⌈from Yoko⌉
     P: ⌊so they ⌋ tell me (.) and I put (1.0) in
        your pigeonhole (.)
     S: right
     P: [you know] (.) a little parcel like that
     S: that's what Magda said ⌈she saw it yeah⌉

The micro-pause after 'nicked' provides an opportunity for the porter to begin speaking. Places at which turns are offered are known as **transition-relevance places** (TRP) and are intonationally marked. But the porter doesn't immediately start a new turn at this point, so the student continues her turn by mentioning the place from which they had been nicked, 'from Yoko'. However, 'from Yoko' is redundant since it is readily inferred as an explicature and since, as the conversation reveals, the porter had been telephoned by a colleague the evening before, presumably on the prompting of the student. This redundant coda finally obliges the porter to begin a new turn.

In fact, the porter begins his new turn as an **overlap**. Overlapped material may be harder to hear but typically contains propositionally less important material, as is the case here: the student's redundant 'from Yoko' and the porter's proform 'so' which stands for the proposition already expressed by the student. Then after a micro-pause, the porter commences an **account** with 'and', whose function seems to be to mark the start of the account. By that I mean that 'and' doesn't conjoin 'so they tell me' and 'I put it in your pigeonhole' – rather, it advises us that an account is upcoming.

Accounts are typical features of talk exchanges. Sometimes their function is remedial, for example, the preferred second pair part in an invitation is an acceptance. Often a refusal, the dispreferred second pair part, takes the form of an account which explains why the invitation cannot be accepted. In this exchange, the porter's account is notable for its deliberate delivery with frequent pauses and its marked word order. Obviously enough, accounts should be truthful representations of events that both parties can agree, hence the pause after 'pigeonhole' which prompts the student's 'right', the porter's overlapped appeal for understanding '[you know]', and the student's confirmation that the porter's account squares with her own understanding of the situation, indicated by 'that's what Magda said' and by 'she saw it yeah'.

The porter's use of 'and' as he continues his account orients to a significant item in the account, that the parcel was damaged:

(4)   s: that's what Magda said ⌈she saw it yeah   ⌉
      P: ⌊and it was a little⌋ bit torn mind
         (.) but I put it ⌈in   ⌉ (.) and when Robin phoned me last
      s: ⌊ well⌋
      P: night (.) I said I remember (.) I can't remember which
         name it was but I knew it was in the first pigeonhole
         ⌈A B⌉ C or D

The state of the parcel is also oriented to by 'mind' and by 'but' – despite its being 'a little bit torn' he put it in the pigeonhole. The student then attempts to interrupt with 'well', which signals her wish to re-base the discussion – perhaps to ask why a damaged parcel was put in the pigeonhole. But the porter refuses to give up the turn and continues his account with 'and', again signalling a further development.

The porter's switch from reported speech 'I said ... I can't remember which name it was' to direct speech 'I knew it was in the first pigeonhole' reinforces the veracity of his account.

The porter's turn also contains a **repair**, in which an intended sequence is replaced by a new one: 'I said I remember (.) I can't remember which name it was.' Perhaps he was going to say that he remembered putting it in the first pigeonhole, but then repaired his account to make it more particular and thus convincing. Most repairs are of this kind, self-initiated and self-completed. Occasionally, a repair is other-initiated, for example when you ask the speaker to clarify something that was unclear to you. Very occasionally indeed, repairs are other-initiated and other-completed, but this sort of correction of what someone else says is obviously rare and distinctly face-threatening.

In (5) below, we can distinguish the student's first 'yeah' as a back-channel confirmation of what the porter says. It has the function of encouraging him to continue. Presumably the student, whose family name begins with 'B', is confirming that the first pigeonhole is the right one. This encouraging use of the back-channel is known as **aizuchi**. As there is no single word for this conversational strategy in English, we borrow the word *aizuchi* from Japanese. Her second 'yeah' confirms that she had 'looked in' the appropriate pigeonhole.

(5)   P: night (.) I said I remember (.) I can't remember which
         name it was but I knew it was in the first pigeonhole
         ⌜A B⌝ C or D
      S: ⌞yeah⌟
      S: yeah that's what me and Magda had looked in ⌜to see our
      P: ⌞ that's right
      S: mail⌝
      P: and ⌟ it was there

The porter then completes his account by asserting that the parcel was indeed in the appropriate pigeonhole.

(6)   P: and ⌟ it was there (..) so after this (.) I mean it's (..) it's
         Durham students going in the bloody place (1.0)
         I caught two yesterday (..)
      S: doing ⌜what   ⌝ (1.0) doing what=
      P: ⌞afternoon⌟
      P: =just walking about (..) [they] don't live there (1.0)
         definitely English students (2.0)
      S: wh wha what hh
      P: in Yoko Hall (1.5)

Accounts are typically followed by **formulations** in which the significance of the account and its consequence are formulated. Often upcoming formulations are signalled by *so* as occurs here in 'so after this'. However, the expected formulation doesn't occur directly because the porter repairs his strategy and instead signals with 'I mean' that a **self-formulation** is upcoming. This self-formulation consists of a causal explanation or attribution of blame, 'it's Durham students going in the bloody place'. He decides that it's more important to attribute blame at this stage in the talk exchange than to explain what measures will be taken in the future.

The causal explanation is immediately followed by the account of another incident which, although not directly related to the disappearance of the parcel, is intended to support the causal explanation. The student's reaction, 'wh wha what hh', shows that she is wrong-footed by the appearance so early in the exchange of a causal explanation.

Although we have examined only the very short opening sequence of a talk exchange, and although we started with no *a priori* theoretical assumptions or categories, we noticed several 'methods' which were highlighted in bold – turn, adjacency pair, latched utterance, pause, transition-relevance place, overlap, account, repair, *aizuchi*, formulation, self-formulation. Such conversational features are called **members' methods** because they are recognized by all those who belong to the community of talkers (members) and are expectable routines (methods). This approach to language is therefore 'ethnomethodological': we begin without assumptions and we notice (the '-ology' of 'ethnomethod*ology*') methodical patterns (the '-method-' of 'ethno*method*ology) which are recognized by group members who share a common culture (the 'ethno-' of '*ethno*methodology').

9.2.1 Talk-in-interaction structure

This section of the chapter describes some of the expectable routines of conversational sequencing, although you are no longer novices having studied several members' methods in the previous section.

In a series of papers written between 1968 and 1980, Schegloff and a number of co-researchers established the basic mechanisms underlying talk-in-interaction.

In their seminal paper 'A simplest systematics for the organization of turn-taking in conversation' (1974), Sacks, Schegloff and Jefferson discuss the way that turns are allocated in conversation. The four paragraphs and Checking understanding tasks that follow are based closely on this paper.

Sacks *et al.* show that a turn projects its own end, or transition-relevance place, and that the speaker may select next speaker or allow self-selection of next speaker to take place in a way that minimizes gaps and overlaps. Because a turn's end is projected, next speakers have an opportunity to prepare their contributions.

Checking understanding (9.1) ————————————————

Working with the interaction in the travel agent's printed in full in the previous chapter (pp. 179–181), do the following.

1. Find a turn whose end is projected and explain how this is effected.
2. Find a place where the speaker selects the next speaker.
3. Find a place where next speaker self-selects.
4. Find a place where there is a gap, and account for it.
5. Find a place where there is an overlap and account for it.

Sacks *et al.* also describe a range of ways in which a next speaker is selected. These include the use of adjacency first pair parts, an address term such as the name of the intended next speaker, repair techniques such as one-word clarificatory questions and repetitions of parts of a prior utterance with question intonation. Tags may also serve as an exit technique for a turn. Sometimes a next speaker is selected as the natural next speaker by virtue of being the understood recipient of some request, comment or suggestion without any overt selection procedure.

Checking understanding (9.2)

Working with the interaction in the travel agent's, find examples of the following.

1. A first-pair part of an adjacency pair.
2. The use of an address term.
3. A one-word or a short *wh*-phrase clarification request.
4. A clarification request involving repetition.
5. A tag used as an exit technique.
6. A place where there is a natural next-turn taker.

Sacks *et al.* show how turn size may vary either because units such as sentences naturally vary in length or because a speaker may have a turn more than one unit long if no other speaker self-selects at a TRP. They show how, in a conversation involving four or more participants, schism may occur so that more than one conversation occurs simultaneously. And they show how conversation can become discontinuous so that lapses occur, although in the case where a next speaker has been selected only pauses, rather than gaps or lapses, are possible.

Checking understanding (9.3)

Working with the interaction in the travel agent's, do the following.

1. Find an example of a long single-unit turn.
2. Find an example of a short single-unit turn.
3. Find an example of a long turn resulting from lack of next speaker self-selection.
4. Can you find examples of pauses and lapses?

Sacks *et al.* also show how turns regularly have a three-part structure, consisting of orientation to preceding turn, business of present turn and orientation to next turn.

Checking understanding (9.4)

Find an example of a three-part turn in the interaction in the travel agent's.

Obviously enough, this is only a beginning, but a beginning that shows the systematic nature of conversation and provides a detailed metalanguage for describing its regularities.

Other important features of conversation include the following.

- Departures from the unmarked norm: for example, in the travel agent's, the whole middle sequence in which the travel agent asks about travel dates could be thought of as an insertion between the first and second parts of the conversation.
- The extent to which conversations are unmarked exchanges between equals or are unequal encounters: both the student/porter and the customer/travel agent conversations are service encounters involving a party with something to trade and a party eager to obtain goods (including information); besides issues of age and gender, there are in-built inequalities in the interaction type itself.
- Audience design, listener behaviour and the co-authored nature of talk-in-interaction.

And then there are (the very small number of) metapragmatic folk terms, such as *topic* and *interruption*. In fact, metapragmatic folk terms are by no means universal, which seems to indicate different cross-cultural awarenesses. In Japanese, for example, there is no single word for *interruption* but, as saw in the previous section, there is a word '*aizuchi*', meaning to use the listener channel in ways that are supportive of the speaker by interjecting expressions like *I see, I agree, yeah, go on*, etc. In English there is no metapragmatic folk term for this phenomenon. There are some languages in which the verb form *interrupt* is in regular use but the nominal *interruption*, although feasible, is felt to be awkward – this is generally the case in Slavonic languages, for example.

And even when two languages appear to have a common metapragmatic folk term, it is not necessarily used to describe the same phenomenon in an identical way. So that what a member of another culture understands by *pause* or *topic* may not be the same as your understanding.

This section of the chapter will conclude by drawing your attention to three or four of the features of the travel agent exchange discussed in the previous chapter, but this time from a CA perspective.

You will recall that when we considered the three opening turns of the exchange, I asked who should speak first and what the effect of the customer speaking first is. Notice that we could not usefully begin to consider the pragmatic effects of what was uttered without discussing the sequential ordering of the exchange.

I then asked you to consider whether the customer's comparatively long four-unit opening might overwhelm the travel agent. Again, I asked you to consider the significance of the sequential properties of the exchange irrespective of the propositional content of the utterances that make it up and their illocutionary force.

The third question I asked you to consider was whether it was a good strategy for the customer to give a reason for asking for information. Notice that even this question, which appears to be about the best strategy for achieving a purpose, is also about sequential preference. Is the customer falling in with or departing from the preferred or most expectable sequential structure in giving a reason for making a request for information?

And in discussing the customer's second turn, *oh I see*, as an indication that the preceding utterance was unsatisfactory, we were treating *I see* not only as short on Quantity (a pragmatic explanation of its function) but also as a dummy turn obliging the travel agent to recycle her previous turn (a sequential explanation of its function). You may recall that, after discussing the three opening turns, I then set out a strategic summary of the interaction that had taken place:

CUSTOMER: request for information (reason given).
TRAVEL AGENT: refusal to supply information (reason given).
CUSTOMER: indication that this is not a sufficient response.

Notice how this summary could be re-analysed as a series of adjacency pairs which show how the initiative (i.e. initiating function) switches between the two parties. Looked at from this perspective, the first five turns of this encounter exhibit the following adjacency pair properties.

CUSTOMER: First pair part of adjacency pair – request for information (*Can you help me...*)
TRAVEL AGENT: Dispreferred second pair part – request not met (*Well we're not British Rail agents...*)
CUSTOMER: Invites a less dispreferred second pair part (*Oh I see*)
TRAVEL AGENT: Responds with an offer – a first pair part (*I can tell you what it is to go to Edinburgh*)
CUSTOMER: Preferred second pair part – accepts offer (*yes*); new first pair part – seeks clarification of the offer (*by plane*).

Thus we see how the initiative swings from the customer to the travel agent and back to the customer, as the customer succeeds in getting the travel agent to agree to provide him with at least some of the information he is seeking, despite her initial refusal to help.

9.2.2 Transcription issues

You will have noticed in the data discussed in this chapter that I have used a minimal set of transcription conventions to indicate only pauses, turn constructional units, unrecoverable items, and places where turns are latched or overlap. I've avoided conventional punctuation because it is necessarily interpretative. I could have gone to the opposite extreme and tried to provide a transcription which fully represented the intonation contours of the talk – but this would have been immensely difficult for me to produce and for you to follow. All transcription is interpretative to some degree, but the researcher's aim is to try to find a minimal, or most parsimonious, standard representation which presents the data with as little interpretation as possible.

When I say that all transcription is interpretative, I mean that the transcriber has always to make a choice between alternative representations of data. Consider the following exchange from the conversation between the porter and the student:

(7) P: ⌞so they⌟ tell me (.) and I put (1.0) in your
              pigeonhole (.)
     S: right
     P: [you know] (.) a little parcel like that

In this transcription, I decided that the pause after 'pigeonhole' marked a TRP, that 'right' was a distinct turn rather than a back-channel *aizuchi*, and that the barely recoverable and therefore putative '[you know]' looked forward to the upcoming 'a little parcel' rather than backward as a gloss on 'pigeonhole'. One alternative would have been to have treated the pause after 'pigeonhole' as a processing pause and 'right' as an *aizuchi*, in which case the transcription might have looked like this:

(8) P: ⌞so they⌟ tell me (.) and I put (1.0) in your
              pigeonhole (.)
     S: right
     P: [you know] (.) a little parcel like that

This example shows that transcription and analysis cannot be entirely separated – indeed, transcription is a research activity in its own right and involves decisions about what count as data and how they are to be represented. Consequently, any analyses of (7) and (8) would take different directions.

This raises a wider problem for the analyst which I first mentioned in Chapter 5 when we saw how difficult it was to determine the salient meanings in the conversation between the restaurant owner in Florence and myself, although no doubt they were entirely clear at the time our conversation occurred. The interpretations suggested in this chapter for the porter/student conversation are necessarily tentative, therefore, and fall far short of the interpretations which will have occurred tacitly to each of the two parties in the exchange. Fauconnier echoes many previous observations when he writes of natural language data that the '*illusion of simplicity*' it presents is a well-known consequence of our double status as observers and competent performers' (1997: 32). Because we are competent performers, we think that talk is easy to understand. But as soon as we begin the serious business of analysis, we find ourselves suggesting interpretations in which we probably have only limited confidence. There's no doubt in my mind that the student understood exactly the sequential function of *and* in the porter's utterance '⌞so they ⌟ tell me (.) and I put (1.0) in your pigeonhole (.)', but we can never be sure that our analysis of such examples is right.

9.3 Talk and context

In CA a distinction is often drawn between 'macro' and 'micro' contexts. Macro contexts are said to be 'distal' in the sense that they exist outside the talk exchange. Thus in Chapter 8 I described the male manager/young female employee with limited office-fronting responsibilities scenario as a distal context, and suggested that this context was remade in the service encounter when the customer pressed his enquiry. Although I didn't use the term 'distal' in Chapter 7, we can now see that Matsumoto's argument that deference characterizes Japanese interactions is an argument for the recognition of social hierarchy, an obvious distal context. In contrast, micro contexts are created within the micro domain of the talk exchange. The question is whether talk is determined or constrained by distal contexts, with context seen as presumptive, or whether in fact it is talk which creates context. You may well have noticed that I didn't tell you the macro context in advance of discussing the porter/student data. This was because I wanted relevant aspects of this context to become clear through our analysis. The significance of this decision will become apparent as you read further in this section.

Until the late 1980s there was no real challenge to the received view, summarized (but not accepted) by Zimmerman and Boden, that 'since social structure forms the presumptive context of activities of lesser scale, such as social interaction, it is ultimately the fundamental explanatory resource' (1991: 5). In other words, the received view was that context constrains talk. But by 1992, Duranti and Goodwin were writing, 'context and talk are now argued to stand in a mutually reflexive relationship to each other, with talk, and the interpretive work it generates, shaping context as much as context shapes talk' (1992: 31).

Schegloff (1992) has a more radical perspective. He argues that a distal context can only influence a talk exchange to the extent that it is made relevant in it. Therefore, there is no such thing as a distal context: if macro contexts aren't relevant we can discount them, and if they are relevant, they will be appear as micro contexts oriented to in the talk itself. Imagine a conversation with your doctor which begins with the doctor saying *How are you*: how do you know whether this is a social greeting inviting a response such as *Fine thanks! How are you* or whether it is a professional enquiry inviting a response such as *Much the same I'm afraid*? Although the existence of extra-interactional phenomena such as professional status and setting is not in doubt, demonstrating that such aspects of context are oriented to is much more problematical. Perhaps for this reason, it has even become fashionable to talk as Schegloff does of the occasional non-consequentiality of context, and of interactions in which context is 'just a context' (1992: 214).

However you choose to resolve the macro/micro issue yourself, there can be no doubt that we all bring a potentially infinite number of contexts to conversations: our age, sex, ethnicity, social class, occupational background, family status, etc. And of course, each of these contexts is made up of many parts, several of them apparently incompatible. Thus students may be intelligent, young, irresponsible, serious-minded, rebellious, radical, uninitiated, poor, etc.

With these thoughts about the role of context in mind, recall the porter's opening turn in the conversation we studied earlier in the chapter:

(2)   P: hello young lady=
      S: =hiya

Notice how the porter encodes elements of the macro context, that the student is female, of a certain social class (perhaps not the same class as he is), and that he is older than her. The question for the analyst is why the porter chooses to orient to these aspects of the distal context in the opening turn of an interaction. Why is it relevant that the speakers are of different sexes, ages and classes? Or to ask the question from a political correctness perspective, is it legitimate to treat their different sexes, ages and classes as relevant? These questions become all the more interesting when we know another element of the distal context, that the porter is responsible for the security of parcels and that the person to whom he is speaking has come to talk to him precisely because he has this role and a package addressed to her has gone missing. Thus the porter sees to it that the conversation is not just between a porter and a student, but between an older male and a younger female. Perhaps now the student's latching of the second pair part of her greeting is more explainable and makes known her exasperation with the context being created.

9.3.1 Talk, context and society

Chapter 4 began with a quotation from Pope's *Essay on Criticism*

'Words are like leaves; and where they most abound,
Much fruit of sense beneath is rarely found.'

In the context of the discussion of implicature which it preceded, this quotation reminded us that less elaborated sentences often have implicit meanings when used as utterances. One might go further still and observe that it would be possible to say very little indeed in a situation where the context itself constituted all the necessary premises for inferring a meaning. Thus it is 'not done' for most of us to speak when we are presented to royalty unless invited so to do. And when invited to speak, we used honorifics like *Sir, Ma'am* and, I'm told, *Your Royal Highness* to reflect that context at the level of the sentence.

In the more usual way, with which we have been largely concerned in this book, meaning is conveyed by drawing an inference from two kinds of premise, the utterance we hear and our knowledge of the world. The question that then arises is whether, in different cultures, utterances (language) and knowledge of the world (context) have the same weight in determining what meanings are conveyed, or whether in some cultures either language or context plays a more deciding role than in others. At the societal level, therefore, whole cultures may be placed at different positions on the continuum sketched in Figure 9.1.

| Premises drawn mostly from knowledge of the world: language used to reflect context | ⟷ | Premises drawn mostly from utterances: language used to reflect context |

Figure 9.1

This distinction between cultural types was elaborated by Hall (1976) who distinguished 'high context' cultures in which relatively little language is needed to establish a basis on which to proceed and 'low context' cultures in which relatively more language is needed (see Chapter 5). Language functions both to reinforce externally perceived social structure (typical for high context cultures) and to create new social structure for the purposes at hand (typical for low context cultures). These two functions relate to what Hofstede (1980: 94) described as 'status consistency' (high context) and 'overall equality' (low context).

It is sometimes claimed that there is a set of properties which go with each cultural polarity, such that high context cultures will be shame driven (an individual's behaviour is conditioned by the opinions of others), and characterized by deference and the maintenance of relative position, and low context cultures will be guilt driven (individuals are accountable to themselves for their behaviour), and characterized by courtesy and the possibility of social mobility.

In the encounter we have been studying in this chapter, the porter invokes 'status consistency' elements of context such as age and gender in an 'overall equality' culture as part of his bid to determine the relevant events that occurred and to attribute blame in a way that is favourable to his position.

9.3.2 Talk, convention and context

This chapter has examined talk in its own right rather than as an illustration of types of pragmatic meaning such as implicature and illocutionary force. While categories of pragmatic meaning are sometimes important to our understanding of the utterances that make up extended talk, the sequential properties of talk are central in any characterization of the nature of the talk-in-interaction.

Our description of pragmatic uses of language in the previous chapters has assumed, following the received position, that pragmatic meaning is 'non-conventional'. But in fact we can see that the interaction in the travel agent's is, if not conventional, at least expectable in many very obvious ways, and that sequential ordering and even pragmatic meanings are much more obviously expectable than they are unconventional. In fact pragmatic meanings are non-conventional only to the extent that they are not literal, truth-conditional or invariably associated with particular forms. Given a context, it makes about as much sense to think of pragmatic meanings as non-conventional (or even conventional, come to that) as it does to think of any other linguistic level as non-conventional in its context. The use of the term 'non-conventional' to describe pragmatic meaning can be seen as an unfortunate consequence of judging utterance meaning by the criterion of sentence meaning.

The perception that an assemblage of pragmatic values in a form we call the utterance is insufficient to account for the meaning of utterances arranged sequentially as accounts and formulations, as preferred and dispreferred contributions, as more or less procedurally consequential, and in a form we call talk enables us to confirm the difference between the function a category has as the sum of its components and the role it plays as a component in a larger category.

This insight may be profitably applied to some of the issues that have been implicit in many places in our earlier discussions. For example, in the very first chapter we saw that *I'm tired* can have as many meanings as it has contexts of use. In one context, it might mean *I want to go to bed*, in another *I want to go to bed alone*, in another *I want to go to bed with you (now)* and in yet another *I don't want to get out of bed*. Yet we still sense that it has a core literal meaning, although this meaning is not the meaning conveyed in any of the four examples just given. We now have an explanation for why this should be. The core meaning of *I'm tired* is the meaning it has as a sentence; the real-world meanings of *I'm tired* are the meanings it has as a set of utterances in which distal contexts are oriented to. Thus a single entailment, or sentence meaning, can have many different speaker meanings. And the speaker meanings are more precise and context invoking than the less determined sentence meaning.

9.4 A post-methodic afterword

We began this chapter with Kopytko's distinction between rationalistic and empirical pragmatics. We allowed the work of Austin, Grice, and Brown and Levinson to be treated as rationalistic, although there is every reason to suppose that Austin in *How to do things with words* (1962) and Grice in 'Logic and conversation' (1967a); Brown and Levinson in *Politeness: some universals in language usage (1987)* all thought that they were revealing fundamental empirical facts about the way talk works. And we allowed ourselves to be persuaded that if we wished to understand the way language is really used, theories supported by single-utterance examples were no substitute for data approached with no prior analytic categories or templates in mind. For a brief, heady chapter, we have been studying 'empirical' pragmatics (Bilmes, 1993).

And as it turns out, the study of conversation does indeed reveal orderly patterns of turn taking in which accounts precede formulations and in which there are preferred and dispreferred contributions. These methodic patterns are recognizable to members of a common group and frame sequential communication. CA thus captures the principles of talk-in-interaction. And maybe too CA complements the theories of Grice, and later of Sperber and Wilson, whose principal concerns have been to account for gaps in denotation by showing how inference supplies implicit meaning.

However, I would be failing in my duty, if I overlooked what I will call the 'post-methodic' critique of this position. This critique is very clearly set out in a brief paper by Briggs in *Pragmatics* 7/4 (1997). Briggs criticizes CA for identifying abstract patterns which are applied across a range of cases and for pursuing the everyday in a strictly local context which excludes the historical, social and cultural circumstances in which talk occurs. He mocks the kinds of orderly behaviours that are central in the kind of pragmatics we have been studying: cooperation, rationality, relevance, politeness, turn-taking. According to Briggs, these are all ideologically motivated, reductionist generalizations which deny the broader political context in favour of a narrowly adjacent micro context in which society is stable and orderly. Think for a moment of all the occasions when speakers try to shout each other down or parties use violence, either individual or collective, and you get the point.

Even the short opening of the porter/student dialogue is open to a quite different kind of analysis from the one suggested in this chapter. This different, post-methodic analysis sees not order but underlying chaos and political struggle in the roles of the parties. They are divided by age, sex and class and will use their respective political identities to attribute blame. Truth, and in particular which or what circumstance, immediate or distal, is responsible for the security and subsequent disappearance of the student's parcel will be determined in the talk by the exercise of power. Although I was careful not to inform you in advance of the immediate context, I should perhaps, had you not already known it, have informed you of the wider social and political context in which the parties struggle for survival and where disorderly as well as orderly events and accounts of events occur.

I wonder whether it's too irreverent to suppose that, if we were to pursue the post-methodic line suggested by Briggs, we might in due course end up, like the rationalists and empiricists before us, with an account of what we took to be language use but which had become instead an account of language. When we studied *How to do things with words*, we began brightly with the notion that a sentence in a context of use is an utterance, but now we see that we have ended up knowing only what an utterance is. We might pursue the attractive postmodern notion that talk is fundamentally disorderly, and end up knowing only what disorderly talk is.

Raising pragmatic awareness: talk-in-interaction

1. Working as an individual, listen out for two consecutive utterances which are paired but where the second utterance is a slightly surprising rejoinder to the first. Bring your adjacency pair to your tutorial. Read only the first utterance of the pair and invite your colleagues to guess the second. Discuss the expected and the actual illocutionary forces associated with each adjacency pair.
2. While you are involved in a conversation, watch out for interruptions. Note who interrupts, how they interrupt and how the other speakers react. Report your observations in your tutorial group.

3. While you are part of a conversation, listen out for clarification requests and repairs. Are repairs usually self- or other-initiated and self- or other-completed? Why do these repairs occur? Report your observations in your tutorial group.

4. Observe two people who are deeply involved in a conversation. Record any moments of their interaction that are striking so that you can describe the paralinguistic features of talk-in-interaction which you observed to your tutorial group.

5. Eavesdrop on just five seconds of a conversation. Decide in advance that you will eavesdrop on five seconds from some predetermined moment (such as when someone next puts food in their mouth). Record exactly what is said, paying special attention to its sequential properties, and report your findings in your tutorial group.

6. Each member of your tutorial group should eavesdrop on the beginning of a talk sequence where the first speaker has a reason for talking. Does the speaker introduce the reason immediately or not? Compare your different observations in your tutorial group.

7. Work with a partner and together eavesdrop on a conversation. You should take one speaker and your partner the other: you should each listen carefully for the occurrence of fillers, hesitations and pauses. Compare your observations.

8. How are conversations closed? Is the gist formulated? What sort of agreements are made? How are topics closed? Are they recycled? Do the same systems occur at the end of conversations as apply at the end of topics within conversations? Report your observations in your tutorial group.

Acknowledgement: the student/porter conversation was recorded by Joanne Burdon who carried out a preliminary analysis. I'm very grateful to her for permission to use these data here.

Further reading

Primary texts: Sacks, H., Schegloff, E.A. and Jefferson, G. (1974); Schegloff, E.A. (1992).

Textbooks: Duranti, A. (1997: 245–79); Hutchby, I. and Wooffitt, R. (1998: 38–69); Mey, J.L. (1993: Ch.11, Ch.12); Schiffrin, D. (1994: 232–81); Yule, G. (1996: 71–82).

10 Reflexive language: metapragmatic and metasequential encoding

'He hath indeed better bettered expectation
than you must expect of me to tell you how.'
(*Much Ado About Nothing*, 1600)

Keywords reflexive, procedural encoding, hedge, metalinguistic,
metapragmatic, metasequential, meta-talk, troubles talk

The following letter appeared in *The Times* of 2 June 1999:

(1) Sir, Please would you join me in a campaign to ban the words
     'basically', 'essentially' and 'actually' from media and everyday
     speech?
          Basically, if we could remove those words, it would actually add to
     the time that is essentially available for meaningful language by
     anything up to a third. And you would remove what is actually,
     basically and essentially an irritating substitute for 'um' – which at
     least has the virtue of brevity.

In Chapter 1, I used the term 'reflexive' to describe the way in which one
part of what we say provides a comment on how our utterance fits into the
discourse as a whole or on how the speaker wants to be understood. What
the writer of the letter to *The Times* is objecting to is the over-use of adverbs
with a reflexive function. No doubt the second sentence of his letter would
be just as clear without the adverbs he uses ironically. But, as we saw in
Chapter 1 and again in our discussion of hedges in Chapter 4 and procedural
encoding in Chapter 5, there are times when they have their uses. Indeed,
there are times when they are essential, as we saw in Chapter 5 when I failed
to understand Alice's message for want of a *so*.

When used non-ironically, *basically* usually tells us that the writer is putting something economically and simply, *actually* tells us that the proposition is accurate if unexpected, and *essentially* tells us that the proposition is appropriate or relevant. These adverbs guide our interpretation by telling us how to take the propositions to which they are attached – their function is metapragmatic. And although the letter-writer objects to them, he is rather hoist with his own petard by his own last sentence when he finds *at least* a useful way of advising us of how to take 'which ... has the virtue of brevity'.

Checking understanding (10.1) ─────────────────

Can you find other expressions in the letter to *The Times* which, by the letter writer's notion of what is 'meaningful language', might also be candidates for banning?

In the first, more substantial part of this chapter we will distinguish three kinds of meta-function:

- metalinguistic function, where a linguistic form is used to describe the act of speaking itself or to represent, gloss, or refer to another linguistic form
- metapragmatic function, where a linguistic form is used to guide the hearer's pragmatic interpretation
- metasequential function, where a linguistic form is used to guide the hearer's understanding of the way a turn contributes to a conversation's procedural consequentiality.

In the second part of this chapter, the final theoretical chapter before a concluding chapter on project work in pragmatics, I'll make some brief 'reflexive' comments on the place of pragmatics in our broader study of language seen from a generative perspective.

10.1 Meta-functions

10.1.1 Metalinguistic function

When we study pragmatics, we are naturally more interested in metapragmatic and metasequential phenomena than in metalinguistic phenomena. Nevertheless, language is unique in that it has the ability to refer to itself (the metalinguistic function) as well as to its effects (the metapragmatic function). Thus Lucy writes, 'Speech is permeated by reflexive activity as speakers remark on language, report utterances, index and describe aspects of the speech event ... and guide listeners in the proper interpretation of their utterances' (1993: 11). So just how do speakers do these things?

Among the ways that we remark on language, Lucy notes *mention* as in

(2)   The word 'well' is a hedge

gloss as in

(3)   Pragmatics, the module with four assignments

and *comments* about language as in

(4a) English is all pragmatics

(4b) What is pragmatics about

(4c) Hedging is typical in lecturer-speak

We report utterances both by means of *quotation* as in

(5)   He said, 'You're nuts'

and *gloss* as in

(6)   She insulted me

We may also refer to the *events of speech* as in

(7)   Let's put it this way

(8a) Why do you ask that

(8b) Now you've told a joke, would you like a cup of tea?

Checking understanding (10.2)

Think up several examples of your own of mention, gloss, comment and quotation, and reference to events of speech.

Lucy also discusses indexicals as 'Forms which reflexively take account of the ongoing event of speaking itself, in terms of which we can use and understand their referential and predicational value' (1993: 10). Because understanding what is picked out and referred to by deictics depends upon establishing a relation to the speech event in which they occur, they also implicitly refer to the speech event itself. Silverstein discusses indexicals as multifunctional because they combine 'semantico-referential' properties which are found in all the speech events in which they occur, with indexical functions that are utterance specific and therefore reflexive (1976: 21, 46).

   In her work on 'meta-talk', Schiffrin (1987) discusses 'metalinguistic referents' or discourse deictic items like *the former* and *the next point*, which implicitly refer to the discourse event in which they are grounded. Similarly, metalinguistic operators, functioning either as higher level predicates such as *right* and *wrong* or as discourse connectives such as *for example*, *like* and (!) *such as*, also make implicit reference to the discourse event of which they are a part. Schiffrin also discusses our ability to describe speech acts with metalinguistic verbs of saying such as *say* or *tell* or *ask*, to describe talk functions with metalinguistic verbs such as *clarify* or *define*, and to describe speech events with metalinguistic verbs such as *argue* or *joke*.

Checking understanding (10.3) ───────────────

Think up several examples of your own of metalinguistic referents and metalinguistic operators, and of speech act descriptions, talk function descriptions and speech event descriptions.

You may recall that we also encountered another kind of metalinguistic reference in our discussion of utterance-type meaning in Chapter 4. On p. 96, I mentioned Levinson's observation that Q1- and M-inferences are metalinguistic because they make implicit reference to other, non-present members of a set (Q1-inferences) or to unmarked but non-present expressions (M-inferences).

The purpose of rehearsing Lucy's and Schiffrin's work on the metalinguistic descriptions of talk functions and of reminding ourselves that inferences too may sometimes be metalinguistic is to show that language, even when used propositionally, is frequently reflexive. The question then is: does the meta-function also operate at the level of pragmatic meaning? And as it turns out, yes we can, for example, both ask what a particular expression means (a metalinguistic inquiry), and ask what someone means by using a particular expression (a metapragmatic inquiry).

10.1.2 Metapragmatic function

Do you recall the porter saying to the student in the data we examined in the last chapter

(9)   and it was a little bit torn mind

His use of *mind* advises her of the illocutionary force he intends. His utterance is more than a simple description – he is warning her of the special relevance of a distinctive feature of the parcel, and by implication a feature that might have led to its theft. One frequent metapragmatic function is to draw attention to the intended illocutionary force of an utterance in this way. Thus we may choose to say either

(10) It's me again

or, when we want to indicate the illocutionary force overtly,

(11) I'm afraid it's me again

Because *It's you again* doesn't have the same illocutionary force as *It's me again*, unless we are being sarcastic, we cannot say

(12) ?I'm afraid it's you again

Instead we might indicate the illocutionary force with something like

(13) Oh no it's you again

Checking understanding (10.4)

Starting with *please*, which is used for indicating a request, make a list of several illocutionary force indicating devices and indicate their metapragmatic functions.

In Chapter 4, I used the term 'metalingual' to describe the function of hedges. At that stage in our study, I was looking for a term that was neutral between 'metalinguistic' and 'metapragmatic'. In fact, we can now see that indications of the extent to which maxims are being adhered to are metapragmatic in that they gloss the intended effect of what is said rather than its literal meaning. And procedural encoding, which we studied in Chapter 5, is also clearly metapragmatic because it helps us to understand utterances, and particularly their implicatures, that would otherwise be more difficult to recover.

Checking understanding (10.5)

Study the following examples discussed in Chapter 1. Which of the italicized items have a metalinguistic and which have a metapragmatic function?

(14) P: What's your name *by the way*

(15) PHARMACIST: They make you drowsy *mind*

(16) *I think* we could go in now *you know*

(17) What's your name *again*

(18) Am I ready to go *do you mean*

(19) No, *well*, yes I am

(20) Radion removes dirt *AND* odours

(21) The Conference trade has *literally* helped turn Brighton around

(22) I *really* like your new haircut

(23) *I suppose* today it's especially important to be thinking carefully about what our students say to us

(24) *and er is it* Knowledge and Reality

(25) *Indeed*, I did have a relationship with Ms Lewinsky that was *not appropriate. In fact*, it was *wrong*

10.1.3 Metasequential function

Consider three more of the examples we discussed in Chapter 1:

(26) Right, shall we begin

(27) There must therefore be a very good case for not allowing anyone to proceed to Year 3

(28) Now I've done it

Right in (26) doesn't seem to be metalinguistic. It may well have a metapragmatic function, advising the audience of the intention of the speaker to be business-like. But it also tells us something about the place of the utterance in the wider discourse. It seems to be a conversational method for getting attention, and as such is only appropriate (with the characteristic intonation contour and pitch associated with getting attention) when the speaker wants to begin speaking or to re-assert his or her hold on the floor. In other words, it tells us something about the place of the proposition in the wider talk or discourse context. Its function is metasequential.

Similarly, *therefore* in (27) has a metapragmatic procedural function and helps us to interpret the proposition in an appropriate context. However, *therefore*, also marks a formulation and as such has a metasequential function. We shouldn't be surprised to find that an expression has two functions – after all, speakers are simultaneously conveying pragmatic meanings and ensuring the procedural consequentiality of the talk exchanges (or, in this case, the written discourse) to which they are contributing.

Now in (28) seems to have a *quasi* deictic function. It refers to the event that has just occurred – as you may recall, the breaking of one of the speaker's chopsticks. It would be possible for us to replace *now* with something like *with this action*. But *now* also has a function relative to the discourse – it marks a new topic perhaps. Its function is to claim precedence for the speaker's present contribution even if it interrupts their own or another speaker's turn. Because it tells us about the speaker's contribution to the talk, its function is partly metasequential.

In fact, conversation is very rich in metasequential phenomena as speakers guide their co-conversationalists in how to determine the status of their contributions as members' methods. The remainder of this section will be largely given over to the close examination of a talk exchange which will show the importance of metasequential markers in guiding the participants' understanding. The conversation in question occurs when the warden of a student hostel, known as 'The Doctor' on account of his having recently been awarded a PhD, meets two students, Nicole and Susie, on the staircase one evening. This is how the conversation opens:

(29) DOCTOR: how's it doing
     SUSIE: yeah no erm Nicole wants to no we need a word with you
     DOCTOR: oh ⌈right⌉
     NICOLE: ⌊no ⌋ someone's been nicking stuff out the fridge
            (2.0) so
     DOCTOR: which one

NICOLE: ours (.) well Susie's butter's gone and my cheese has gone
         as well
DOCTOR: right ⌈yeah⌉
NICOLE: ⌊like ⌋ I opened new packets and stuff so=
DOCTOR: =right the whole lot
NICOLE: yeah

Susie's response to the Doctor's opening greeting 'how's it doing' is not the preferred greeting second pair part. Instead she begins with three meta-sequential particles, 'yeah' (= I hear your greeting), 'no' (= but we have business to transact), 'erm' (= how to begin?). (My interpretations are obviously challengeable, so do feel free to think through your own both here and in the continuing analysis.) Her second use of 'no' signals a repair from the relatively informal 'Nicole wants to' to the official trouble reporting regis-ter 'we need a word with you'. The Doctor acknowledges this turn with the metapragmatic 'oh' (= a surprise) and the metasequential 'right' (= I under-stand it's to be troubles talk, so continue).

As Susie had selected Nicole as next speaker after the Doctor, it is Nicole who continues with a metasequential 'no' (= it's not small talk). She then reports 'someone's been nicking stuff out the fridge'. At the end of this brief account there is a long pause, but the expected next speaker, the Doctor doesn't self-select, so Nicole provides the metasequential marker of an upcoming formulation, 'so', and then stops again. Typically the speaker who provides an account also provides a formulation. But in some talk types, including seemingly this one, the authority to whom the trouble is reported is expected to decide the outcome.

However, the Doctor seeks more information before determining what to do next, and asks 'which one', to which Nicole gives a minimal response 'ours' (= which did you expect). She then pauses before signalling metaprag-matically, and maybe metasequentially ('well'), that the upcoming contribu-tion is slightly unexpected. In fact, the agentless passive structure of the upcoming contribution, 'Susie's butter's gone and my cheese has gone as well' is a more negatively polite way of conveying the proposition already conveyed with positive politeness, 'someone's been nicking', in her previous turn. The effect of this repair in the direction of negative politeness is to slightly enlarge the distance between herself and the Doctor, and therefore to stress the official nature of the talk.

The Doctor's metasequential 'right yeah' acknowledges Nicole's turn and invites her to continue, which she does with a metalinguistic and implicitly metapragmatic 'like' (= does what comes next match your expectation?), followed by another element of account, 'I opened new packets and stuff'. Her turn ends with an invitation to the Doctor to formulate, 'so', which he appears to anticipate, and being unwilling to formulate, he delivers a latched turn confirming that he has understood (metasequential 'right'), and contain-ing a first pair part inquiry, 'the whole lot', which Nicole confirms with a minimal second pair part 'yeah'.

You may wish to quarrel in places with my suggested analysis, but the general point is clear – that speakers use a wide range of metasequential markers to help them to make clear to each other what the status, *qua* method, of each of their contributions to the talk is and what they expect by way of contributions from each other. These metasequential methods are available on all occasions of talk. If you listen in an aware way to the conversations that go on around you, you will notice how such metasequential markers usually pass without notice.

One way of looking at the talk exchange up to the moment at which the Doctor determines an outcome is to regard the troubles reporting as a presequence, or preliminary part of the conversation. The Doctor seems keen to extend this part of the talk as far as possible, as his next – and perhaps unexpected ('well') – question shows:

(30) DOCTOR: well do you actually know when it happened
    NICOLE: erm (.) right it was there on Friday and we went to get it
              yesterday and it wasn't there so
    SUSIE: yeah

Although Nicole stops short of formulating what is readily inferred as an explicature, the metasequential marker of the upcoming formulation, 'so', still occurs. Susie's confirmation of Nicole's account, 'yeah', invites the Doctor to self-select and proceed to a determination of what's to be done.

In the next phase of the conversation, the Doctor proposes an outcome:

(31) DOCTOR: right erm (2.0) there not a lot (.) can do about it I can sort
              of like .hh (2.0) have a word with people if you want
              (1.5)
    DOCTOR: erm .hh (3.0) I mean (.) do you do you want to sort of like
              have a word with everyone or just (.) do you want us to put
              a sign up or (1.5)
    NICOLE: yeah a sign'll do won't it
    DOCTOR: on near the fridge
    NICOLE: yeah
    DOCTOR: (..) and on the pantry door it's just the one upstairs isn't it
              next to the showers

The Doctor's proposed outcome is signalled metasequentially with 'right', which acknowledges the student's previous turns and projects his own upcoming contribution, and with 'erm' and a pause, which signals a shift to a new method, which involves determining a consequent course of action. This is followed by a metalinguistic comment on the courses of action open to him, 'there not a lot (.) can do about it'. The first two of the three suggested options are also metalinguistically hedged and the last two tail off with suggestions that there might be alternatives, although these are not explicitly stated and cannot be recovered as explicatures:

(32) I can *sort of like .hh (2.0)* have a word with people if you want (1.5)

(33) erm .hh (3.0) I mean (.) do you do you want to *sort of like* have a word with everyone *or just*

(34) (.) do you want us to put a sign up *or*.

The first suggestion, that the Doctor should have a word with people, is framed as an offer. The 1.5-second pause that follows it invites a second pair part, but neither of the students wishes to accept this offer. Rather than explicitly reject it, a strongly dispreferred strategy especially given the authority status of the warden, they remain silent.

The second proposed course of action, (33), begins with a metasequential pause ('erm'), an in-drawn breath ('.hh'), a further pause, and the Doctor's metasequential signal that a self-formulation is upcoming ('I mean'). This self-formulation is the least 'official' of the three courses of action proposed, hence the signal that it is a self-formulation. It's also the least attractive to the students because they could already have taken this course of action without the Doctor's help. He orients to this least-attractive status of his suggestion by the very short pause before his third suggestion

(34) do you want us to put a sign up or

Although all three suggestions orient to the official nature of the proposed courses of action in their register ('have a word with people', 'have a word with everyone' and 'put a sign up'), only this third suggestion encodes the Doctor's status with the use of institutional 'us' to refer to himself.

There is a further significant pause, but this time the Doctor doesn't take up the turn, and Nicole then accepts his third, and because third presumably his least favoured, suggestion. She orients to the unsatisfactory nature even of this third proposal with the predicate 'do' and the metapragmatic tag 'won't it'. Thus conversational preference conventions oblige her to accept a third suggestion even if she isn't happy with it, as she signals metapragmatically. Having got Nicole's reluctant agreement, the Doctor is then quick to confirm the places where the notices are to be placed, and orients to his relative unfamiliarity with the location of fridges by asking for confirmation that 'it's just the one upstairs' with the metapragmatic tag, 'isn't it'.

So far we've said nothing about the distal context, although early in the conversation this was oriented to by the troubles reporting and by the register chosen for it, and latterly in the register chosen for the outcomes suggested by the Doctor. So the distal context encoded in these parts of the talk involves the Doctor's responsibility for dealing with problems of the kind being reported to him.

There is also another particularly interesting element of the distal context of which the Doctor must be aware: student solidarity. Although students bring complaints to him, there is another code which forbids them to name peers who may be responsible for the anti-social behaviour complained of. In this context, Nicole's use of 'someone' in 'someone's been nicking stuff out the fridge' is likely to be an attributive rather than a referential description, i.e. that 'someone' does not refer to an identifiable person. However, there is always the possibility that 'someone' is a referential description and that the identity of thief is known to or suspected by Nicole and Susie – but student solidarity prevents them from substituting a name for the description 'someone'.

Having determined a course of action, and with this aspect of the distal context in mind, the Doctor's next task is to make a token attempt to discover the identity of the person responsible for the theft. I said that the Doctor would make a 'token' attempt to discover the identity of the thief because if the identity of the thief was really to be discovered, it wouldn't be necessary to put up a sign. Had the Police been called, one could hardly imagine their suggesting putting up a sign and then turning to the task of identifying the culprit. So in the order in which the Doctor turns from one topic to another, he implicitly orients to the distal context, and particularly to student solidarity which obtains even in a situation where the students themselves are victims.

This is how the next phase begins:

(35) DOCTOR: (..) and on the pantry door it's just the one upstairs isn't it next to the showers (2.0) so I mean it's likely [it's] to be someone (1.0) around that area you would've thought wouldn't you (1.5) there's only about one fridge on that floor in't there

     NICOLE: yeah

     SUSIE: mm

     NICOLE: yeah somebody with a cheese toastie machine

     SUSIE: <laughs> yeah

     DOCTOR: ay er do you know anyone who's got one (2.0)

     NICOLE: Wo I've got one but I'm not going to nick my own cheese am I <laughs> so

     SUSIE: mm no

Having asked for confirmation that there is a single fridge on the floor above, the Doctor signals a change of member's method, first by the significant two-second pause, then by signalling an upcoming formulation ('so'), then by repairing this to a self-formulation ('I mean'). The reason for the repair to a self-formulation, or at least to signal metasequentially that it is to be a self-formulation, is that a self-formulation is less face-threatening that a 'logical' formulation, and therefore felt to be more appropriate to a context in which accusations, however implicit, threaten the students' face by virtue of being invitations to abandon the principle of student solidarity. Thus when the self-formulation appears, it's metapragmatically hedged by 'likely', by the hypothetical 'you would've thought' and by the tag 'wouldn't you':

(36) it's likely [it's] to be someone (1.0) around that area you would've thought wouldn't you

In this way, the Doctor invites Nicole and Susie to treat 'someone around that area' as a referential description. The following 1.5-second pause provides an opportunity for them to name a likely culprit. But when this opportunity isn't taken up, he continues his turn by recycling the query about the number of fridges on the floor. Thus his invitation to the students to break ranks and name the thief is inserted between two versions of the same enquiry, an enquiry which is relevant to the agreed course of action of posting a sign.

Nicole and Susie both confirm that there is a single fridge on the floor. Nicole then signals her willingness to pursue the investigation a stage further with metasequential 'yeah', and then provides a more particular description, 'somebody with a cheese toastie machine'. This description appears to be a strong candidate for a referential reading (i.e. 'someone with a cheese toastie machine' = Mary Smith) rather than an attributive reading (= someone with a cheese toastie machine whose identity is unknown). And this candidate determination appears to be validated when Susie laughs and confirms the description. The Doctor also confirms the description ('ay'), signals metapragmatically and metasequentially with the hesitation marker 'er' that what comes next is significant, and then invites the students to name the thief: 'do you know anyone who's got one'. After a pause, Nicole rejects this context by taking 'anyone' in a marked way to include herself. She invites a formulation by another speaker ('so'), metasequentially excuses her contribution with 'Wo' (?=well) and metapragmatically appeals for solidarity with the tag 'am I'. Susie obligingly provides ('mm no').

Having failed to get Nicole to name a culprit, the Doctor then turns to Susie and the theft of her butter:

(37) DOCTOR: and they've taken your butter as well
     SUSIE: yeah
     DOCTOR: what type of butter was it
     SUSIE: Flora light

In doing this, his metasequential use of 'and' indicates that the direction of his talk is still directed to identifying the thief.

Checking understanding (10.6)

The rest of this conversation follows below. Try to identify the function of the metalinguistic, metapragmatic and metasequential markers in lines 3–12 and 40–41 for yourself. You may find it best to concentrate on items in italic script.

(38) SUSIE:	Flora light	1
	(3.0)	2
DOCTOR:	you can go round and have a look *if you want to*	3
SUSIE:	yeah	4
	(3.0)	5
NICOLE:	it's not *like* it'd still be there *is it*	6
	(1.5)	7

SUSIE:	dunno it's *virtually* a full packet	8
NICOLE:	*yeah* mine as well *actually* I know it was	9
	\<Vicky approaches\>	10
DOCTOR:	*yeah* just seeing people using your cheese again	11
	and you cannot really accuse someone cos they	12
	might have bought (.) bought it themselves	13
NICOLE:	I know	14
SUSIE:	mm	15
DOCTOR:	I'll stick a notice up (.) and if it keeps	16
	happening then ⌈(1.0) ⌉	17
VICKY:	⌊what's happened⌋	18
DOCTOR:	we'll call a	19
	meeting ⌈and so forth⌉	20
SUSIE:	⌊getting stuff⌋	21
VICKY:	nicked	22
NICOLE:	somebody keeps nicking stuff from the fridge	23
SUSIE:	uh	24
	(2.0)	25
VICKY:	what in terms of what milk or (.)	26
NICOLE:	cheese	27
VICKY:	cheese	28
DOCTOR:	cheese is quite expensive	29
VICKY:	yeah	30
SUSIE:	Flora	31
	(3.0)	32
VICKY:	it's annoying	33
	(1.0)	34
SUSIE:	mm	35
	(4.0)	36
VICKY:	Susie	37
SUSIE:	yeah	38
VICKY:	will you help me with my ⌈linguistics work⌉ \<laughs\>	39
DOCTOR:	⌊right I'm off ⌋	40
SUSIE:	*all right then* Doctor	41
NICOLE:	I'll just go and get a load of ⌈my washing ⌉	42
SUSIE:	⌊see you later⌋ pet	43
	(1.0) yeah yeah that's fine ⌈yeah ⌉	44
VICKY:	⌊are you⌋ about to call	45
	somebody	46
SUSIE:	no no no no	47

Summary

In this chapter we have been studying three kinds of diacritic or gloss, those on the propositional or semantic content of utterances and utterance types, those on the force of utterance tokens, and those on the sequential methods of turn tokens. What this evidence shows us is that we frequently need help under-standing the semantic, pragmatic and sequential properties of talk. This is a natural fall-out of the general indeterminacy, and hence economy, of language and of the one-to-many property of forms to functions. This procedural or instructive function applies at the level of propositional meaning, pragmatic function and conversational method. It also neatly explains why diacritic expressions such as *basically*, *essentiality* and *actually* to which *The Times* letter-writer objects do not typically appear in reported speech. On those rare occasions when a reporting speaker feels it appropriate to convey their force, they are represented in the speech act description the reporting speaker provides. Thus when we report an utterance or written communication which contains the sentence adverb *basically*, we either ignore it or provide a descrip-tion such as 'the speaker summed up her position by saying . . .'.

What the data examined in this chapter tell us is that one of the most frequent pragmatic functions is to mark the meta-function. The pragmatic categories that we studied in the earlier chapters – deixis, speech acts, impli-cature, presupposition – were for the most part first drawn to linguists' atten-tion by philosophers of language, but now we see that shifters/indexicals, illocutionary force indicating devices, maxim hedges, Gricean conventional implicatures, speech act descriptions, and procedural encoding generally share a common reflexive function that prompts our understanding of what is meant by what is said. It almost tempts us to begin our study of pragmat-ics from a different perspective.

10.2 The place of pragmatics in a theory of language

This book began with a quotation: 'We all know what light is; but it is not easy to tell what it is'. Of course physicists now find it quite easy to tell what light is, and no doubt one day we will have an equally developed understanding of language and of the usage principles that we study when we study pragmatics. But our present situation with respect to pragmatics is a bit like Dr Johnson's with respect to light: we know what pragmatics is, but it is not easy to tell what it is. This is why, rather than starting out with a bold definition, in Chapter 1 I made several comments about what pragmaticists are interested in. Nor am I going to boldly define pragmatics now, although I will try to draw out the significance of the ground covered in the intervening chapters.

In that first chapter, I enumerated the pragmatic features of language use (appropriacy, indirectness, indeterminacy, relevance, reflexivity) and language understanding (inference based on the use of language in context). Each of these observations about language was of special salience at some stage in the chapters that followed. For example, in Chapter 7 we considered politeness phenomena relative to hearer expectations of appropriacy. In Chapter 3 we problematized the notion of indirectness (and of directness for that matter). In our discussion of Relevance Theory in Chapter 5 we noted that an implicated meaning is an inference based on two kinds of premise, fully explicated propositional form and knowledge of context. And in this chapter, we have seen how pervasive reflexive language is and how it serves metapragmatic and metasequential functions.

Most pragmatics textbooks follow a different strategy from the one taken in this book and typically begin with a definition of pragmatics. Levinson, for example, begins by describing the historical origin of the term 'pragmatics' before rehearsing a number of candidate definitions (1983: 5–35). These include:

- the study of language from a functional perspective
- the study of the context-dependent nature of language use and language understanding
- the study of the effects of language use on the grammar of language
- the study of non-conventional, or, more narrowly perhaps, non-truth conditional meaning, possibly to be understood as speaker- or utterance-meaning rather than sentence-meaning.

In a similar way, Green begins by defining pragmatics as 'the study of understanding intentional human action' (1996: 2), and Mey as 'the science of language as it is used by real, live people for their own purposes and within their limitations and affordances' (1993: 5).

Although it may seem odd to begin a book as we did without defining its subject, the fact of the matter is that the wide range of phenomena we have been investigating do not fit neatly under a single definition. What is for sure is that pragmaticists take a special interest in language as it is used, which is why the term *utterance*, a metapragmatic folk term used to describe sentences as they occur in discourse has been a key word in so many of the chapters.

More difficult even than defining pragmatics is the task of delimiting its domain. Broadly, we have been distinguishing between what we might call 'conventional' sentence meaning and pragmatic speaker meaning, taking 'conventional' sentence meaning to be a meaning associated with linguistic expressions whenever they are used, and pragmatic speaker meaning to be the meaning that is associated with them in particular contexts.

In deciding what to include in this book, I have had to draw lines in ways that are to some degree arbitrary. For example, although we have discussed deixis as a relation between a point of origin and a referent, we skated very rapidly over the actual process of reference assignment – surely a pragmatic phenomenon, and one which Green, for example, discusses in some detail.

So if we accept that definitions of pragmatics are elusive and that no treatment aims to exhaust the pragmatic domain, what have we been doing together? We have certainly been attempting a systematic description in which a wide range of data has been brought together and shown to have common properties in each area treated. A cynic might say that this is all we have been doing – just providing labels for categories of phenomena that seem to share common properties. But in fact we have gone some way beyond that: just as a syntactician is interested in criteria for syntactic category membership, so we have been trying to determine not just what data is presupposition triggering but, more importantly, what we mean by 'presupposition' – not what examples of use appear to be presuppositions, if you like, but what presuppositions appear to be. Pragmaticists are interested not only in the actual use of language, but also in usage principles, in trying to find a 'grammar' that accounts for the way language is put to use, on the assumption that language would not be as it is if it were not used to communicate with.

10.2.1 Explanation or description

If we were to achieve not merely a description of pragmatic phenomena as they occur when language is used but a proper 'grammar' of pragmatics, we would expect such a usage theory to have explanatory power, to be able to account for the way things are, and indeed have to be. Thus Horn claims for the Quantity maxim, 'make your contribution as informative as is required', that it has 'generality, explanatory power and consequences for simplifying grammatical and lexical description' (1988: 117). And in Chapter 4, we saw how Quantity-based implicatures account very neatly, as Horn (1972) shows, for the lexical gap indicated in Figure 10.1.

some	all
sometimes	always
permit	oblige
or	and
none	*nail
never	*nalways
forbid	*noblige
nor	*nand

Figure 10.1

It is data such as these which suggest that pragmatics not only provides a coherent description of the way we use language, but also provides usage principles.

There is another sense in which pragmatic systems are explanatory, and in some ways this is a more telling one. In Chapter 3, we saw how Mr Logic systematically responds to propositional content and not pragmatic meaning. We could therefore use the principles of Mr Logic-speak that we identified to generate predictable ('grammatical') 'Mr Logic' utterances for other contexts. And in Chapter 4, we saw how teletext subtitling can be accounted for and predicted on the basis of pragmatic criteria. Again, we could use the principles that we identified to generate predictable, and hence 'grammatical', subtitles algorithmically from spoken text. And perhaps most telling of all, in Chapter 4 we were able to show how the natural process of language change sometimes depends upon pragmatic inference.

By way of contrast, in Chapter 8 we considered the Chomskyan argument that, in relation to syntax, pragmatics is an epiphenomenon. This argument is put very clearly in *Knowledge of language*, where Chomsky writes

> We must distinguish between the literal meaning of the linguistic expression produced by S and what S meant by producing this expression ... The first notion is the one to be explained in a theory of language. The second has nothing particular to do with language; I can just as well ask, in the same sense of 'meaning', what S meant by slamming the door. (1976: 76)

However, the reflexive features of the utterances we considered from the television chat-show required a syntactic characterization too, although their motivation was 'essentially' pragmatic and intended to guide the interpretation of 'what S meant by producing this expression'. It therefore seems hard to maintain the notion of a syntax that takes no account of what is meant by what is said.

Conclusion

When the first edition of this book was originally conceived, as is the custom, the publisher asked me for a proposal indicating the structure of the book, and how it would sit among existing books in the same field. And, again as is the custom, the publisher then sent the proposal to three outside anonymous readers for their comments. The least enthusiastic of the three concluded his – or was it her? – report with the following sentence: 'I see no great harm in this book and it could even be quite fun.' At the end of the next chapter, you will have to (or do I mean 'you must'?) decide whether your judgements coincide with those implied in the reader's sentence. Why, one wonders, do we feel such a need to be implicit?

Raising pragmatic awareness: reflexive language

1. Position yourself somewhere where you expect purposeful talk to occur – perhaps your departmental office. Try to identify whether there is a movement from pre-sequence to main business in the talk you overhear and how this is metasequentially signalled.
2. Eavesdrop on a conversation and make a list of some of the authentic metalinguistic, metapragmatic and metasequential phenomena you overhear. Bring them to your next tutorial and share them with your colleagues.
3. Observe a typical talk-type, such as an instruct sequence or an information enquiry sequence. What metasequential phenomena occur?
4. Listen to or record a conversation and select a number of metalinguistic items. Do they also have a metapragmatic function?
5. Observe and record an unequal encounter – do the two speakers differ in their use of metasequential phenomena and in particular in their acknowledgement of the end of the previous turn and their projection of their own turn?
6. Make a close study of the metapragmatic phenomena a member of your family or a close friend displays and report your findings to your tutorial group.

Acknowledgement: the troubles reporting data were collected by Susan Millington, who conducted a preliminary analysis. I'm very grateful to her for permission to use these data here.

Further reading

Primary texts: Lucy, J.A. (1993: 9–32); Schiffrin, D. (1987).
Textbooks: Mey, J. (1993: 269–74); Verscheuren, J. (1998: 187–95).

11 Doing project work in pragmatics

Keywords experiment, data, hypothesis, findings, variables, analysis, quantitative, qualitative, collecting data, ethical issues, informant's consent, pilot, sample, transcription, topics, empirical pragmatics, literature

This chapter contains suggestions for project work with a pragmatic orientation. It discusses the types of project which are viable and the issues involved in successful data collection and transcription.

11.1 The nature of pragmatic investigation

Many linguists, although not by any means all pragmaticists, view their subject as a science. They see the purpose of linguistics as bringing order to the untidy set of data that we call language. Rather as we might observe the apparently untidy revolution of known planets around a star and form the hypothesis that their motion suggested the presence of a further, as yet undiscovered planet, and then set out to test this hypothesis, so in linguistic investigation too, a favoured method is to frame and then test hypotheses. To take a quite arbitrary example, I once overheard someone say to a two-year-old

(1)   Why don't you use your spoon

whereupon the two-year-old obligingly picked up her spoon and tried to feed herself with it. If two-year-olds can understand indirect speech acts, it seemed reasonable to hypothesize that my then fifteen-year-old son shouldn't have any trouble with them either. And so when I next saw him eating with his fingers, I said, trying to capture the intonation pattern of the original utterance:

(2)   Why don't you use your knife and fork

Unfortunately the perlocutionary effect was not as I had intended – he responded to the propositional content rather than to the illocutionary force of my utterance.

We can easily imagine potentially investigable topics in this area that might well, given a little thought, be turned into testable hypotheses. These topics might include:

- family members show that they are displeased with one another by responding to the propositional content rather than the illocutionary force of each other's utterances, typically treating indirect speech acts as though they were direct speech acts
- some indirect parental requests are complied with by children and some are not, the determining factors perhaps being age of child, gender of child, gender of parent, time of day, subject of request, etc.
- when two-year-olds are not compliant with indirect requests, this is a matter of choice rather than a result of lack of pragmatic understanding
- when parents and children talk to each other, indirect requests are more commonly associated with money talk than with personal hygiene and bedroom tidying talk.

Each of these topics is potentially investigable. A typical way to proceed would be to try and frame a testable hypothesis. For example, we might hypothesize that two-year-olds respond equally (un)cooperatively to indirect and direct requests. And then we might set out to test this hypothesis by designing an experiment in which a sample of two-year-olds was selected and stimulated to action by a series of requests, some expressed directly and some expressed indirectly. The data resulting from such an experiment might be best collected on videotape. Once the data had been collected, they could be analysed and a finding would emerge, either that the hypothesis was proved or that it failed. If it turned out that the sample of two-year-olds complied more readily with direct than with indirect requests, this finding would presumably have implications for the way adults should talk to two-year-olds on occasions when they wanted to get them to do things. And the research might suggest follow-up experiments: for example, it might be useful to try and design an experiment to determine whether two-year-olds failed to respond to indirect requests because they were failing to understand their pragmatics or because they did not like being talked to indirectly.

This kind of research is usually called 'empirical' because it studies real, observable phenomena, in this case the reactions of two-year-olds to a series of direct and indirect requests. The research method outlined above is typical:

- frame a testable hypothesis (or series of hypotheses) suggested by some observation about the way the world appears to work
- design an experiment which will enable you to collect data which test this hypothesis

- collect the data under experimental conditions
- quantify the data in order to determine whether or not the hypothesis is proved
- consider the implications of the findings and whether follow-up experiments would be useful.

Very often empirical research of this sort tries to determine whether there is a significant, as opposed to a chance, association between two variables. So that, for example, you might try to establish whether there is a significant association between age and understanding of indirect speech acts as demonstrated by compliance with indirect requests.

Recognizing the scientific basis of linguistics has important consequences for the way we investigate language. But this does not mean that all pragmaticists think of the area of linguistics they are interested in as essentially scientific. Nor does it mean that every aspect of pragmatics readily lends itself to such methods of investigation. In fact, precisely because pragmatic meaning depends so much on inference, which is not a directly observable phenomenon, there are lots of ways of investigating language use that are not contrived experiments of the kind suggested for the investigation of two-year-old responses to indirect requests.

If you were interested in conversation, for example, you would rarely want to design an experiment to collect sets of data that would be easily comparable. In fact, you could argue that we got further in our analysis of the conversation in the travel agent's or between the warden and the students by trying to understand it in terms of the sequential properties of talk rather than by investigating how frequently the speakers made use of particular pragmatic strategies. In this case, the conversations were not collected as part of a controlled experiment at all. And they challenge us to provide an exhaustive analysis capable of accounting for all the contexts oriented to in the data.

Obviously very different techniques are involved in researching two-year-old talk by means of hypothesis testing as suggested above and researching the structure of conversation in the ways demonstrated in Chapters 8, 9 and 10. The first approach is often called 'quantitative' because it requires a substantial quantity of data whose regularities can be determined, often by detailed statistical means. The second approach is often called 'qualitative' because its results rely more on the interpretative insight of the researcher than on objectively measured associations between sets of variables.

Pragmatic research makes use of both of these approaches. And when you identify the area you wish to research, it is usually fairly clear which method is likely to give the better result.

11.2 Collecting data

You may be collecting your data because you wish to test a hypothesis. In this case, your data will usually be elicited, as in the hypothetical two-year-old project discussed above. When this is the case, you will need to design elicitation experiments very carefully to make sure that you are collecting data that enable you to measure what you seek to measure rather than some other phenomenon. This means that all the non-relevant variables need to be eliminated. It wouldn't be very useful, for example, if a linguist measured two-year-old responses to indirect requests only to realize afterwards that the results reflected the extent to which the requests themselves were palatable.

More often in your own work, you will probably collect your data first and have only a fairly general idea of what you hope they will show before you have collected them. The researcher who obtained the travel agent data, for example, was investigating contexts in which enquiries didn't lead to purchases. As it turned out, the data were valuable for many other reasons.

There are some fairly well established *dos* and *don'ts* when it comes to data collection. One of the most obvious relates to the so-called 'Observer's Paradox', or effect that the observer or collector has on the nature of the data itself. If you tell someone you would like to ask them a number of questions, they will provide you with data that reflect this situation and are very unlikely to represent their natural speech style. So it's important to find a means of collecting data which is not influenced by the collection procedure itself.

Similarly, if you tell your friends to have a natural conversation while you record it on tape, you will get anything but a natural conversation. I'm not saying that it isn't interesting to analyse data in which speakers orient to their situation as data providers, and maybe even to a supposed overhearing audience such as a tutor to whom you may eventually submit your work. However, in most situations you are unlikely to be able to collect representative data if your informants know that they are being recorded. On the other hand, there is an ethical issue: it is widely agreed that we ought not to make use of revealing data provided by informants without their consent. And indeed we often need to know things about our informants (such as their ages or nationalities or status in an organization) that may well not be directly revealed in the data they provide, so we will need to talk to them anyway. Therefore we have to decide whether:

- to obtain the prior consent of our informants before we collect data from them
- to ask permission to use the data after they have been collected
- not to ask permission at all.

The decision we make will typically depend on the circumstances in which the data are collected and the kind of talk that is expected to occur.

Asking permission before collecting data: we obviously need to ask permission before collecting data if we are hoping to record our own job interview, or if we are recording a business meeting or a doctor–patient encounter.

Asking permission once the data has been collected: some years ago a colleague and I conducted a small-scale research project in which we decided that reliable data could only be obtained if permission was not sought until after the data had been obtained and that the nature of the project and the transaction involved were such as to justify this. Every afternoon for four weeks we recorded every transaction that occurred between 4 and 5 p.m. in our local tourist information office. We were hoping to find out whether native and non-native speakers and native and non-native members of the culture used the same pragmatic strategies to achieve the same ends, such as finding overnight accommodation in the local area. Although the staff of the tourist information office knew they were being recorded, if we had told the visitors as they walked through the door that they were going to be recorded, the data would obviously have been distorted. So the transactions were recorded covertly.

As each informant left the counter, they were approached by a research assistant who explained to them that they had been recorded as part of a research project whose purpose was to study the ways in which people make requests, with the ultimate aim of developing teaching materials that would help non-native-speaker visitors in the future. They were asked whether they would agree to the conversation they had just had being analysed or whether they would prefer the tape to be erased. As it happened, only two informants asked for their conversations to be erased. Both were non-native speakers who said that if they had known they were being recorded they would have spoken better English! In the case of all the rest who gave their consent, we were then able to ask about their native/non-native-speaker status, their language learning backgrounds, ages, etc.

Recording without asking permission: many researchers would consider it acceptable to record short anonymous bursts of talk without obtaining the speaker's consent. For example, I might pretend to be an innocent bystander if I happened to be fortunate enough to be passing with my pinhead microphone and concealed tape-recorder and saw a motorist returning to their car just as a traffic warden was attaching a parking ticket. Because this material is in the public domain and might equally be recorded by a passing television crew, and since the identities of the informants will remain unknown and therefore no one can be damaged by the analysis of the data, this might be considered the type of situation that it would be ethical to record without the consent of the informants. Unlike the other situations discussed, it is also uncertain that data being obtained in this way are going to be used at all – pragmaticists collect masses of data rather as tourists take masses of photographs, but only a small part of all the data we record in this way will ever be transcribed, let alone analysed.

You may be wondering about how the data analysed in this book were obtained. The travel agent data were collected one busy Saturday morning by a researcher standing in a queue with a hidden microphone behind the customer. The travel agent's consent to use the data was obtained the following Monday. The warden/student data was obtained by a student collecting data for her pragmatics project by simply allowing the cassette-recorder to run as she went about her business. She obtained the consent of the three other people involved when she decided to use the data for her project. The student/porter data studied in Chapter 9 were recorded entirely by chance. The researcher had a tape-recorder in her bag and was on the way to the station to collect data according to a pre-arranged plan. She didn't realize that her tape was running until she reached the station and found she had collected gold on her way there. Subsequently I asked the porter for permission to use the data in this book.

There are a number of other points to keep in mind when you collect data. These include the following.

- Whenever possible, do a pilot collection exercise first. This will enable you to see whether the data you are collecting are: (a) audible and therefore transcribable; and (b) useful for the purposes you have in mind.
- Give some thought to whether you need to use all the data or just some part of them. There are circumstances when excluding any of the data you collect would render them an incomplete record of the speech event recorded. There are other occasions on which some random sample, such as the second ten minutes of a classroom interaction, might be preferred just because it is a random sample and directly comparable with other samples selected according to the same criterion. There are still other occasions when you are looking for particular types of data, such as inserted sequences between a question and the eventual answer, which probably means that you will have to transcribe all the data collected and then select your target data from the whole. If you have thought these issues through before you begin your data collection exercise, you will probably be able to collect your data more economically and are likely to collect only data that are genuinely useful.
- Don't be too ambitious: one hour of conversation involving several speakers can take many days or even weeks to transcribe. So limit the amount of data you set out to collect to what you can practically transcribe and usefully analyse – two or three minutes of talk will keep you occupied for many hours.
- If you collect data featuring more that two or three speakers, when you come to transcribe it, you are guaranteed to have problems in some places determining who the speaker is. This problem can sometimes be overcome by recording your data on video, but this is usually impractical. Another option is to be present during the speech event and note the opening words of each speaker. To do this, you will need to number the speakers, perhaps according to their locations around a table. But even this method is far from foolproof, as you will quickly discover. There are also practical problems associated with recording a many-speaker event: inevitably some speakers will be nearer the microphone than others, so some will be harder to transcribe. And the transcription will be harder still in the sections where several speakers talk at the same time, such as at points of agreement or when schism occurs, i.e. a larger group becomes two smaller groups for a number of exchanges so that two conversations run concurrently.

Once you have tried to collect your own data, you will become aware of the need to plan carefully – nothing is more frustrating than to have data which do not really reveal what you had hoped they would or which are so difficult to hear that you can never get an accurate enough transcription to work with.

11.3 Transcription conventions

When you make a transcription, you will need to make decisions about the notation conventions you employ and about how to set out the transcription on the page.

11.3.1 Notation

Conventional transcriptions of conversations use standard orthographic script rather than phonemic transcription. This is fortunate since the task of transcription would be overwhelming otherwise. (Of course, you are always able to give a phonetic representation of an item in your subsequent analytic discussion if you need to.) Most standard orthographic transcriptions are adapted to show how items like *and* and *your* are actually spoken since their realization may vary in obvious ways. So you might expect to use representations like *n* and *yer*. You also need to indicate hesitations like *er* and *um*, other fillers and uptake signals like *uh*, *uh-uh* and *yeah*, and audible breathing (*hh*) and indrawn breath (*.hh*). You may decide to indicate any particularly marked representation of a lexical item. In the travel agent data, for example, the travel agent's version of *but it* was transcribed as *burit*.

A more difficult issue is whether and how to represent intonation and pitch. Many transcribers avoid standard punctuation marks altogether because they can only represent broad interpretations of the functions of utterances and are in many ways ambiguous. The easiest solution is only to indicate very marked examples, so that distinctive pitch prominence might be marked by capitalizing the appropriate segments (e.g., you WHAT) and the louder of two simultaneous utterances where the speakers are competing for the floor by underlining. There are more elaborate systems for marking intonation contours such as the one worked out by Crystal and Davy (1969: 24–40), but they are very laborious to employ and require a degree of skill to interpret too.

More important in many ways than marking intonation is marking features of conversational sequencing. For example, you will almost always need to mark pauses in talk. The most widely used convention is parentheses, with the length of pause indicated in tenths of a second, so that '(2.5)' would represent a pause of two-and-a-half seconds. Short pauses can also be marked with parentheses and points, with '(.)' equal to a one-syllable length pause, and '(..)' equal to a two-syllable length pause, as we saw in Chapter

8. Sometimes the micro-pause that we expect at transition relevance places (TRP) does not occur, so that the utterances of the two speakers are *latched*, a phenomenon which is usually indicated by an '=' sign.

Another sequencing phenomenon that needs to be marked is the *overlap* of two speakers. The start of an overlap may be marked by a double slash '//' and the end of the overlap by an asterisk '*', which may be indicated in both speakers' utterances. An alternative is to use deep brackets, as I have been doing in this book.

(3) TA: we're not British Rail ⌈agents⌉
     C: ⌊you're⌋ not a ⌈gents I see⌉
     M: ⌊but I'll   ⌋ give you a
           rough idea

Notice how double slashes and asterisks have different implications for the appearance of the transcription on the page:

(4) TA: we're not British Rail //agents*
     C: //you're*not a//gents I see*
     M: //but I'll*give you
           a rough idea

Because the customer both overlaps the travel agent and is himself overlapped by the manager, this exchange illustrates how using different symbols to mark the start and the end of an overlap (such as slashes and asterisks or right- and left-facing brackets) makes a transcription clearer.

You will also need a convention to indicate that the transcription is uncertain or that there is a contribution which you are unable to transcribe. This may be done with single or double parentheses or with square brackets. As you'll have noticed, I've been using square brackets.

You may also want to indicate an important non-linguistic feature. This may be done with square or angled brackets as in

(5) NICOLE: yeah somebody with a cheese toastie machine
     SUSIE: <laughs> yeah

Although these are relatively widely agreed conventions, there is considerable minor variation in the way that different linguists use and adapt them to their own purposes. There is nothing to prevent you using conventions that are especially suited to your own data as long as you provide a key indicating how the conventions are to be understood.

Before you begin your own transcription, you would be well advised to study two or three examples. The *Handbook of pragmatics* (Verschueren *et al.*, 1995: 646–54) also provides a useful summary of transcription principles and Schiffrin (1994: 422–33) provides a comprehensive summary of the conventions used by Jefferson, Tannen and others. Another useful source is Atkinson and Heritage (1984: ix–xvii), reprinted in Jaworski and Coupland (1999: 158–66). Hutchby and Wooffitt (1998: 73–92) also have an informative chapter.

11.3.2 Setting out the transcription on the page

This is a much trickier area than it might appear to be. You only realize the complexities of the problem and the effects of the decisions you make once you have tried a few ways. Five possibilities are discussed below.

1. Start each new speaker at the left-hand margin. If you have an adequate way of indicating latched utterances and overlaps, in theory a transcription in which all new speakers began at the left-hand margin, even when overlapping the previous speaker, would be transparent. However, as soon as you have more than two speakers, this becomes problematical, as the following example shows:

   (6) TA: we're not British Rail//agents*
       C: //you're* not a//gents I see*
       M: //but I'll*give you a rough idea

   This is not only difficult to follow, but might also give the impression that the customer and the manager simultaneously overlap the travel agent.

2. Wherever there is a TRP, start the new turn at the left-hand margin. This convention not only solves the problem highlighted in (6), it also shows where TRPs occur. Notice how this means that a speaker who self-selects at a TRP will also start a new line at this point. In the travel agent data, when the customer tries to get the travel agent to take the turn and eventually has to continue himself, the data were represented as follows:

   (7) TA: I can tell you what it is to go to Edinburgh
       C: yes (1.0) by plane
       TA: by plane

   I chose this method of representing the data when you first came across them in Chapter 8 because they are easy to read in this form when you are unfamiliar with transcription conventions, but a more accurate representation perhaps would have been

   (8) TA: I can tell you what it is to go to Edinburgh
       C: yes
           (1.0)
       C: by plane
       TA: by plane

   This convention also enables a transcriber to distinguish a TRP from a genuine in-turn pause such as occurs when the manager searches for the right continuation:

   (9) M: er yeah the flight's a standby guarantee (..) yeah you you turn
          up and you've got to er (1.0) if they can't get on one flight they'll
          put you on the next any of the next two

   Some transcriptions that start a new line at each TRP also employ a capital letter at the start of each turn.

3. Start the next speaker at the point in the line where the previous speaker terminates. This method has the advantage of capturing the notion that talk continues naturally but has the disadvantage that it does not enable TRPs to be unambiguously transcribed. Both this and the first method may be suitable for very short examples of data but are not as satisfactory for longer conversations.

4. Use running lines for each speaker. This method has the advantage that it enables *aizuchi* to be marked as they occur without breaking the record of the speaker's talk. It works rather as music for an orchestra would be scored. There are clearly some advantages to this method which allows *aizuchi* to be marked in a natural way and captures the notion of continuing talk. It is particularly suited to talk where the contributors offer very unequal contributions, such as an instruction giving or an explanation sequence in which the instructed party does little more than indicate understanding. However it is a rather cumbersome method which becomes very wasteful of space as well as difficult to follow as soon as three or more speakers are involved.

5. Use columns for each speaker. This is an uncommon method of transcription but can be used quite effectively where the encounter is very unequal. For example, a teacher–pupil exchange which followed a question-answer format might lend itself to this method of representation. One advantage of the method is that utterance types as well as data can be represented in this format. So if we had transcribed the opening of the travel agent encounter in this way, we would be able to parallel the transcription with a typification of the contributions in the same format:

(10) C: can you help me I have to go to Edinburgh (.) somebody told me it was cheaper to go by plane than by train (.) is that right

TA: (1.5) well we're not British Rail agents so I don't know the difference

C: oh I see

TA: I can tell you what it is to go to Edinburgh

(11) C: request for information

TA: refusal to supply information

C: indication that this isn't a sufficient response

TA: responds with a part offer

Whichever method you choose for transcribing your data and however you adapt it to your own needs, you will discover how time-consuming making a good transcription is. We are unfortunately still many years away from having a computer program with voice recognition capable of turning multi-speaker natural talk into a transcription for us, so meanwhile we have to make do with existing technology.

In this respect, you will find the transcription task much easier if you work with a transcriber rather than a tape-recorder. A transcriber usually comes with a foot control. Each time you use the control to stop the tape, the tape automatically rewinds a few words so that you can hear the problem passage again. This also means that your hands are free to type the transcription as you control its pace with the foot control.

There have been attempts to write computer programmes which allow you to insert new material or delete misheard original material while at the same time adding or taking away the appropriate number of spaces on linked lines. Imagine, for example, that as I listen to the travel agent data again, I discover that I had misheard the customer's contribution in

(12) TA: that's a saver (0.7) burit it's a standby
      C: a st ⌈andby ⌉
      TA: ⌊you ha⌋ve to book it in advance but um (.)

As I listen again, I realize that the customer actually says not *a standby* but *it's a standby*. If I insert *it's*, the travel agent's overlap will no longer be in the right place. Software has been written which enables the relative positions of utterances to be maintained when insertions and deletions are made to linked lines. Such software obviously makes the task of revising a transcription much easier, but isn't a substitute for the really hard work involved in the first draft.

It should be repeated that making a good transcription is very time-consuming indeed and that you can only find out by trial and error which kind of notation represents your data most accurately. Expect to listen to your tape many times – you will be surprised to find that even with the clearest tapes there are tiny things that you misheard or had never noticed before. This is especially noticeable if you switch between different tape-recorders or transcribers. And, just for security, always work with a copy of the original tape.

11.4 Investigable topics

It may seem rather odd to come to discussing possible topics for project work after discussing technical issues. But now that you have considered the nature of pragmatic investigation and the problems associated with data collection and transcription, you may have a better idea of what topic areas are practical.

This section should not be taken as prescriptive or constraining. Indeed, there are many other areas that can be investigated besides the few suggested below and in many ways other than those outlined above. What follows is a short list of investigable areas.

1. Conversational strategies: how does turn-taking work – in general terms and in a particular conversation? According to what principles and by what means does the speaker select the next speaker? Who self-selects at TRPs and with what effects? How does a potential speaker show their intention to be the next speaker? What sort of interventions occur:

requests for clarification, confirmations of understanding, *aizuchi*, repair – both self- and other-initiated and self- and other-completed? What are the mechanics of interruption – is interruption projected? If so, how far ahead is the intention to interrupt signalled? Are there interruption markers? What determines whether the existing speaker or the interrupter secures the floor? And relatedly, how does topic shift occur – is it natural or contrived? Is it preceded by a formulation of the gist of what had gone before? Is an agenda adverted to? Is topic a viable unit of analysis? Do discussions of topic have internal structure? The units of conversation – insertion sequences, adjacency pairs, presequences. How are contributions cued and how does any contribution project beyond its moment of utterance?

2. Activity types and the institutional use of language: the structure and pragmatic properties of seminars, interviews, etc. Also talk types: the structure of telephone conversations, ordering sequences in restaurants, contributions to radio phone-ins, etc. To what extent are these speech events goal-oriented and to what extent do they determine their own structures? How are expectations signalled and how are prototypes, or best examples, implied and referred to? How is talk constrained and how do participants indicate constraints on allowable contributions? Determining the functional role assumed by a speaker and assigned to other speakers.

3. Focusing on power and distance, 'relation indicating devices' (Matsumoto, 1988): how speakers encode these; how speakers get their own way. Facework – how speakers use politeness strategies to acknowledge the face wants of others.

4. Audience design: how speakers signal that they take their audiences into account and how an audience is constructed by the speaker.

5. Co-authorship: how conversations and speech encounters are co-authored by participants; signals of agreement and mutual recognition of ends; successful negotiation.

6. The acquisition of pragmatics: what is to be acquired and how it gets acquired – studies of infants and their recognition and production of pragmatic effects; the role of pragmatics in enabling first language acquisition. The acquisition of a second pragmatics – pragmalinguistic knowledge and sociopragmatic skills (Leech, 1983: 11), honorific language, achieving pragmatic effects.

7. Intercultural pragmatics: how members of different cultural groups accommodate and react to socio-pragmatic differences.

8. Adding to pragmatic description: can you add a term of your own to the growing list of terms such as 'account', 'formulation', 'cue', which have been borrowed from everyday use and applied to conversational phenomena as descriptions of members' methods? Showing how your term is motivated and how it accounts for a typical and repeated pragmatic effect.

9. Adding to pragmatic description: can you add a term of your own to the

growing list of terms such as 'instruct', 'meetings talk', etc. which have been used to describe recognizable talk types?

10. Context: does the external social structure determine the way talk is organized and the type of contributions that occur, or is the context created by the talk itself?

11. Ethnomethodological accounts of language use: showing how language use is expectable, regular and recognizable by members of a community. Providing an ethnographic account of the way that talk and life are entwined. Showing how membership and cultural affiliation are oriented to and have both including and excluding functions.

12. Metapragmatic and metasequential phenomena: how these are used by particular speakers and for what reasons.

13. The explanatory nature of pragmatics: show how some pragmatic feature such as a maxim hedge or an indirect speech act can account for systematic language behaviour.

14. Folk views of talk: investigating the extent to which people's beliefs about pragmatic uses of language (politeness, interruption, etc.) are oriented to in the talk and reflect the phenomena that are actually observed. The degree of match between metapragmatic folk terms and pragmatic metalanguage.

15. When talk goes wrong: what is unexpectable but occurring and what might we hypothesize would never occur. Recognizing the regulative aspects of talk. Coping with pragmatic misunderstandings. How lasting are the effects of misunderstandings in talk-in-interaction and how are they repaired?

11.5 Learning by doing

In this final part of the chapter I'll make some comments about ways of learning pragmatics by doing data-driven pragmatic analysis.

In order to do this kind of 'empirical' pragmatics, it certainly helps to have a grasp of the kind of terminology associated with 'rationalistic' pragmatics – in fact, it makes one kind of sense to study rationalistic pragmatics of the kind presented in the earlier chapters in this book in your first year studying pragmatics and then to move on to empirical pragmatics later.

On our courses, students 'do' empirical pragmatics in their second year (although we don't necessarily call it by this name). Their work consists of recording naturally occurring data such as conversation, meetings talk, institutional talk, media talk, an instruct sequence, classroom talk, an interview – in fact, whatever interests them. They select two minutes of this recording and describe both the distal context and the immediate talk context in which it occurs. I listen to their tapes, and if I think the data are transcribable and analysable, they move to the next stage – actually transcribing it. Inevitably, the transcription goes through several drafts, during which process they begin to work out the approach they are going to take to their data. Often they bring their data to class to try out suggestions on their classmates and to get feedback. When their approach is decided, they write about the analytic parameters they intend to use and, if they are fortunate, uncover a key which helps them to understand their data. Let me give a couple of examples.

One year, a student had recorded a visit to her flat by first-year students looking to take it over the following year. As she worked on the data, she found several orientations by her flatmate to her status as a final-year student. This was confirmed by the first-year students who were also orienting to this status. And then she got the idea – what she had in front of her was 'seniors talk'. She had added a new semi-technical term to the inventory that includes 'instruct', 'meetings talk', etc.

Another student recorded a mother/small child exchange in which the child was complaining vigorously about having to leave a place she was visiting earlier than she had expected in order to go home. Amid the shouting and the tears, two things became clear – the mother was constantly presupposing that they were going to leave and the child was constantly striving for different ways of making what had been implicatures in the early part of the exchange more and more explicit. So you could see a constancy in the mother's contribution and a progressive development in the child's contribution as she became more and more enraged. Put like this, it seems simple, but it takes a lot of hard study and careful analysis to uncover such patterns from complex data. So let's take a case and study it.

Imagine you had collected the data involving the porter and the student whose opening sequence we studied in Chapter 9. The question then is: how can you find a key to unravel what's going on in it?

The first thing to realize about this method of collecting data, is that you don't know what you're going to get until you've actually got it and are faced with task of accounting for the talk that occurs. In the case of the porter/student data, two things we did notice in our preliminary study in Chapter 9 were the use of accounts and the participants' interest in determining who or what is to blame for the event that occurred. Perhaps we'll be able to analyze these in more detail. Let's look more carefully at the first two minutes of this six-and-a-half-minute conversation.

Participants
Present throughout: P = Head porter; S = Female student
Present from line 70: P1 = Postman

(13)
P: hello young lady=	1
S: =hiya (1.5) em I was round yesterday I've had some CDs	2
nicked (.) ⌈from Yoko⌉	3
P: ⌊so they ⌋ tell me (.) and I put (1.0) in your	4
pigeonhole (.)	5
S: right	6
P: [you know] (.) a little parcel like that	7

```
S:  that's what Magda said ⌈she saw it yeah    ⌉              8
P:                         ⌊and it was a little⌋ bit torn mind  9
    (.) but I put it ⌈in (.)⌉ and when Robin phoned me last    10
S:                  ⌊well  ⌋                                   11
P:  night (.) I said I remember (.) I can't remember which name  12
    it was but I knew it was in the first pigeonhole           13
    ⌈A B⌉ C or D                                               14
S:  ⌊yeah⌋                                                     15
S:  yeah that's what me and Magda had looked in ⌈to see our   16
P:                                              ⌊that's right  17
S:  mail⌉                                                      18
P:  and ⌋ it was there (..) so after this (.) I mean it's (..)  19
    it's Durham students going in the bloody place (1.0) I    20
    caught two yesterday (..)                                 21
S:  doing ⌈what      ⌉ (1.0) doing what=                      22
P:        ⌊afternoon⌋                                          23
P:  =just walking about (..) [they] don't live there (1.0)     24
    definitely English students (2.0)                        25
S:  wh wha what hh                                            26
P:  in Yoko Hall (1.5)                                        27
S:  all right hh                                              28
P:  and I chased them out (1.0)                               29
S:  what were they doing there just                          30
P:  well they're just wandering about cos (..) what the Durham  31
    students have given (.) load (.) give the number (.) the  32
    code number to anybody (..) loads and loads of Durham     33
    students                                                 34
S:  well I'm sure I've come in before and there's been a note  35
    on the door you know so-and-so I'm in room whatever (.) the  36
    code number is                                           37
P:  that's right (.) and for that we have no control whatsoever  38
    (.) so after this (1.8) what I intend to do (.) is any    39
    parcel or anything (.) we leave in here                  40
S:  right                                                    41
P:  and we put a note in the pigeonholes                     42
S:  thanks ⌈erm  ⌉                                            43
P:        ⌊that's⌋ all we can do Joanna                       44
S:  I know                                                   45
P:  but I definitely put it in yesterday morning darlin I     46
    remember it                                              47
S:  so hh I mean I don't know what to do now to [be honest] cos  48
    I've phoned (.) em (.) the company                       49
P:  that's right                                             50
S:  and all I can get is this (.) bloody (.) answerphone if you  51
    want if you want to make your payment press one if you want  52
    to check ⌈your balance press two⌉ so that's all I        53
P:          ⌊that's right that's right ⌋                      54
```

```
s: can get from there                                              55
P: because Robin told me he says oh the other girls (.) some       56
   of the other girls from (.) they saw it in the pigeonhole       57
   (1.0) I says I put it in                                        58
s: yeah                                                            59
P: and it was a little bit (.) it was was brown paper pet (..)     60
   and it was a little bit torn                                    61
s: yeah                                                            62
P: (1.5) and I left it in the pigeonhole (.) cos if it's           63
   recorded delivery or anything you see ⌈we  ⌉ we leave them      64
s:                                        ⌊yeah⌋                   65
P: in here (..) and we put a note on the pigeonhole (..)           66
   ⌈on the door        ⌉                                           67
s: ⌊okay I don't quite⌋ think you know where I stand do you        68
   (.) cos I mean (.) if they're going to sting me for (1.0)       69
P1: <enters> evening Reg                                           70
```

11.5.1 Doing accounting – first thoughts

Once we notice the importance of accounts in our data, a sensible course of action is to think through in a preliminary way what an account is for and then, once we have an idea of the field we are interested in, to do a literature survey. So what is an account for and how do accounts contribute to talk? Let me have a go at summarizing in a slightly more academic way what we already know about accounts and their contribution to talk based on what you read earlier in this book.

The purpose of negotiated talk is to arrive at a set of mutually agreed propositions which are an accepted outcome for all parties. It is in this sense that talk is consequential. Each turn in talk is expected to be procedurally consequential, i.e. to forward the purpose of the negotiation. When a first pair part such as a question cannot be satisfactorily answered, an account is frequently provided as a next-best second pair part. Accounts are dispreferred to the extent that it is their veracity rather than their explicit procedural consequentiality that is at stake, but are remedial to the extent that they prevent a breakdown in communication. Thus, accounts privilege veracity over procedural consequentiality.

Perhaps at this stage and before our literature search, it's worth returning to the data to see just how accounts do privilege veracity over procedural consequentiality. When we return to our data, we straightaway see that the porter makes the proposition that he placed the parcel in the pigeonhole into a 'validity claim', i.e. orients to its veracity, in a variety of sequential environments:

- by providing contextual detail: *I left it in the pigeonhole* (1.63)
- in contrast to the previous part of the account: *but I put it in* (1.10)
- when reflexively indicating a shift in members' method to accounting: *but I definitely put it in yesterday morning* (1.46)

- within reported speech: *but I knew it was in the first pigeonhole* (1.13) *they saw it in the pigeonhole (1.0) I says I put it in* (1.57)
- when confirming an earlier account: *and it was there* (1.19).

11.5.2 Doing accounting: reading the literature

You'll probably want to read as much as you can find in order to develop your understanding of the theoretical background. Often it's good to start with (a) an early classic and (b) a recent state-of-the-art work and then fill in as much of the ground in between as is appropriate to your needs. If you had read Scott and Lyman's (1968) paper as your early work and Firth's (1995) paper as your more recent one, you would have discovered that accounts are variously seen as follows.

1. 'Statement[s] made by a social actor to explain unanticipated or untoward behavior' (Scott and Lyman, 1968: 46).
2. Remedial – they repair or prevent norm violations (Firth, 1995: 200).
3. Ways of responding to reproaches. For example, in our data, the porter takes the student's assertion that she doesn't know what to do (1.48) and her following account (1.48–55) as an indication that her wants aren't satisfied by his account, i.e. as a reproach. He therefore recommences his own account with *because* (1.56), overtly signalling his obligation to account. And he embeds within this account (1.56ff) the account of his colleague which confirms the accuracy of his own original account.
4. Selective, i.e. they may be used to represent events in a way favoured by the speaker. For example, in our data, the porter goes on record as representing events from his own perspective: *that's all we can do Joanna* (1.44). Although this validity claim is theoretically challengeable, given the unequal distribution of power, the challenge isn't easy to make.
5. Negotiable/co-constructed, so that an account may be modified through questioning, prompting, etc. 'In that the account cannot "tell the whole story", its detail, veracity and implied prudence will often be "probed" by the account's recipient' (Firth, 1995: 212). For example, in our data, as we saw in Chapter 9, in the opening of the conversation (1.2–8), the porter acknowledges the student's account before commencing his own, which she acknowledges and then confirms as consistent with her own knowledge of events. In the co-construction that follows, the student's use of the past perfect, *that's what me and Magda had looked in* (1.16), refers to a time before Robin's telephone call, thus co-constructing an agreed sequence of events.
6. Acknowledging that there is something to be accounted for by the speaker. Thus the porter reflexively orients to his need to account with *because* (1.56) and *cos* (1.63).

As you can see, we've already gone a long way down the road of explaining our data. However, in considering accounts as speaker-favoured representations, we noticed the difficulty the student has in challenging the validity claims made by the porter. And since the veracity of both accounts and outcomes needs to agreed by all parties, the question then is whether both parties in this speech event are equally well placed to agree or determine the 'truth' of the propositions which an account contains. This suggests that it would be useful to read in this area too. If your search had led you to Harris's (1995) paper on 'Pragmatics and power', you would have discovered that '"Truth" comes to be defined pragmatically as what is accepted explicitly as "shared knowledge"' (Harris, 1995: 117). In our data, for example, the porter uses *I* in the accounts that describe his own actions. His affiliation to institutional membership encoded by *we* occurs in virtually all non-accounting talk (ll. 38, 40, 44, 64).

Harris also states: 'Conflicting goals in the institutional contexts selected are power-laden and related to knowledge claims that must be negotiated linguistically' (1995: 120), as we saw above, and it is 'difficult for the less powerful participant to raise validity claims relating to the "truth" of the utterances of the more powerful participant' (1995: 129). This further reading suggests that we have found a key which will help us to unlock our data.

Summary

The investigative method sketched out above involves the collection of data whose analysis we expect will make a small contribution to knowledge. Preliminary analysis suggests a productive area for further study – in this case, the use of accounts. This is followed by background reading which reveals further productive lines of analysis, in this case the relationship of the representation of events to the power status of the participants in the talk exchange. An obvious next step would be to study the way the situation is resolved in the continuing conversation. This further study would be likely to raise our awareness of how particular outcomes arise, and, by implication, how such outcomes might be worked towards or avoided in future contexts.

11.5.3 Doing causal explanation: first thoughts

Why did the package go missing? Who, if anyone, is to blame? And what are the consequences for the porter and the student? The porter clearly has an interest in attributing the disappearance of the package to some cause other than his own actions and he clearly has his own ideas as to how to do this. These factors are immediately apparent from the data.

At this point, a wise researcher would stop and realize that further analysis along these lines couldn't proceed without knowing more about the attribution of blame. We wouldn't expect linguistics to provide such knowledge, but it seems reasonable to suppose that psychologists, anthropologists and sociologists would all be interested in the attribution of blame. The best strategy in such situations is often to talk to experts or to fellow students in these fields and ask for their advice on basic reading.

11.5.4 Doing causal explanation: reading the literature

If a helpful social psychologist had recommended Hewstone and Fincham's comprehensive textbook chapter on attribution theory and if you had found Hilton's (1991) paper on conversation and causal explanation, you would have discovered that causal explanations rely on counterfactuality: if the event which did occur can be compared to a contrast case in which the event would not have occurred, then a cause is identified. Potential causes include:

- the person (in this case, the porter's actions) – test for High/Low *consensus*
- the stimulus (in this case, the parcel) – test for High/Low *distinctiveness*
- the circumstance (in this case, the disappearance of the parcel) – test for High/Low *consistency*.

Diagrams may make it easier to understand these 'tests': look at Figures 11.1, 11.2 and 11.3.

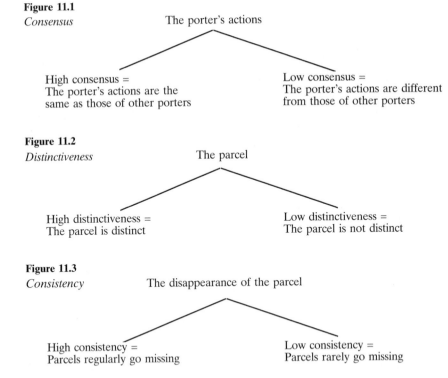

Figure 11.1
Consensus   The porter's actions

High consensus =
The porter's actions are the
same as those of other porters

Low consensus =
The porter's actions are different
from those of other porters

Figure 11.2
Distinctiveness   The parcel

High distinctiveness =
The parcel is distinct

Low distinctiveness =
The parcel is not distinct

Figure 11.3
Consistency   The disappearance of the parcel

High consistency =
Parcels regularly go missing

Low consistency =
Parcels rarely go missing

It is therefore in the porter's interests to establish High *consensus* (Low *consensus* = his actions could be at fault), High *distinctiveness* (something about the parcel attracts the thief) and either High *consistency* (the situation is common and thus by implication uncontrollable) or Low *consistency* (this is a new situation and thus couldn't have been foreseen).

The literature demonstrates that High *consensus* + High *distinctiveness* + High *consistency* configurations are associated with *dispositional attributions*. This means that the event is likely to occur anyway because the porter's actions are like anyone else's in his position, the parcel attracts attention and parcels regularly go missing. Dispositional attributions work on the principle of agreement – the situation is like others in which the event is likely to occur. In his talk, the porter may therefore be expected to orient to the characteristic nature of the event – as indeed he does.

A High *consensus* + High *distinctiveness* + Low *consistency* configuration makes the package the *causal explanation* since the porter's actions are like anyone else's in his position, the parcel attracts attention and parcels rarely go missing. Causal explanations work on the principle of difference between this and other events. In his talk, the porter may therefore be expected to orient to the exceptional nature of the event (as indeed he does), the particular characteristics of the parcel (as indeed he does), and to counterfactual cases where the event would not have occurred (as indeed he does).

The porter's orientation to the characteristic nature of the event occurs just over two-thirds of the way through the conversation when he says:

(14) P: an' you see in Yoko (.) I've said it over and over again you've got two keys (l.166–7)

This is followed by an explanation of the significance of the keys and then an account reflexively signalled by *but what happens* (l.175). This is followed by a formulation (*so our hands is tied*) (l.178) and a judgement (*but they're punishing their own (2.5) their own students*) (l.180):

(15) P: an' you see in Yoko (.) I've said it over and over again   166
        you've got two keys (.) one for the main door and one for   167
        their own door   168
     S: yeah   169
     P: that main door's supposed to be locked all the time (.)   170
        that stops anybody else getting in (2.0) Yoko   171
     S: yeah   172
     P: who hasn't got a key   173
     S: yeah   174
     P: but what happens (.) we go up and telling them lock it and   175
        lock it all night at half past ten [what have you] we go   176
        over at quarter to eleven (.) an' it's wide open again   177
        (1.5) so (.) our hands is tied   178
     S: (0.5) okay   179
     P: but they're punishing their own (2.5) their own students   180

The porter's orientation to the exceptional nature of the event is shown by his repeated formulations of future intentions involving a new strategy: *so after this* (l.19); *so after this (1.8) what I intend to do (.) is any parcel or anything (.) we leave in here* (1.39). The need for a new strategy implicitly orients to the exceptional nature of what has occurred.

The porter's orientation to the distinctiveness of the parcel is reflexively signalled by *and it was a little bit torn mind* (1.9). Its distinctiveness is again oriented to at 1.60: *and it was a little bit (.) and it was brown paper pet (..) and it was a little bit torn.*

The porter invokes a counterfactual case where the event would not have occurred (1.63–7). He also suggests that events like this would not occur if the proper procedures were adhered to (1.170–3).

Summary

In this second investigation of our data our preliminary analysis suggests a productive area for further study – in this case, causal explanation. This is followed by background reading in a related discipline which enables us to explain significant portions of our data. An obvious next step would be to study the way the situation is resolved in the continuing conversation and in particular whether the causal explanation/dispositional attribution agreed on reflects the power status of the participants in the talk exchange or whether the outcome is favourable to one or the other party.

One more thing: our background reading in this case reveals the true value of our data. Not surprisingly, it turns out that the literature on causal explanation represents abstract cases rather than actual real-world instances. Although convincing, it isn't supported by empirical data of the detailed kind that we have been investigating. In other words, we have been *doing* causal explanation with a real instance transcribed in front of us. You will very often find in your own project work that you are able to show with a real case that a theoretical construct is sustainable – or, sometimes, that it needs to be modified.

Conclusion

I hope the relatively detailed work that we have been doing in the final part of this chapter will inspire you to work on your own pragmatics project, either within a regular class or as an individual project within your overall course. Although it's slightly unnerving to collect data while still unsure of just what you are going to be able to do with it, you can be certain that all naturally occurring talk is pragmatically rich and offers opportunities for detailed analysis and explanation. Take heart from a student whose final-year project I supervised in Hong Kong. She was extremely worried about collecting data first and only later deciding what to do with it. However, she plucked up courage and went to the airport where she had a useful airline contact who made it possible for her to record transactions at a check-in desk. One of the first passengers she recorded was *en route* from Shanghai to Sydney *via* Hong Kong. But instead of getting his Hong Kong–Sydney boarding pass at the air-side transit desk, he had made a mistake and passed through immigration to the land-side. At the check-in desk, he was accordingly asked to pay the Hong Kong departure tax, and he was not happy . . .

The student's analysis of the resulting data earned her an A grade.

Checking understanding: solutions and suggested answers

1 Using and understanding language

(1.1)

PHARMACIST: Do you usually have this sort

The pharmacist presupposes that I've had cold capsules before. Given the speaker, I'm much more likely to understand her utterance as a professional rather than a social enquiry.

PETER: Yeh I think so

My informal 'Yeh' shows that I'm being friendly. I know that I usually have the sort I've asked for (and so, probably, does the pharmacist), but I hedge my reply with 'I think' because it's more friendly to pretend to be a bit uncertain. My use of 'so' is anaphoric and refers back to 'have this sort' – she and I are beginning to co-construct our conversation.

PHARMACIST: They make you drowsy mind

I take the pharmacist's 'you' to refer not to me in particular but to people in general (unlike her 'you' in the first utterance). Her use of 'mind' signals that she is warning me of something. Her utterance also makes sense of what she had said before: if she had just given me this warning straight away, it might have sounded rather abrupt.

PETER: Oh are there others that don't

My use of 'Oh' shows that I'm a bit surprised by what she has just said. My question 'are there others that don't' shows that I think she is trying to find an indirect way of recommending a different kind of capsule, and so I invite her to give me the information that I assume she has.

(1.2)

Even Presidents have private lives

Appropriacy – Clinton obviously thought this was the most appropriate way to deal with the revelation that he had had a relationship with a White House intern.

Indirectness – This seems to be an indirect way of saying that it was no one else's business.

Inference – I infer that Clinton is implying that he can do things like this if he wishes.

Indeterminacy – 'have' = are entitled to.

Context – The meaning we infer depends on Clinton saying it rather than you or me saying it.

Relevance – In order to understand this utterance, I need to consider what would make it relevant – for example, he is talking about himself rather than some other president and his affair with Monica Lewinsky is a newsworthy story.

Reflexivity – Clinton's use of 'even' tells me that what he says may be contrary to the general view and surprising.

I don't know how you say this in English but for me it was ooh-la-la-la

Appropriacy – Peslier obviously thought this was the most appropriate way of expressing his delight.

Indirectness – Peslier does not say directly what he feels.

Inference – I infer from the third 'la' that Peslier is very happy indeed.

Indeterminacy – It's hard to imagine anything more indeterminate than a meaningless segment 'la' which is added to the more conventional but still strictly meaningless expletive 'ooh-la-la'.

Context – It would clearly need to be as exceptional a context as winning a major race for the speaker to add the third 'la'.

Relevance – The most relevant way to take this utterance is not as a request for language tuition (as it might be in the context of a second-language class-room) but as an expression of delight.

Reflexivity – Peslier begins by commenting on his inability to convey the meaning he feels. His use of 'but' then contrasts this comment with his attempt to express what he feels, which he does in a mixture of English and pastiche French.

(1.3)

Ich bin ein Berliner

Deixis – *Ich* is deictic because the person it refers to can only be determined by identifying the speaker on this occasion.

Speech Act – President Kennedy reassures the Berliners.

Implicature – President Kennedy implies that he will stand by (West) Berlin when the city is threatened by the Wall, and perhaps that he empathizes with the people of the city. He implies that anything that happens to them, happens to him too.

We would have come to different conclusions if the speaker and/or the location had been different. Since we know that President Kennedy is not literally a Berliner, we know that he is conveying an indirect meaning and we therefore look for the likeliest or most relevant inference.

2 Deixis: the relation of reference to the point of origin of the utterance

(2.1)

1(a). Gesturally

Which finger did he bite?/*This* little finger on the right

Are you ready? Wait for it! Wait for it! *NOW*

It's *behind* (pointing to the location to help someone who can't find the item referred to by *it*)

1(b). Non-gesturally

I bet you weren't expecting *this*

I know more about pragmatics *now* than I did before I read this chapter

I always hide *behind* a tree (i.e. behind in relation to the seeker)

1(c). Non-deictically

And *this* strange guy walks in and vomits

Now that wasn't a very nice example

I hide my money *behind* the bookcase (the back of the bookcase does not require any context to be fully determined because bookcases have backs and fronts, so the use is intrinsic)

3. If you took *the last example* to refer to the most recent example discussed, the use would be deictic because without knowing where in the discourse the phrase occurred, it would be impossible to identify the example referred to. But if you took *the last example* to refer to the upcoming, final example in the chapter, the use would be intrinsic.

(2.2)

1. How about *We're not all daft you know* or *Our understanding of history will always stand us in good stead*?

2(a). How about *Look at him over there – I bet he drinks Carling Black Label*?

2(b). In more primitive times, *Let him have it, Chris* led to the execution of Derek Bentley for supposedly instructing his accomplice to fire the gun he was holding. *Him* refers to the policeman who was shot and *it* refers to the gun used to shoot the policeman – these look deictic in the sense that one could only identify the referents if one knew the context.

3. If Salman Rushdie is using *we* and *us* exclusively, he means that only he should be tolerant. But if he is using the pronouns inclusively, he means that those who have declared the *fatwa* should also show tolerance. The exclusive reading is apologetic and the inclusive reading is more accusatory. If the use is non-deictic, then he is treading a middle course between apology and accusation – but it's difficult to see why he should have used *we* and *us* at all if he intended this meaning. It clearly isn't easy to determine the status of the pronouns here.

(2.3)

1. At first sight it appears that *go* is used for movement away from the speaker and *come* for movement towards the speaker as we saw in (1) and (2). But this example shows that when the addressee is at the location to which the speaker is travelling, the addressee rather than the speaker becomes the deictic centre. Thus movement towards the addressee triggers the use of *come*.

2. I would normally say (22), but I would say (23) if I was talking to someone who lived in the same house as John or who was very close to him. And if I was asking John for an invitation, I would always use *come*.

3. I'm indebted to Zhang Qian of South-East University Nanjing for posing this neat problem and to Kelly Glover for helping me to tidy up the explanation. It seems to me that

(24) To the left of Mark

is deictic because it will always be interpreted as to the left from the speaker's (or addressee's) perspective (= Sue)

(25) On the left of Mark

could be deictic (left from speaker's or addressee's perspective) (= Sue) or non-deictic (left from Mark's perspective) (= Dave)

(26) On Mark's left

is typically regarded as non-deictic, i.e. identifying the referent does not depend on knowing the point of origin of the utterance.

If you agree with this verdict, you need to think about why it should be the case. One solution could be to do with English being a Head + Adjunct order language, i.e. we expect the head word (for example, the preposition in a preposition phrase) to come first. *On the left* is the head in *on the left of Mark* so the order is expectable. But in *on Mark's left*, the head word *left* comes second. When this word order occurs in a predominantly Head + Adjunct language, the whole phrase will tend to be viewed as a single compound word, a head in its own right as it were, so that *Mark's left* becomes a new non-deictic term to describe what is on the left in relation to Mark irrespective of the speaker's perspective.

4. The two expectable utterances for me are *this side of Durham* meaning between the speaker's location and Durham, and probably closer to Durham than to the present location, and *the other side of Durham* meaning beyond Durham in relation to the speaker's location. *Yon* and *yonder* are relics of a former third proximal indicating greater distance from the speaker than indicated by *this* and *that*. I took the speaker to mean *the other side of Durham*, although I don't recall having heard the expression before.

5. It seems that we designate locations around us as though they were extensions of our bodies. This suggests that our language is a conceptualization that depends on our experience. Notice also the many non-demonstrative expressions involving body parts, for example, *afoot, eye up, cheek by jowl, yard-arm, brow of a hill, toe the line*, etc.

(2.4)

1. I suggest
(36a) Now what have you found to say of our past
(36b) What have you now found to say of our past (but barely grammatical in this position)
(36c) What have you found now to say of our past
(36d) What have you found to say of our past now
In fact, Hardy actually wrote (36b).
2. (36a) could be non-deictic; (36b), (36c) and (36d) are deictic and (36d) is gestural in the sense that it is prosodically marked.
3. It seems that the use of *now* is progressively more gestural when it occurs towards the right-hand end of the sentence. Since we place elements we want to focus on at the right-hand end of sentences, this is not surprising.
4. The change is from a deictic to a non-deictic expression. It wasn't strictly necessary because it's unlikely that the time of writing (intended by my use of *now*) and the time of reading (how you will understand *now*) will make any difference to the claim I'm making about referring to the 1966 World Cup. But notice that sometimes it is important to distinguish the time of writing and the time of reading. For example, in a book like this, I would be much more likely to write *about a year before writing this* (which, although deictic, enables you to identify the time picked out by looking at the publication date of the book) than to write *about a year ago*. Although in principle you could equally easily identify the time picked out by *about a year ago*, I want to save you the trouble of reasoning that the time of reading isn't the time in relation to which *about a year ago* is to be interpreted.
5. The purpose is to shock drivers into taking more care by warning them of the likelihood of being involved in a future accident. Part of the effect comes from the use of *tonight* in an apparently anomalous way as though a time yet to come is already in the past.

(2.5)

The British announcement is the most direct in that it lexicalizes those who the announcement is aimed at, i.e. the illocutionary target: *Passengers for Sunderland...* (see Chapter 3 for an explanation of 'illocutionary target'). Both the British and the MTR versions are more direct than the KCR version as they give advice (*should*) rather than suggest an option (*may*). It seems that *there* co-occurs with a more indirect way of giving information or advice.

I might be persuaded that *there* is anaphoric, with either *the next station* or, more probably, *Kowloon Tong* as its antecedent, but *here* seems to me to be deictic. This makes me think again about (42) – perhaps it's less natural to get an anaphoric reading for a proximal than for a distal deictic. What do you think?

(2.6)

Heritage writes:

> Consider our example, 'That's a nice one', being said by a visitor to a host while both are looking at a photograph album ... It is obvious that 'nice' could mean a number of things in such a context. The visitor could be admiring the composition of the shot, or suggesting that the photograph was a good likeness of the host, or indeed that the host looked particularly well in the photograph ... Quite a differently organized search [for an appropriate meaning] will be initiated if the utterance is directed by a girl to her boyfriend in front of a jeweller's window. Once again, the referent may be identified by the girl's pointing to a particular ring, but the ring's property of niceness must be looked for in quite a different way. And different properties again will be looked for in a greengrocer's if a lettuce is described as 'nice'. (1984: 143)

3 Speech acts: language as action

(3.1)

1. You will have listed lots of situations and speech acts. One of my favourites is the contrast between the use of *Sorry* to invite the speaker to repeat their utterance and the use of *I'm sorry* with an accompanying scowl to dare the speaker to do this. Here the same proposition seems to be used for entirely opposite purposes.
2. My former student was perhaps re-establishing our acquaintance. As she went on to remind me who she was, she perhaps did not expect me to remember her. Hamlet's father's ghost was urging Hamlet to avenge his murder.
4. Hiroko misheard *it's OK* and thought instead that I had said *OK*. The same proposition conveyed in minimally different ways can thus be used both to accept and to reject an offer.

(3.2)

1. Literal meaning: a bunch of flowers is delivered to a recipient on behalf of a sender. This might count as many things, including thanking or apologizing or expressing sympathy or indicating affection or expressing the wish that the person receiving them should recover from illness. In each case there are expected but not necessarily occurring effects.
2. Locution: conveying the proposition that the addressee has returned to a place they were in on a previous occasion.

Illocution: likely to be an expression of the speaker's irritation with the addressee.
Perlocution: variable, perhaps causing the addressee to go away, feel insulted, make a retort of some kind, etc.

(3.3)

Examples of explicitly performative utterances that are often cited included:

- I second the motion
- I name this ship *QE2*
- I promise you won't regret it
- I bet you £5 you can't eat a kilo of chocolate
- I apologize
- I refuse to accept your explanation
- I plead not guilty.

(3.4)

The counter clerk takes *Do you sell postage stamps* as an indirect speech act requesting a stamp or stamps. In fact Mr Logic asks whether one of the felicity conditions on buying stamps obtains, from which she infers that he wishes to buy some. Whilst she responds to the illocutionary force of his utterance, his 'logic' consists in treating it only as a locutionary act. The absurdity of this strategy is confirmed by the question mark that appears over her head when he does this a second time. Mr Logic could hardly have calculated the perlocutionary effect of treating the address term *smart arse* as a mistaken attempt to use his name.

(3.5)

1. *Could we have some more coffee* is a conventionally indirect way of requesting. Notice that there is a scale of politeness which includes *might* (most formal), *may*, *could* and *can* (least formal). This kind of politeness encodes greater distance between speaker and hearer as you move up the scale. She obviously felt that her husband wasn't quite formal enough with the waitress, as indicated by *You should say may we*.

When challenged, she tries to justify her objection to *could* by appealing to its literal meaning. This is really more or less beside the point since he uses the literal meaning to refer to a felicity condition on having more coffee. Moreover, her preferred replacement, *may*, merely makes reference to another felicity condition, whether it is permissible to have more coffee.

She is quite right to protest that he didn't mean it literally, but then if he had used *may* to begin with, who is to say that she would not have protested that 'it could mean' *have you got permission?* In fact they are just having a quarrel, which followed from her not liking the way he was encoding his attitude to the waitress.

Later she made a lot of fuss and said she could not eat toast and so asked for some bread. But when it came, she did not like the look of that either and ended up eating the toast. This enabled him to get his own back with the observation *you had a piece of toast in the end*, clearly an indirect way of scoring a point.

2. You are supposed to say *No* with fall-rise intonation, which counts as inviting the assistant to tell you. But it was late, I was tired and thinking of sorting the children out when I got home, and why should I have heard of their miserable oil anyway, and so I rather rudely said *No* with falling intonation, to which the assistant replied *I see I can't interest you.* This interesting example shows how the same lexical item can have quite opposite illocutionary forces and consequential perlocutionary effects depending on the intonation pattern assigned to it.

A week or two later I stopped again at the same garage. There was a different assistant this time, but she tried just the same utterance on me. I didn't feel keen to go through the charade of fall-rise *No*, nor did I want to repeat the rudeness of falling *No*, so I decided to try *Yes* instead. It had just the same perlocutionary effect as falling *No*. Why didn't I think of it the first time!

3. Not only are the formulas interesting here (e.g., my first utterance counts as an indirect instruction to stop smoking) but the sequential properties of the three interactions are very similar: I begin with information about the smoking status of the location, which is inevitably responded to with a checking question. Either these two turns are sufficient to bring the smoking to an end or, more usually, I have to make some broader comment about smoking in the area, which is sufficient to ensure compliance with the illocutionary purpose of my first utterance. These data show how a series of speech acts in a predictable sequential structure constitute a recognizable speech event.

4. I felt reprimanded by (43). It was as though I was partly to blame for my daughter's untidy bedroom. Perhaps if my wife had said *her room* instead of *that room of hers* I would not have had this feeling. In (44), the chairman finds a witty way of telling the speaker to stop talking. I process Eleanor's utterance in (45) as the presequence to 'asking' a favour and indicate that I may not be enthusiastic about agreeing to it.

4 Implicit meaning: Grice's theory of conversational implicature

(4.1)

(8) If I knew that everyone believed in God, I should have said so. Thus *Some people believe in God* implies that not everyone does.

(9) Because I don't say the more expectable *made a good job*, I imply that it wasn't as good a job as I'd hoped it would be.

(10) If I had more than £100, I should have said so, so *I've got £100 to last me until the end of the month* implies not more.

(11) If I knew that Maurice Greene could run 100m in less than 9.8 seconds, I should have said so, so *Maurice Greene can run 100m in 9.8 seconds* implies not less.

All these implicatures result from the Quantity maxim.

(4.2)

Quantity – a helper will pass just one light bulb rather than two to their colleague on the stepladder.

Quality – a helper will supply a light bulb of the appropriate quality (i.e., new rather than burnt out) and kind (bayonet-type or screw-type, as required).

Relation – a helper will supply assistance that is relevant to the stage in the operation (e.g., will secure the stepladder when their colleague is climbing it rather than before or after).

Manner – a helper will make the nature of their assistance clear (e.g., will make it evident that they are really securing the stepladder rather than being ambiguous or dilatory about it).

(4.3)

1.

(22) flouts Quantity by saying that the competition survives because it survives. However, it's not very difficult to recover the implicature that the competition is a social institution despite being difficult to justify in terms of political correctness.

(23) is not a sincere question (my wife knows that I haven't see the room) and it therefore flouts Quality. Once again it's not very difficult to recover the implicature that the room is untidy and not fit to be seen.

(24) By providing a response which is not an answer to the question asked, my daughter intends to direct me away from an unwelcome line of questioning. It is an attempt to flout relevance. Many pragmaticists doubt whether any utterance can ever be irrelevant as an addressee will always attempt to work out how even an apparently irrelevant utterance, such as this one, is related to what has gone before. Perhaps we should say of Eleanor's contribution that the relevance is given but not obvious.

(25) flouts the maxim of Manner since *take lead from* is ambiguous. There are therefore more perspicuous ways of indicating that dogs' behaviour is like their owners'. Newspaper headlines, advertisements and jokes are often understanding tests of this sort.

2.

(26) Quantity – tautology.

(27)–(31) Quality – metaphor, overstatement, understatement, rhetorical question, irony.

3.

(32) *Current* is ambiguous. *Ahead* is given a particularly literal sense by the television advertisement which shows human-like pylons striding 'ahead' across open country.

(33) *We have the lead* is ambiguous, with one sense contradicting what is entailed by *cordless*.

(34) The second multiplication symbol is used in a less than maximally perspicuous way to represent the lexical item *by* in the phrase *by far*.

(35) Again, the multiplication symbol lacks perspicuity in this newspaper advertisement for second-hand Land Rovers.

(36) The spelling of *fourmost* suggests the number *four* and reminds us that a Land Rover is a four-wheel drive vehicle.

(37) This advertisement combines the two notions of *a class of its own* and *a glass and a half of* milk, which other advertisements state goes into every bar of Cadbury's milk chocolate.

(38) Since the power of computers is measured in *megahertz*, the homophone *hertz/hurts* is an obscure way of suggesting that this company makes buying a computer easy.

(39) The name *Walter Wall Carpeting* suggests the idea of *wall-to-wall carpeting*.

(40) This advertisement is obscure because of the syntactic ambiguity involving readers' using their eyes to be critical judges of beauty and the advertisers' treating their eyes as a critical (i.e. valuable) property.

(41) This advertisement plays on the ambiguity of helplessness in the face of temptation (i.e. one can't stop oneself taking a piece of pizza) and helping oneself to food.

(42) Two ambiguities: *BA* and 'Be a', and the ambiguity between connotations of *better connected* – connected to more flights and having an impressive social network.

(43) *On the spot* means both 'immediately' and, literally, 'on the spot or pimple'.

It seems to me that if we can pass the understanding test that newspaper headlines and advertisements sometimes pose, we feel good about ourselves and, by association, we are motivated to read the stories or have positive feelings towards the products advertised. Passing these understanding tests is a kind of initiation rite which makes us members of the privileged group of those who get the message.

4.

It's the taste flouts Quantity (insufficient information) and Manner (obscure) and therefore triggers an inference process in which the addressee looks for the likeliest meaning that is relevant in the context that obtains – that the taste is good for something being advertised on television and bad for a school dinner.

(4.4)

2. Here are some tentative suggestions – do they coincide with your ideas?

Well – hedge on Quantity.

if you asked me for a straight answer, … I shall say that … in terms of the averages of departments … you would … find that … there … wasn't very much in it one way or the other – the proposition.

as far as we can see – hedges Quality.

looking at it by and large – ?hedge on Quality, ?intensifies Quantity.

taking one time with another – ?intensifies Quantity, ?has truth value.

then – intensifies Relation.

in the final analysis – intensifies Manner.

it is … true to say that – intensifies Quality.

… probably … hedges Quality.

at the end of the day – intensifies Relation.

in general terms – ?hedges Quality, ?hedges Manner.

… probably … hedges Quality.

not to put too fine a point on it – ?intensifies Relation, ?intensifies Manner.

… probably … hedges Quality.

as far as one can see – hedges Quality.

at this stage – hedges Quantity.

(4.5)

Because (71) appears at the beginning of the academic year and because of the pictorial representation, we infer that WH Smith sells everything necessary for study except uniforms. (72) implies that the videos sold at WH Smith are tear-jerkers for which you will need a handkerchief; and because the advertisement appears just before Christmas, it might also be inferred that if you buy someone a weepie video from WH Smith as a present, you will have to go somewhere else to buy them handkerchiefs too.

We say that implicatures are non-conventional because they are not part of the meaning of the expressions that trigger them. These examples show the non-conventional nature of implicature in a particularly obvious way because the reasoning processes that enabled us to calculate the implicature in (71) will not work algorithmically for (72): i.e. you would be wrong to infer that (72) implies that WH Smith sells everything necessary for Christmas except hankies. Thus the implicatures recovered from (71) and (72) are non-conventional just because they are implicatures – and even recovering one of them fails to provide an algorithm by which the other can be recovered.

(4.6)

(73) flouts Quality and Manner. The question isn't a sincere question and the utterance is a deliberately obscure way of drawing attention to the misspelling of *necessary* by highlighting the homophone in *seeing double/double 'c'*. The speaker might be taken to imply that the optician does not inspire confidence.

(74) flouts Manner. The speaker implies that the manufacturer of the fireworks is less than successful by suggesting that the brand name is inappropriate. The speaker is obscure in the sense that he treats the brand name as a description. I found myself doing the same thing after we had a new boiler fitted bearing the brand name *Ideal*, or, as I put it after one or two mishaps, *far from ideal*.

(75) flouts the maxims of Quality and Manner. The graffiti suggest that the car is dirty by implying that it is not white. This is an obscure way of recommending that the car should be washed.

(76) flouts Manner. It might be taken to imply that the dessert menu is a kind of afterthought, or that diners are entitled to a dessert (i.e. it's what they deserve, even maybe as a kind of punishment – cf. *just deserts*). So both *just* and the homophone *desserts/deserts* are ambiguous.

(77) flouts Manner by making a pun with *note.*

(4.7)

The assignment of contrastive or any other non-natural stress typically results in an implicature because the unmarked, most perspicuous realisation of the proposition does not occur. (78) implies that other washing powders may remove dirt but will leave your washing smelling unpleasant. You might like to think of other examples of non-natural stress assignment and consider their effect.

(4.8)

When he gets to *in*, and although the utterance is not complete, the speaker realizes that what he intends to say will imply that David Smeaton, a BBC reporter, is a prisoner in the gaol on Dartmoor. He therefore uses *rather more precisely* to intensify Quality and to intensify Manner, so that the listeners are assured of the appropriacy of *on*.

(4.9)

The implicatures I get are that Durham students are better than Cambridge (79) students, and that the previous question was asked by a different speaker and is not taken by this speaker to have been serious (80).

The implicature recovered from (79) is surprising because there's no obvious reason why stating that the students aren't of the same calibre should imply that the second- rather than the first-named institution has the better students. But in related examples, it seems always that the second entity is the benchmark by which we judge – so that even when we state that *John is better/worse than Mary*, it's Mary who is the standard of comparison. It looks as though we get the implicature that Durham students are better by Manner – it's simply the most perspicuous way to resolve the indeterminacy as to whether the first- or the second-named institution is understood to have the better students.

The implicature recovered from (80) is also surprising because we might expect *more serious* to imply or even presuppose that the first question had been serious. But in fact we often use comparatives when we want to imply that the object of comparison has the contrary property as in *I wish she was more intelligent* (implies she is stupid) or *I hope to be more industrious next term* (implies I was lazy this term). Perhaps it's partly a matter of politeness – to say *I wish she was intelligent* is more critical than *I wish she was more intelligent*.

(4.10)

1. The Skoda advertisement implies that the base price, the one to consider first, is the highest rather than the lowest, and that therefore Skodas are very good value. This effect occurs in this advertisement because the usual pragmatic directionality – fast times are better when running 100m, low scores are better when playing golf, more money is better, low prices are better when buying cars – is reversed. Therefore the most relevant way to understand the advertisement is that Skodas are good value.
2.
(81) England fail to lose
Normally we talk about teams *failing to win*, with the default expectation that a team plays to win. But after a recent series of defeats, this headline implies that England are expected to lose. Like all the examples in Checking understanding (4.10), there is a flout on Manner. There is typically a further relevance-derived implicature, here probably that the England team are of poor quality.
(82) Normally we expect things to improve so that they become *better than ever*. Here Manner is flouted because *worse* is 'better' when assessing a museum of horrors. The relevance-derived implicature is perhaps that you should really visit the museum now.
(83) Normally we expect our investments to increase in value. The relevance-derived implicature is perhaps that we should think carefully before buying the financial product on offer.
(84) *But* advises you that I'm going to say something that contrasts with the first stated proposition. The default expectation is that I am going to contrast my stupidity with Alister's cleverness. Manner is flouted because *If you're as clever as me* is more obscure than the expectable *If you're as stupid as me*. The relevance derived implicatures are that really clever people get someone else to do the task for them and that the addressee should follow my example.

(4.11)

(85) *Even* conventionally implicates that the proposition to which it is attached, in (85) *the Labour Party front bench*, is at one end of a scale. Knowing who the speaker is enables us to work out which end of a scale the

Labour Party front bench is at, and further to infer the conversational implicature that the Labour Party front bench is nothing special.

As in (85), *even* in (86) gives rise to the conventional implicature that the
action of bringing a wife into Horley Town Hall is at one end of a scale.
Thus *I have not even brought my wife into Horley Town Hall* conversation-
ally implicates that Horley Town Hall is nothing special. (85) shows that such
implicatures are psychologically real since the speaker goes on to confirm it
by saying *That's what I think of Horley Town Hall.*

(4.12)

Implicature recovered from Hugh's message: the election will reveal which
of us is the better candidate for the position. (This is by no means the only
implicature.)

Calculation Although Hugh says that the best person will win, we cannot
know the outcome of the election in advance. And given that our colleagues
form the electoral college, we expect them to judge wisely. There is also the
default set expression *May the best person win!* which suggests that elections
are reliable ways of selecting better candidates. Therefore the most relevant
way to take what he says in the context in which he says it is that the outcome
will determine who is the better candidate.

Implicature recovered from my comment: this is obviously obscure and therefore flouts Manner, and possibly Quantity and Quality as well. Am I implying that I want to win the election or that I don't want to win the election?

Calculation For a start, my comment suggests that I don't accept the default
assumption implicit in Hugh's message that elections do determine who is
the better candidate. So in order to understand what I meant, first it's necessary to recover an implicated premise. But which of the two possible implicated premises, *Hugh is the best person* and *I am the best person,* is the one
I intend Sara to recover? Unless you have sufficient contextual information
about Hugh and me, you cannot determine this. However, I calculate that
Sara knows enough about both of us to be able to determine it (if I didn't
make this assumption, there wouldn't be any point in making the comment).
If we take *Hugh is the best person* as the implicated premise, then *I hope not*
implies that I want to win. If we take *I am the best person* as the implicated
premise, then *I hope not* implies that I don't want to win. Again, it would
help you a lot in determining what I might mean by *I hope not* to know
whether I am an ambitious candidate or have been put forward by a sponsor
and have reluctantly agreed to stand. Or whether I am the kind of person
who is boastful, or falsely modest, or genuine and sincere, etc. Again, I
expect Sara to be able to recover this contextual information. So we see that
calculating implicatures depends on being able to adduce appropriate contextual knowledge.

(4.13)

The subtitler typically (although not invariably) excludes items that do not add truth value to the utterance, such as NOW in (1) and BUT in (3). Maxim hedges like SORT OF THING in (6) and intensifiers like JUST in (11) and (12) are excluded. Another principle is to delete lexical items whose entailments can be recovered as implicatures: good examples are the deletion of BOTH in (2), ALSO in (4), IN BETWEEN in (7) and FOR ME in (30). This also applies to the conventional implicature OH in (19), which must be recovered as a conversational implicature in context. Notice that the auxiliary assertion WHICH WAS LOVELY in (21), which is not included in the main proposition, is also excluded. The principles guiding deletion of spoken language can be determined by comparing (1), where *didn't you* survives, with (14), where COULDN'T YOU does not. Neither contributes propositional content but, unlike (14), (1) is a genuine question in which *didn't you* is necessary to indicate illocutionary force.

These data may suggest that speakers have the option of allowing an implicature to arise or conveying what would have been the implicated meaning explicitly. The explicit version, *her son and her daughter by her first marriage had both left home*, allows the speaker the option of stressing *both*, which would then act as a trigger to the addressee advising them of an implicated meaning to be recovered. One can even think of examples where stress is hardly required, such as *Tim and Julia went to the cinema together*, where *together* seems to trigger the implicature that this is significant in some way beyond the stated meaning. This analysis suggests that implicitness is a natural and unavoidable property of language. So if I decide to try and make explicit what is an implicature in *Tim and Julia went to the cinema* (implicature: together) by uttering *Tim and Julia went to the cinema together*, another implicature arises.

(4.14)

1. *I don't drink alcohol* is an utterance-type inference, at least as far as British culture is concerned. However, we see from (102) that the Chinese community of Hong Kong do not appear to draw this inference from *I don't drink* and therefore the more explicit full propositional form is required to convey the same meaning. However, in both Cantonese and English *I don't smoke cigarettes* in an utterance-type inference recovered from *I don't smoke*. Being a null-subject option language, Cantonese invites the subject (here *I*) to be recovered as an utterance-type inference. There are interesting differences in word order between the two texts, and the English text also exhibits conjunction reduction, whose effects will be discussed shortly.

2. Like *do something, say something* is relatively inexplicit, and so it often invites an inference. This makes it look like an utterance-type, but in this case the co-text helps us to draw an utterance-token meaning. This example shows that the boundary between utterance-type meanings and utterance-token meanings is fuzzy and that there are cases where we could argue both ways.

(4.15)

1. We understand *after death* to refer to a state that commences when life has ended – cf. *in life*. As a default Q2-inference, the death is taken to be that of the speaker or addressee, whichever is more appropriate in the illocutionary context. Although the most relevant inference in *What to do after a death* is that the dead person is not the addressee, in *What to do after an accident*, one might infer that the accident had happened either to the addressee or to someone else.

2. The marked reply invites the M-inference that the speaker is not going to work.

(4.16)

1. Clearly the joke turns on requiring us to re-analyse *a husband* in such a way as to replace the default Q2-inference *someone as yet unmarried and willing to become a husband*. Although the speaker's father intends the default Q2-inference, the joke turns on the speaker's drawing (or pretending to draw) a marked M-inference.

2.

(117) Q2-inference: good because loud

(118) Q1-inference: both good and loud

(119) M-inference: various, could include *despite being loud, and loud as a bonus, and loud – as was required.*

5 Implicit meaning: Sperber and Wilson's Relevance Theory

(5.1)

1. The more problematical items include:

- determining the modality of *attend* – was I obliged or recommended to attend?
- determining the meaning of *attend* – be physically present at meetings and keep quiet or be physically present at meetings and contribute to them?
- *course planning and examiners' meetings* – a single type of meeting at which two different kinds of business were conducted or two different types of meeting?
- was *in future* in Alice's ideolect equivalent to *in the future* in my ideolect, i.e. from the time the message was written onwards? Or did *in the future* imply that there had been a meeting in the past that I was expected to attend?

2. The explicatures that help trigger the recovery of each of the two implicatures include:

- the relation of *my* to *book* – one of ownership or authorial proprietorship?
- the sense of *seen* – awareness of physical presence or knowledge of contents?
- the sense of *book* – physical object or contents?

The higher-level explicatures will provide us with speech act descriptions such as (put very crudely) 'the speaker is asking about the whereabouts of property she wants returned' or 'the speaker is advising of the need to become familiar with the contents of a book she has written'.

(5.2)

1.
(10) You need to know that 'alcohol in moderation' is not harmful and that large quantities are.
(11) You need to know that there is a risk of mad cow disease spreading to sheep and that slaughtering infected animals is an allowed policy. It might also help to know that sheep do not, so far as we know, have higher cognitive functions.
(12) You need to know that the Equitable Life is unique among life insurance companies in never paying commission to agents.
2. This is an intriguing question. We would expect a relevance theoretic account to require *Tim and Julia went to the cinema* and *Tim and Julia went to the cinema together* to be explicated to the same full propositional form. However, as we saw in Chapter 4, *Tim and Julia went to the cinema* and *Tim and Julia went to the cinema together* trigger different implicatures. So in order for the right implicatures to be recovered, the theory will need to distinguish, presumably at the level of explicature, between propositional forms that are enriched and identical propositional forms that are not enriched. This looks too like postulating underlying forms to be a happy solution to me.

(5.3)

The speaker's utterance is guaranteed relevant (1). She has used an idiomatic expression because she thinks I have the abilities and resources to provide a relevant interpretation of the metaphor (2). But I have a problem explicating *life* (3): am I to infer *life span* – in which case the speaker is stating that the person referred to will cause her to die ten years earlier than she would otherwise have done? Or am I to infer *stage in life reached at present* – in which case the speaker is stating that the person referred to has added ten years to her life expectancy. I certainly need non-linguistic information (such as knowing the mood of the speaker and the circumstances she is referring to) and paralinguistic information (such as the tone in which the utterance is delivered) to help me determine which of the two explicatures I am intended to recover. Having determined this, there will be an accessible assumption (the speaker is unhappy with the person she is speaking about or the speaker is happy with the person she is speaking about) (4, 5). Thus by recovering the appropriate context, I'm able to prove the relevance of the utterance (6).

(I'm grateful to Laurence Brushi for this very neat example.)

(5.4)

Without more of the surrounding conversation, it's not possible to know whether the speaker of (17) wanted to convey only what is entailed in her utterance or whether she intended an implicature. However, *only* in (16) tells the addressees that it will be worth their while processing the utterance for an implicit meaning and that the speaker's purpose is not merely to convey neutral information. First there are several explicatures to be inferred: does *we* refer to the speaker and her partner only or to the speaker, her partner and other members of their family? Since the conversation takes place in Florence, *are* cannot denote present location and must be conceptually enriched to *reside* or some equivalent. *London* is presumably *the city named London in UK*. These explicatures are necessary because this same utterance might have occurred 30 miles from London, Ontario, with very different explicatures.

Having enriched the utterance appropriately, we need to consider relevant contextual factors – the addressees are American visitors to Europe and are thus likely to spend time in London. Perhaps they are being offered a place to stay or being invited to visit the couple's home. On the other hand, it's possible that the speaker is boasting and intending to convey to the addressees that she is no ordinary tourist. Once again, you need more of the surrounding conversation to be sure. As I had been eavesdropping for some while, I knew instantly that the speaker was boasting and was seeking to convey to her addressees that she was more cultured than they. But without the help of *only* I would not have been able to recover the implicature conveyed by the speaker.

(5.5)

1. Part of the explicating process is to disambiguate *handed down*, which appears to be used here as a phrasal verb meaning 'bequeathed'. This explication is presumably based on the inference that when *handed down* occurs in close proximity to someone referred to as a 'dear old grandfather', the phrasal verb reading is the most relevant. Thus one implicature of the explicated utterance is that the joke-teller's grandfather is no longer alive. There is then a pause just long enough to cause the studio audience to think the sentence is complete and therefore to confirm to themselves that the explicature and implicature recovered are the most relevant understandings. But the joke-teller then continues *the other night as he was clearing out our attic.* Discovering that the joke-teller's grandfather is still alive causes us to revise

the original explicature and substitute the new explicated meaning that *handed down* is not a phrasal verb at all but a regular verb followed by an adverb. Unless you got the inappropriate explicature the first time (i.e. the phrasal verb determination), you could not get the joke, which consists in denying an implied meaning. It turned out that the informant group were not able to process *handed down* before the continuation of the joke confirmed it as verb + adverb, and therefore did not get the crucial explicature.

(5.6)

Although the first part of this sequence up to the pause implies that the joke-teller was a successful entertainer, the second part requires the implicated premises that scrapbooks containing large numbers of rave reviews are heavy, that this scrapbook is not heavy and that therefore it did not contain (m)any rave reviews. Without these implicated premises, the implicated conclusion that the joke-teller was an unsuccessful entertainer is not recoverable. The informant group did not succeed in recovering the implicated premises necessary to understand the joke, presumably because they were satisfied that the first part of the sequence up to the pause had conveyed what the joke-teller actually intended them to think.

(5.7)

The group did not have the contextual resources to know what sort of place Scarborough is and that Rugby players would not usually choose it as a holiday destination.

(5.8)

The informant group were not able to recover the explicatures that Ivan is terrible in bed and hence Blodwen is disappointed. We can only speculate about the reasons. Perhaps they are to do with language abilities – they are unaware that *terrible in bed* is a permitted colligation. Perhaps there was insufficient time to revise the first reference assignment and recognize that it isn't the Ivan who was a savage ruler who is referred to – or, at least if it is, it's not his savagery that is salient.

(5.9)

1. Clearly quite a lot of processing effort is required to draw the inference that the tooth was knocked out by a scene shifter who felt insulted by the joke-teller. But since any other conclusion would require more effort, the studio audience therefore assumes that this is the relevant inference. However, the informant group has problems with this utterance – the effort required to process it was too great for the implicature to be recovered.

Perhaps the reference to *the BBC emergency dental service* was taken at face value and therefore the relevance of what followed was especially difficult to prove.

2. That *she's doing very well* can only be understood to be ironic when what follows the pause is understood. Therefore the first pass reading has to be rejected and an extra processing burden is placed on the audience. Moreover, the audience is required to infer that she is not doing very well, although the joke-teller appears not to draw this inference himself.

- The non-standard use of English is regarded as humorous by the regular native speaker audience, but the non-native speaker informant group first have to identify it as non-standard; even if they do this satisfactorily, they lack the native speaker context in which it is comic because incongruous.
- In *you'll be forgiving*, the *au pair* treats *forgive* as dynamic rather than stative; for speakers of languages where there is no co-occurrence constraint such as that on progressive form and stative verb in English, it is by no means intuitive that *forgive* is a stative verb.
- The audience needs to explicate the non-native speaker errors in two ways – both in their own right (i.e. *bad language* = swearing) and by inferring likely intended meanings (i.e. *bad language* = ungrammatical English). Similar explicatures are required for *grandmaster* and *touching up*. The humour partly derives from the implicature that the speaker does not know what she is saying.
- As well as the innuendo associated with *touching up*, there is also the association with painting, so that *my grandmaster needs touching up* maintains a consistent, if unlikely, colligation.

The processing effort required to infer all these meanings is very considerable. This is an understanding test that even native speakers find challenging.

(5.10)

The first pause is an on-record invitation to take sufficient time to process *she's been doing a bit of work for us this weekend at home* to recover the implicature that the speaker has been taking advantage of her. This inference is then confirmed by the time allowed for processing by the second pause after *and*. Having led his audience up the garden path in this way, the joke-teller then denies that this implicature is well-founded (*no*) and insists (*it's true*) that the purpose of her stay is to learn the language. So it turns out that 'the first hypothesis consistent with the principle of relevance', that there is something going on between the joke-teller and his *au pair* girl, is inappropriate, or at least it is a contrivance of the joke-teller. The informant group were not able to infer this implicature at the pauses, perhaps through lack of contextual resources, perhaps because pauses give rise to 'weak implicatures'. Thus they were not able to construct 'the first hypothesis', were consequentially unable to understand the significance of *no* and *it's true* as denials of that hypothesis, and could not therefore understand the joke.

6 Presupposition

(6.1)

(6) The speaker has paid for something and tendered more than the sum required; the addressee is going to give change amounting to more than twenty pence; the addressee will be sympathetic to a request to give the change in particular denominations and has a variety of coins available.
(7) Some people will want to smoke; the person who wrote the notice does not want these people to smoke; these people will be sympathetic to a request not to smoke.

(6.2)

1.
(11) My son exists/existed (definite description); the speaker had a husband before (*second* is iterative).
(12) My varlet exists (definite description); the speaker was unarmed before (*again* is iterative); the speaker had armed (*un-* presupposes an action had been completed).
(13) The three referred to had met before (*again* is iterative) and will meet again (question introduced by *when*).
(14) Someone keeps the gate (question introduced by *who*); *the gate* exists (definite description).
(15) Someone is there (question introduced by *who*).
(16) The king exists (definite description); the king escaped our hands (embedded question introduced by *how*).
(17) The food of love exists (definite description); the musicians were playing before (*play on* is a continuing state description).
2.
Entailment(s) – Joanna has used the telephone to convey a message.
Semantic presupposition(s) – Joanna exists; her telephone calls exist; she had made telephone calls before;
Pragmatic presupposition(s) – These might include the notion that there is some point in saying this, that the addressee will understand it and be interested in it, etc.
Implicature(s) – These might include the implicature that her telephone calls do her no credit, or that making a call on this occasion was predictable.

(6.3)

My friend exists (definite description); my friend didn't have a bank account before ('open' in the sense intended here is a change-of-state verb); opening bank accounts is troublesome (*bother* is an implicative verb – 'didn't bother' asserts that she did not open the account and presupposes that it would have been troublesome to have done so); she didn't earn money before ('start' is a change-of-state verb); she earned money (temporal clause introduced by '[not] until').

(6.4)

Former Prime Ministers exist/existed (*the*)
There has been at least one successor to the Prime Minister referred to (*former*)
The former Prime Minister was removed from office by her colleagues (*who* + non-restrictive relative)
Her colleagues exist/existed (*her*)
The former Prime Minister stopped taking notes (*regrets*)
The former Prime Minister once took notes (*stopped*)
The former Prime Minister allowed exports to Iraq (*when* + temporal clause)
Iraq exists (definite description)
One of the former Prime Ministers was in office (*removed from office*)

(6.5)

These are my suggested examples – are yours as good or better?
Temporal – I chickened out before I got married
Factive – The Prince never ignores the fact that his plants like being talked to
Definite descriptions – The straightforward pragmatics book can never be written
Change-of-state – The second time I began to learn Russian I found it even harder

(6.6)

These are my suggested examples – are yours as good or better?
(10') I wonder what you are thinking about, or even if you are thinking at all (suspension).
(15') Whenever I see the curtains move in my bedroom, I shout 'Who's there?', and in a way I half hope that one day there will be someone there (?suspension/?negation).
(19') I began jogging after a visit to the doctor, although to be honest I'd jogged a bit before then (negation).
(23') Her successor managed to win the election that followed – not that it was a problem given the opposition (negation).
(30') It was the Scots who invented whisky – in as far as anyone can be said to have invented it (suspension).
(31') If you had sent me a Christmas card last year, I would have sent you one this year. As you got one from me this year, you must have sent me one last year (negation).

(6.7)

The potential presuppositions pre-empted metalinguistically are:
(10') *you are thinking about something*
(15') *there is someone there*
(19') *I had not jogged before my visit to the doctor*
(23') *winning the election was difficult* (metalinguistic negation)
(30') *someone invented whisky*
(33') *you sent me a Christmas card last year.*

(6.8)

(86) *Urged* is a plug because its complement sentence is not presupposed.
(87) *Remember* is a filter because on one reading the question seems to presuppose that the witness's lawyer told the magistrate that the witness had married a Hong Kong resident, but on another reading this presupposition does not go through.
(88) *At the time* is a hole because it allows the presupposition that the addressee appeared in the magistrate's court.
(89) *Tell* is a filter because on one reading the question seems to presuppose that the addressee came to Hong Kong (here) in order to take care of her husband's 92-year-old mother, but on another reading this presupposition does not go through.

7 Politeness

(7.1)

If you make only the minimal corrections necessary to turn the message into standard English, it seems to me that the message loses some of its sincerity. And if you can compose a more successful apology than Lam's, I'd be interested to see it.

(7.2)

1. I would certainly have written a more informal, less distance-encoding message. I guess that older people and people of higher social status would find the formal message more appropriate. As we'll see later in the chapter, the over-classes tend to favour distance-encoding strategies.
2. Some of the striking politeness features of these texts include:

Text A
The redundant *I know* is a way of expressing empathy; *but it was very helpful to me* gives a reason for imposing; *I appreciate* is an overt expression of gratitude, and *what you did*, because it is verbal rather than a nominal such as *your action/your help*, is strongly on record; *I feel indebted to you* makes a

small act of assistance look more than it is. Going on record as incurring a debt is very rarely meant sincerely in a non-debt culture like Britain. Why does the writer say *for agreeing to register* rather than *for registering* – does this imply that I had a real choice in the matter?

(I did not feel good when I got this letter. I thought it was over the top.)

Text B

This letter makes use of the powerful *we*. The level of formality also distances the writer from the reader, so that she uses *we acknowledge receipt of* rather than *thank you for* and *regarding the above* instead of *your flights*. Imagine I get home from work and my wife tells me the washing machine isn't working (i.e. implies I should do something about it) and I reply *We were extremely concerned to learn of the problems you encountered, but trust you will appreciate that we are unable to comment before an investigation has been made*. Well, you would not be reading this now because I'd have been permanently hospitalized. This sentence is a good illustration of the distancing effects of politeness. We talk to our friends in plain language (*as soon as we find out what happened*) and to those we know less well in a more formal register (*As soon as we are in possession of the facts*). The use of *would* in the conditional sentence (which is frequently prohibited in pedagogic grammars for learners of English as a second language) expresses a remote possibility and therefore tries to be as non-coercive as possible. Apology is two-sided in the sense that it not only costs the apologizer something to apologise, especially when it is *most sincere*, but it obliges the recipient to accept it. This imposition is moderated by referring to it as a *kind* act.

(When I got this letter, I did not expect to get much out of the promised follow-up letter because too much distance was already being placed between the airline and myself. But I did enjoy the letter because it contained a most unfortunate typing error: the typist hit the key to the left of the one aimed at in the last letter of *grateful*.)

Text C

The employer is the powerful *we* whose actions are mostly expressed verbally rather than nominally (*we place, we provide, would appreciate* – but *a value*), thus stressing that the employer is the agent of action; the employee is a powerless *temporary worker* whose actions are expressed entirely nominally (*workers, opinions, comments*). It is unclear what the employer's underlying motives are in asking the employee to complete the survey form that came with this letter, although a reason is given and stressed with the use of *therefore*; *would appreciate* invites or coerces the employee to earn the employer's gratitude.

(My wife did not fill in the questionnaire.)

Text D

Although purporting to address residents in an impersonal way by suggesting a general rule (a politeness strategy), the illocutionary targets are casual non-residents who are being told indirectly that drinks are not served after

10.30. This is done rather crudely: the verbal *drink* often has the connotation of drinking to excess. *Must* expresses an on-record imposition of obligation without any redress.

(If I had been a resident, I might have been quite pleased to see that the riff-raff were to be chucked out at 10.30. There is a certain directness about this notice, which does not treat addressees and illocutionary target as quite as important as they might like – the inclusion of some formula like *respectfully reminded* might make them feel better.)

3. This postcard, which we get all too frequently where we live, brings very bad news (no water for several hours) but is set out to look more like an invitation to a Buckingham Palace garden party with a variety of font sizes and types. The latest version is also in three colours. One notable feature is the movement towards a less formal register, perhaps suggesting that the culture increasingly favours less distance encoding strategies.

Comparison of Texts 1 and 2

The nominal *INTERRUPTION OF WATER SUPPLY* is replaced by the much more informal elliptical *WATER OFF*. In Text 1, the capital 'W' and 'S' in line 2 and the full date in line 3 are more formal and therefore distance encoding. Text 1 prefers *period* to *time* and mentions *drawing* rather than *using* hot water – because these are inflated terms, they are deferential. In Text 1, there is an attempt to minimize the inconvenience with the warning that using water would be *inadvisable*. Text 1 also implies a powerful position with the use of *It is essential*. The impersonal structures in this sentence and in the previous sentence in Text 1 are typical politeness strategies which try to give the impression that things have to be as they are and happen without any responsible agent. Text 2 contains an overt apology for a situation whose imposition is played down by the minimizing use of *any* and *may*. *Help* in Text 2 is a natural, friendly term – in the final line of Text 1, distance is encoded by the use of *please* which suggests that getting advice is an imposition.

Comparison of Texts 2 and 3

Text 3 begins by explaining why the water will be disconnected and in this way treats the customers as equals entitled to know why they are being inconvenienced. By beginning with an apology, replacing *regret* with *apologize*, and omitting *this may cause you*, Text 3 is more friendly and natural than Text 2. Again, Text 3 favours the more down-to-earth *turned off* rather than *remain shut* as well *so that the water does not run* rather than *to prevent the risk of flooding*. If you imagine someone speaking to you, Text 2 sounds much more formal than Text 3 which, having provided a reason for the imposition, offers advice.

(7.3)

Notice that in both cases *no* would, strictly speaking, have been a satisfactory answer propositionally speaking, but that in both shops the assistants felt obliged to elaborate for reasons of politeness. Dillons makes an offer to compensate for my disappointment and Waterstones explains the situation that has caused my disappointment. Notice that even in my question, I'm careful not to state directly that the book isn't on the shelf.

(7.4)

1. Social distance
(32) treats you as an equal by claiming kinship (*mate*). The elliptical structure *Got* (rather than *have you got*) implies closeness.
(33) begins with an apology (*Excuse me*) and is pessimistic about whether the request will be met (*would you by any chance*).
   The speaker of (32) encodes much less distance between himself and the addressee than the speaker of (33) does. I might make the assumption that the speaker of (32) was 'working class' and the speaker of (33) 'middle class' since it is in the interests of those who suppose themselves to be 'under' to claim equality and those who suppose themselves to be 'over' to try to maintain distance between themselves and others. This is why the kind of politeness middle-class parents teach their children is like that of (33) rather than that of (32), hoping by these means to give their children a head-start in life.
2. Power differentials
(34) is a direct order made all the stronger by the use of *up*, which has the effect of making the verb *eat* perfective, so that it means 'eat until you have finished'. (35) is an indirect way of telling the adult to eat. In (34) the parent shows how much more powerful they are than the child, and in (35) the child shows how much less powerful they are than the parent.
3. Imposition
I don't know what you decided to say. I might say something like

(36) Would it be all right if I left Honey with you on Wednesday morning – I'd like to go shopping by myself for a change
(37) I don't know how to put this. I don't suppose you could do me an immense favour, but we've been invited to stay with the Troll's on Saturday night and you know how they hate babies. I don't suppose there's any chance that we could possibly leave Howler with you is there? I can let you have everything you'll need.

What is being requested in (36) is much less of an imposition than what is being requested in (37).
   Taken together, these three pairs of utterances show that the social distance between speakers, the extent to which their power statuses are equal or unequal and the degree to which one speaker imposes on the other all affect the way we talk to each other.

(7.5)

1. Positive face – *as an Englishman* invites me to think that I will have a special and valued perspective, and one likely to coincide with that of the extremely engaging person to whom I'm talking.

Negative face – *I don't know if I can ask you this question* directly encodes upcoming imposition; *It is very difficult* encodes the face threat the speaker experiences in imposing on my expectation of being uncoerced; the past tense in *did you think* recognizes that a present form, *do you think*, would be more face-threatening; because it is face-threatening to say disparaging things about someone, the speaker minimizes the imposition with *just a little bit*.

2. Now that we know about face, we can see that the British announcement is closest to the way a friend would talk to us (*should*) and is therefore addressed to our positive face. The KCR announcement is more careful not to impose on us (*may*) and therefore respects our negative face to a greater degree. All the announcements respect negative face in not addressing their illocutionary target directly. In not even lexicalizing the illocutionary target, both the KCR and MTR announcements are especially respectful of negative face.

(7.6)

1. The hotel wants to avoid guests stealing items from the bedrooms. But to suggest that hotel guests are thieves is very face-threatening, so this is minimized by the scalar implicature triggered by *should*, by the term *collect* and by offering items for sale. Do you agree that *souvenir* can mean both something paid for and something taken as a kind of trophy?

2.

Agentless passives – *who are required to provide samples for analysis; Patients...are reminded; they may only be accepted; if they are presented; which are presented in non-sterile containers...and therefore cannot be accepted.*

Deference strategies – elevated uses of language, some of which are euphemistic – *samples; are reminded; on request; hazard.*

Impersonal statements of general rules – such as the first and third sentences.

Powerful first person plural – *our staff.*

Reason/explanation – such as the third sentence.

Basically this message encodes power and distance – since doctors have the power to cure us when we cannot cure ourselves and since we only visit them when we are in a weaker state than usual, it may not be surprising to find them behaving towards us in this high-handed way. Try talking to your friends like this and see what happens.

3. These are some of the ways I thought of.

On record without redress – *shut up; don't shout; talk more quietly*

Positive politeness – *if you shout, you'll strain your voice; how about quietening down, Jimbo; let's talk quietly for a change; if you talk quietly, I won't tell your boyfriend about last night; I know you'll quieten down for me*

Negative politeness – *could you possibly talk a bit more quietly; I know I'm out of order, but would you quieten down if I asked you nicely; I'm sorry to ask, but could you talk more quietly; shouting isn't allowed today*
Off record – *everything sounds very loud today; I've a terrible headache; doesn't this room echo*

(7.7)

2. Here are some more suggestions.

Text A
Positive politeness – *I know it must have made a very difficult day even more fraught* (writer can see the world from addressee's perspective); *it was very helpful to me* (gives a reason for imposing)
Negative politeness – *I appreciate what you did and I feel indebted to you* (goes on record as incurring a debt)

Text B
Positive politeness – *We were extremely concerned to learn of the problems you encountered* (expression of sympathy); *you will appreciate that we are unable to comment* (asserts a common perspective)
Negative politeness – *receipt* (without the definite article) (an impersonalizing strategy); *we would be grateful if you would ...* (does not presume addressee's compliance); *kindly accept our most sincere apologies for the inconvenience caused* (apology)

Text C
Positive politeness – *we place a high value on our temporary workers' opinions* (expression of approval); *we ... would appreciate your comments* (shows interest in addressee); *therefore* (gives a reason for imposing)

Text D
Negative politeness – *Residents wishing to drink ...* (imposition stated as a general rule)

8 Speech events

(8.1)

1. In A's first utterance, *OK* signals that the reasons for calling have been dealt with, and *well* signals that the speaker is shifting ground and is likely

to produce an utterance that the addressee might not have expected, or might not have expected at that stage in the exchange. *I'd better go* is a pre-closing device – the speaker is taking care of his own interests and thereby signalling that he hopes to bring the telephone conversation to a speedy close. He could equally have taken care of the addressee's interests by saying, for example, *I'd better let you go now*. In A's third utterance, *OK* signals his agreement that the conversation is all but over and that it's appropriate to proceed with his sign-off, *bye-bye*.

2. My guess is that B's first utterance is a reminder of some kind that her son should get someone known to both of them to do something. This sort of utterance often 'types' an earlier part of the conversation by summarizing what should happen next. But as it happens, what B thought was to be done has already been done, so perhaps B's second utterance is something like *That's OK then*, which A acknowledges with *OK*. Did you come to the same sort of conclusion?

(8.2)

(26)
Redundancies/repetitions – *yourself; the; to*
Hesitations – *er; er*

(27)
Repairs/reformulations – *were you a better climber than anybody else or were you physically stronger; or what*
Redundancies/repetitions – *yourself; in; to to*
Hedge – *I mean*
Hesitations – *er er; er*

(8.3)

(28) *if I remember arightly was it* – the parenthetical question is used as a request for reassurance that the right question is being asked; *did you not* – this provides the interviewee with a let-out and indicates that the questioner thinks he already knows the answer to the question he is asking, thus flouting the Quality maxim.

(29) the reduplication suggests that the question is tentative.

(30) *what* suggests a question is coming, although it is immediately followed by the repair *you I mean you had to;* the tag *had you* turns a statement into a question so that a suggested answer is already provided for the interviewee.

(31) *what frightens you* is a question that threatens the positive face of the addressee. So the fact that a face-threatening question is coming is signalled a long way ahead (*I'd like to ask you; I've always wanted to ask this of somebody*), and the threat is minimized by the interviewer typing his question as *daft*.

9 Talk

(9.1)

Some suggestions follow. You will probably have found other, equally good, examples of your own.

1. TA: (1.5) well we're not British Rail agents so I don't know
           the difference (l. 4–5)
So projects the imminent end of the turn by indicating the beginning of its final, consequential part.

2. TA: ⌊Ron with the shuttle saver (l. 25)
The term of address selects the speaker.

3. C: (0.2) and h ⌈and ⌉
    TA: ⌊[   ]⌋
    C: how often do they go (l. 38–40)
The customer has to compete for the turn and thus self-selects.

4. M: (0.8) yeh (l. 26)
The manager delays confirming that he has been included in the conversation. By virtue of being an incomplete proposition, the previous turn (*Ron with the shuttle saver*) had asked him to confirm the openness of the channel of communication before the travel agent resumed her turn. Perhaps the manager resents his employee's strategy. Or perhaps he thinks he is too important to answer her immediately.

5. TA: we're not British Rail ⌈agents⌉
    C: ⌊you're⌋ not a ⌈gents I see⌉ (l. 97–8)
The customer does not want the travel agent to complete a turn which contains a proposition that the customer has earlier categorized as an unacceptable contribution.

(9.2)

1. First-pair part of an adjacency pair:
    C: are you guaranteed a seat (l. 22)

2. Use of address term:
    TA: Ron what happens if he wants the last flight (l. 75–6)

3. One-word or short *wh*-phrase clarification request:
    TA: 0.3 what weekend= (l. 14)

4. Clarification request involving repetition:
    TA: that's a saver (0.7) burit it's a standby
    C: a ⌈standby⌉ (l. 19–20)

5. Tag used as an exit technique:
   TA: and coming back they er (3.4) er (0.4) you're coming back
       Sunday aren't you (l. 63–4)

6. Place where there is a natural next-turn taker, here the manager:
   TA: what happens if he wants the last fl ⌐ight⌐
   C: ⌊if I⌋ want to come back
       on the ⌐last flight on the Sunday night⌐
   TA: ⌊[   ] they don't put   ⌋ on an extra plane
       do they
   M: (1.4) well theoretically if it's full they're supposed to
       put a back-up plane on (l. 79–85)

(9.3)

1. Long single-unit turn:
   C: ah ha (.) so it's 40 either way and it starts at 7.40 on
       Saturday from London and 9.40 from Edinburgh on Sunday (.)
       until what time on Sunday night (l. 67–9)
The absence of a verb in the *until* 'clause' indicates that this is a single unit.

2. Short single-unit turn:
   C: oh I see (l. 6)

3. Long turn resulting from lack of next speaker self-selection:
   C: 19.40 (.) now what happens if you turn up for the 19.40
       flight and they get you on any of the next two does that
       mean Monday (1.5) or do they guarantee to do something
       about it on Sunday night (l. 71–4)

4. There are many pauses, especially while the travel agent looks up the information which she needs to complete her turn. Although there are no lapses because this is an event with a clearly defined purpose rather than incipient talk, there are a number of what might be termed potential lapses where the initiative rests with the customer but he seems undecided as to how to proceed. For example:
   M: in theory (2.1) whether or not it works in practice I don't
       know
   C: (3.0) now if I buy a ticket from you then it costs I I pay
       you £100 ⌐ (.) n ⌐ (l. 87–90)

(9.4)

Three-part turn:
   TA: (13.0) well there's a shuttle service (0.4) um (.) £60 one
       way (2.5) er (2.3) when do you want to go (l. 11–12)
well is oriented to the preceding turn and *when do you want to go* to the succeeding turn.

10 Reflexive language: metapragmatic and metasequential encoding

(10.1)

The letter writer seems to be unhappy about procedural encodings, so how about his opening word, *Please*, which tells us of the illocutionary force of his first sentence (a request)? And what about *anything* and *up to*, each of which hedges the accuracy of the expression that follows it?

(10.5)

(14) *by the way* has a metapragmatic function because it informs the addressee about the degree of relevance of the utterance to what went before in the conversation.

(15) *mind* has a metapragmatic function because it indicates to the addressee the illocutionary force or propositional attitude intended by the speaker.

(16) *I think* has a metapragmatic function because it informs the addressees that the speaker isn't totally committed to the proposition she voices; *you know* has a metapragmatic function because it appeals for the addressees' agreement.

(17) *Again* has a metapragmatic function because it turns the proposition into a grudging apology.

(18) I think it's rather difficult to know what function *do you mean* has. It seems essentially metalinguistic because it asks the speaker to explain whether his utterance has a particular meaning. On the other hand, the question seeks to establish what the speaker meant by what he said, and hence it seems to have a metapragmatic function. Of course, it's quite common for metalinguistic comments and queries to have a pragmatic function too.

(19) The discourse particle *well* usually has the function of preparing the addressee for a contribution they were not expecting. This unexpected contribution may be linguistic, pragmatic or sequential. The use of *well* here is quite exotic because it's most often found first word in a turn. Here the speaker prepares his addressee for a change from polite agreement with staying longer (her presumed wish) to a direct statement of his own preference. Although *well* often marks mild disagreement, its real function is to re-base the turn in a less expectable direction, as this very interesting exchange I recently heard on a radio interview shows. The interviewer said to a Cabinet Minister of the way his department was working, 'That's an appalling record, isn't it?' And the Minister replied somewhat surprisingly, 'Well it is ...'.

(20) The stressed AND is metalinguistic in the sense that it draws attention to the way a particular linguistic item is to be taken, but its effect is metapragmatic in that it causes us to draw an inference that we wouldn't otherwise have drawn.

(21) *literally* is metalinguistic because it glosses the predicate 'helped turn Brighton around' even if not in a very illuminating way.

(22) *really* is metapragmatic because it conveys to the addressee that the speaker is sincerely committed to the proposition.

(23) *I suppose* is metapragmatic because it conveys to the audience that the speaker isn't totally committed to the proposition.

(24) *and er is it* is metalinguistic because it informs the audience that the speaker isn't sure of the appropriate expression. Like the earlier meta-linguistic examples, it also has a metapragmatic function – in this case, the assertive force of the utterance is lessened.

(25) The two higher-level predicates, *not appropriate* and *wrong*, are metalinguistic in that they provide a comment on the topics to which they act as predicates. The discourse particle *Indeed* is metapragmatic because it tells us that the speaker is making an admission. *In fact* appears to have a metalinguistic function advising us that the original higher-level predicate, *not appropriate*, needs to be repaired.

(10.6)

Line 3 *if you want to* – a metapragmatic indication of the illocutionary force of the utterance as a suggestion with the authority of the speaker.

Line 6 it's not *like* it'd still be there *is it* – we might explicate this utterance to give something like *the existing situation is not like the situation in which it would still be there*. Thus *like* is metalinguistic. The tag, *is it*, is a metapragmatic indication of the propositional attitude of the speaker.

Line 8 *virtually* – a metalinguistic gloss on 'a full packet'.

Line 9 *yeah* – a metasequential indication of an upcoming contribution with a supporting propositional content; *actually* – a metapragmatic indication that the proposition is well founded, if unexpectable.

Line 11 *yeah* – as in Line 9.

Line 12 *and* – a metapragmatic indication of how the propositions either side of *and* are to be taken.

Line 40 *right* – a metasequential marker of the speaker's intention to break into a conversation from which he had been excluded.

Line 41 *all right then* – a metapragmatic acceptance of the previous speaker's proposal, with *then* marking the present speaker's agreement.

Glossary

activity type (or speech event)   a goal-directed, culturally recognizable routine (Levinson, 1979).

adjacency pair   a fundamental unit of talk consisting of a sequence of two paired units produced by different speakers so that the 'first pair part' triggers an appropriate 'second pair part'. Examples include greeting + greeting, invite + acceptance/refusal (Schegloff and Sacks, 1973).

anaphora   a reference to a previous item, or 'antecedent', in a discourse.

communication   the act of conveying a meaning from one party to another.

context   any relevant element of the social structure. Context may impinge on or be created by the use language. Presumptive contexts are said to be 'distal' or 'macro' and contexts created in talk are said to be 'micro'.

contextual resource   the term Sperber and Wilson (1995) use to describe the knowledge schema(ta) required by a hearer in order to understand an utterance.

conversation   a series of utterances exchanged between two or more speakers which follows a regular pattern of turn-taking.

cooperative principle   the central presumption underlying Grice's theory of conversational implicature (1967a) which enjoins speakers to make relevant, expectable contributions to conversation.

defeasibility   the term used to describe the cancellability status of a meaning. Some meanings are defeasible (e.g., that I have only one child in *I have a child*), others are not defeasible (e.g., that I have at least one child in *I have a child*).

deixis   the 'indexical' property of a closed class consisting of demonstratives such that their reference is determined in relation to the point of origin of the utterance in which they occur. Examples include *I, here* and *now*.

E-language, I-language a distinction drawn by Chomsky (1986) between language which is externalized (E) and internalized knowledge of language (I).

entailment a meaning that is always associated with an expression so that on every occasion when the expression occurs the meaning occurs. For example, I can never say that one football team *beat* another without entailing that the first team scored at least one goal more than the second.

ethnomethodology the study of social behaviour, including linguistic communication, which looks for regularities common to members of a particular group.

explicature a term used by Sperber and Wilson (1995) to describe the 'full propositional form' of a sentence whose indeterminacies have been resolved by a process of inference.

face a person's sense of self-esteem (positive face) and desire to determine their own course of action (negative face) postulated by Brown and Levinson ([1978], 1987) as the psychological feature addressed by politeness expressions. Hence face-wants (= need to have face respected), face threat (threat to self-esteem or to freedom of action), facework (= language addressed to the face-wants of others). Brown and Levinson suggest face is a universal feature of personality which politeness addresses, but some commentators think this view of face too western-oriented.

factivity the property of a set of predicates in whose domain subject or complement clauses are presupposed (Kiparsky and Kiparsky, 1971).

felicity conditions the conditions which must be in place for a speech act to be performed appropriately (Austin, 1962; Searle, 1969).

form linguistic structure (as opposed to function). Thus a sentence is a form, while an utterance is a sentence put to use, i.e. given a function.

grammaticalization the process by which an item comes to have a systematic relation to other items.

higher level explicature a term used by Sperber and Wilson (1995) to describe the propositional attitude of the speaker of an utterance, including speech act descriptions, which the addressee must recover inferentially.

historical pragmatics the study of the role that pragmatics, and particularly pragmatic inference, plays in language change.

honorific language forms used to encode the (high) social status of the addressee.

implicature an inferred meaning (Grice, 1968), typically with a different logical (i.e. non-truth-preserving) form from that of the original utterance. In Grice's theory, the inferential process by which a hearer derives a conversational implicature is calculable, and the implicature is defeasible and nondetachable (if the context holds, any item with the same meaning will have the same implicature); according to Grice, implicatures may be 'generalized' (inferred irrespective of context – i.e. *some* will always implicate *not all*) or 'particularized' (particular to the context of the utterance in which they arise).

indeterminacy   a property of linguistic forms such that their semantic value is underspecified and needs to be enriched in ways particular to the contexts in which they occur.

indexicality   the encoding of points of reference relative to the speaker and the time and place of the utterance.

indirect speech act   a functional use of language effected by the use of a form other than the one prototypically associated with the function concerned. For example, 'Would you mind opening the window' is a request expressed in an interrogative form.

inference   a conclusion derived from premises. A deductive or 'logical' inference is necessarily valid; inductive inferences 'project beyond the known data' (Honderich, 1995) and are probabilistic, i.e. an inductive inference may not yield the same conclusion when additional premises are adduced. Pragmatic inferences are usually presumed to be inductive, although Sperber and Wilson argue that explicatures and implicatures in relevance theory are deductive inferences. A hearer will frequently be led to infer a meaning as the result of a 'trigger', a feature of the utterance or its correspondence to known facts that leads the hearer to suspect that the literal meaning is not the (only) meaning that the speaker seeks to convey.

intentionality   according to some accounts, pragmatics is the study of the way that intentionality is reflected in language use. Speech acts very obviously reflect intentionality.

literal meaning   it is generally (but not universally) held that words and sentences have an invariant literal meaning.

logical form   the underlying representation of the propositional content of a sentence in a form that may be adjudged true or false.

maxim   the term Grice uses for the four sub-principles of his cooperative principle. The four maxims enjoin the speaker to strive to provide appropriately informative, well-founded, relevant contributions to conversation in a perspicuous manner. These may be 'hedged' by metalingual glosses which indicate the extent to which the speaker is abiding by one or more of them. Examples include *I mean* and *by the way*.

meaning   the sense that is conveyed in a communicative act. Conventional linguistic meaning is usually thought of truth-theoretically, i.e. if you know whether a sentence is a true or false description of some state of affairs, then you know what it means (truth-conditional semantics). Grice distinguishes conventional meaning and non-conventional or inferred meaning.

membership   a central notion in ethnomethodology reflecting the extent to which a person shows cultural affiliation. Hence members' method, a generic term used in Conversation Analysis for the knowledge of conversational 'methods', such as turn-taking, accounting, formulation, etc., which are demonstrated in conversational practice.

metalanguage   the use of language in a self-reflexive way to comment on or gloss itself. Hence metapragmatic uses of language gloss the pragmatic function of (parts of) an utterance and metasequential uses of language gloss the conversational function of (parts of) a talk sequence.

negation   negation maps one value (false) on to another by means of a negative particle; the negative particle is also used metalinguistically as a way of objecting to some aspect of an utterance on any grounds except its conventional, semantic meaning.

performative   the use of language to accomplish action.

politeness   the relationship between how something is said and the addressee's judgement as to how it should be said. In Brown and Levinson's model, politeness phenomena are seen as redressive and computed as a function of speaker–hearer power–distance differential and degree of imposition.

pragmatics   the study of language used in contextualized communication and the usage principles associated with it.

preference theory   contributions to talk are said to be preferred and dispreferred. When it's necessary to make a dispreferred contribution, such as refusing an invitation, this may well be linguistically redressed.

presupposition   a meaning taken as given which does not therefore need to be asserted; variously defined as 'semantic presupposition' (non-defeasible, contributes to the truth-conditional meaning of the sentence), 'conventional implicature' (non-defeasible, non-truth-conditional) and 'pragmatic presupposition' (cancellable where inconsistent with speaker/hearer knowledge about the world).

presupposition projection   the property of some complex sentences to inherit the presuppositions of the component sentences embedded within them.

procedural encoding   an indication of how to process the proposition to which it is attached in order to determine its relevance. Distinguished by Blakemore (1987) from the 'conceptual encoding' of propositions.

proposition   a linguistic representation of a state of affairs with a truth value. Utterances may also encode the attitudes of speakers to the propositions which they contain.

reference   most descriptions refer to different referents (persons, objects, notions) on each occasion when they are used. The function of picking out an object in the world which matches a linguistic description is called referring.

relevance   according to Sperber and Wilson (1995), every utterance is relevant merely by virtue of being uttered. If we know how it is relevant, we know what the speaker means.

repair   a term used in conversation analysis to describe the correction or adjustment by speaker or hearer of some part of what is said.

sentence   the formal output of a grammar in which constituent items are combined in a limited set of rule-derived configurations.

sequence   a term used to describe the grammar of conversation as a variety of sequentially ordered turn-types and members' methods.

speech act   the performative, or action-accomplishing, aspect of language use, and particularly the (illocutionary) force associated with an utterance.

speech event   see 'activity type'.

talk/talk-in-interaction   a term used to describe conversation, which draws attention to the underlying principle of turn-taking.

turn (turn constructional unit)   the principal unit of description in conversational structure.

usage   the principles which underlie allowable 'use'.

utterance   a sentence used by a speaker for some purpose. Thus 'I'm Peter' is both a sentence (it has a determinate grammar) and an utterance (I use it to introduce myself).

References

Alexander, J.C., Giesen, B., Munch, R. and Smelser, N. (eds) 1987: *The macro-micro link*. Berkeley: University of California Press.

Atkinson, J.M. and Heritage, J. (eds) 1984: *Structures of social action*. Cambridge: Cambridge University Press.

Atkinson, M., Kilby, D.A. and Roca, I. 1988: *Foundations of general linguistics* (2nd edn). London: Allen and Unwin.

Austin, J.L. 1962: *How to do things with words*. Oxford: Clarendon Press.

Austin, J.L. 1970: *Philosophical papers*. Oxford: Oxford University Press.

Austin, J.L. 1971: Performative-constative. In Searle, J.R. *Philosophy of language*. Oxford: Oxford University Press, 13–22.

Basso, K.H. and Selby, H.A. (eds) 1976: *Meaning in Anthropology*. Albuquerque: University of New Mexico Press.

Bauman, R. and Sherzer, J. (eds) 1974: *Explorations in the ethnography of speaking*. Cambridge: Cambridge University Press.

Bilmes, J. 1993: Ethnomethodology, culture and implicature: toward an empirical pragmatics. *Pragmatics* 3/4, 387–409.

Black, M. (ed.) 1965: *Philosophy in America*. London: Unwin Hyman.

Blakemore, D. 1987: *Semantic constraints on relevance*. Oxford: Blackwell Publishers.

Blakemore, D. 1992: *Understanding utterances*. Oxford: Blackwell Publishers.

Briggs, C.L. 1997: From the ideal, the ordinary, and the orderly to conflict and violence in pragmatic research. *Pragmatics* 7/4, 451–9.

Brown, P. and Levinson, S.C. 1978: Universals in language usage: politeness phenomena. In Goody, E.N. 1978, *Questions and politeness*. Cambridge: Cambridge University Press, 56–311; reprinted with new introduction and revised bibliography as *Politeness: Some universals in language usage* (1987). Cambridge: Cambridge University Press.

Burton-Roberts, N. 1989: *The limits to debate*. Cambridge: Cambridge University Press.

Carston, R. 1988: Implicature, explicature, and truth-theoretic semantics. In Kempson, R.M. 1988: *Mental representations*. Cambridge: Cambridge University Press, 155–81.

Chomsky, N. 1976: *Reflections on language*. Glasgow: Collins.

Chomsky, N. 1986: *Knowledge of language: Its nature, origin, and use*. New York: Praeger.

Cole, P. (ed.) 1978: *Syntax and semantics 9: Pragmatics*. New York: Academic Press.

Cole, P. (ed.) 1981: *Radical pragmatics*. New York: Academic Press.

Cole, P. and Morgan, J.L. (eds) 1975: *Syntax and semantics 3: Speech acts*. New York: Academic Press.

Comrie, B. 1976: Linguistic politeness axes: Speaker-addressee, speaker-reference, speaker-bystander. *Pragmatics Microfiche* 1.7.

Crystal, D. and Davy, D. 1969: *Investigating English style*. London: Longman.

Davis, S. (ed.) 1991: *Pragmatics: A reader*. Oxford: Oxford University Press.

Diessel, H. 1999: The morphosyntax of demonstratives in synchrony and diachrony. *Linguistic Typology* 3, 1–49.

Dirven, R. and Ilie, C. forthcoming: *Language and ideology: Cognitive descriptive approaches*. Amsterdam: John Benjamins.

Drew, P. and Heritage, J. 1992: *Talk at work*. Cambridge: Cambridge University Press.

Duranti, A. 1997: *Linguistic anthropology*. Cambridge: Cambridge University Press.

Duranti, A. and Goodwin, C. 1992: *Rethinking context*. Cambridge: Cambridge University Press.

Fauconnier, G. 1997: *Mappings in thought and language*. Cambridge: Cambridge University Press.

Firth, A. 1995: 'Accounts' in negotiation discourse: A single case analysis. *Journal of Pragmatics* 23, 199–226.

Foley, W.A. 1997: *Anthropological linguistics: An introduction*. Oxford: Blackwell Publishers.

Gazdar, G. 1979: *Pragmatics: Implicature, presupposition, and logical form*. New York: Academic Press.

Gladwin, T. and Sturtevant, W.C. (eds) 1962: *Anthropology and human behavior*. Washington, DC: Anthropological Society of Washington.

Glover, K.D. 2000: The sequential analysis of proximal and distal deixis in negotiation talk. *Journal of Pragmatics* 32/7.

Glover, K.D. and Grundy, P. 1996: 'Why do we have these': When reconstructing the indexical ground is disfavoured. In Romary, L. and Reboul, A. (eds) *Time, space and indentity*. Nancy: CRIN-Loria, 117–33.

Goody, E.N. (ed.) 1978: *Questions and politeness*. Cambridge: Cambridge University Press.

Green, G.M. 1996: *Pragmatics and natural language understanding* (2nd edn). Mhawah, NJ: Lawrence Erlbaum Associates.

Greenberg, J.H. (ed.) 1978: *Universals of human language*. Los Angeles: Stanford University Press.

Grice, H.P. 1967a: William James lectures: Logic and conversation. In Cole, P. and Morgan, J.L. 1975: *Syntax and semantics 3*. New York: Academic Press, 41–58.

Grice, H.P. 1967b: William James lectures: further notes on logic and conversation. In Cole, P. 1978: *Syntax and semantics 3*. New York: Academic Press, 113–28.

Grice, H.P. 1968: Utterer's meaning, sentence-meaning, and word-meaning. *Foundations of Language* 4, 1–18.

Grundy, P. 1998: Parallel texts and diverging cultures in Hong Kong: Implications for intercultural communication. In Niemeier *et al*. *The cultural context in business communication*. Amsterdam: John Benjamins, 167–83.

Grundy, P. and Jiang, Y. 1998: Deictic reference and cognitive semantics. *HKPU Working papers in Chinese and Bilingual Studies* 1, 85–103.

Grundy, P. and Jiang, Y. forthcoming: The bare past as an ideological construction in Hong Kong discourse. In Dirven and Ilie.

Gu, Y. 1990: Politeness phenomena in modern Chinese. *Journal of Pragmatics* 14/2, 237–57.

Hall, E.T. 1976: *Beyond culture*. Garden City, NY: Anchor Press.

Hanks, W.F. 1992: The indexical ground of deictic reference. In Duranti, A. and Goodwin, C. *Rethinking context*. Cambridge: Cambridge University Press, 43–76.

Harris, S. 1995: Pragmatics and power. *Journal of Pragmatics* 23, 117–135.

Hawkins, J.A. 1978: *Definiteness and indefiniteness: A study in reference and grammaticality prediction*. London: Croom Helm.

Heritage, J. 1984: *Garfinkel and ethnomethodology*. Cambridge: Polity Press.

Hewstone, M. and Fincham, F. 1996: Attribution theory and research: Basic issues and applications. In Hewstone *et al. Introduction to social psychology*. Oxford: Blackwell, 167–204.

Hewstone, M., Stroebe, W., Stephenson, G.M. (eds) 1996: *Introduction to social psychology: A European perspective* (2nd edn). Oxford: Blackwell Publishers.

Hilton, D.J. 1991: A conversational model of causal explanation. In Stroebe, W. and Hewstone, M. *European review of social psychology*, Vol. 2. Chichester: John Wiley, 51–82.

Hofstede, G.H. 1980: *Culture's consequences*. Beverley Hills: Sage.

Holmes, J. 1986: Compliments and compliment responses in New Zealand English. *Anthropological Linguistics* 28, 485–508.

Holmes, J. 1995: *Women, men and politeness*. London and New York: Longman.

Honderich, T. (ed.) 1995: *The Oxford companion to philosophy*. Oxford: Oxford University Press.

Hopper, P.J. and Traugott, E.C. 1993: *Grammaticalization*. Cambridge: Cambridge University Press.

Horn, L.R. 1972: *On the semantic properties of logical operators in English*. PhD dissn. University of California, Los Angeles.

Horn, L.R. 1984: Toward a new taxonomy for pragmatic inference: Q-based and R-based implicature. In Schiffrin, D. *Meaning, form, and use in context*. Washington, DC: Georgetown University Press, 11–42.

Horn, L.R. 1985: Metalinguistic negation and pragmatic ambiguity. *Language* 61/1, 121–74.

Horn, L.R. 1988: Pragmatic theory. In the *Cambridge Survey*, Vol. 1, 113–45. Cambridge: Cambridge University Press.

Horn, L.R. 1989: *A natural history of negation*. Chicago: University of Chicago Press.

Hutchby, I. and Wooffitt, R. 1998: *Conversation analysis*. Oxford: Blackwell.

Hymes, D.H. 1962: The ethnography of speaking. In Gladwin, T. and Sturtevant, W.C. (eds) *Anthropology and human behavior*, Washington, DC: Anthropological Society of Washington, 13–53.

Jaworski, A. and Coupland, N. 1999: *The discourse reader*. London: Routledge.

Kaplan, D. 1978: On the logic of demonstratives. *Journal of Philosophical Logic* 8, 81–98.

Karttunen, L. and Peters, S. 1979: Conventional implicature. In Oh, C.-K. and Dinneen, D.A. (eds) *Syntax and semantics* 11. New York: Academic Press, 1–56.

Kasper, G. 1990: Linguistic politeness: Current research issues. *Journal of Pragmatics* 14/2, 193–218.

Kempson, R.M. (ed.) 1988: *Mental representations: The interface between language and reality*. Cambridge: Cambridge University Press.

Kiparsky, P. and Kiparsky, C. 1971: Fact. In Steinberg, P., Jakobovits, L. *Semantics*. Cambridge: Cambridge University Press, 345–69.

Kopytko, R. 1995: Against rationalistic pragmatics. *Journal of Pragmatics* 23, 475–91.

Lakoff, G. 1971: Presupposition and relative well-formedness. In Steinberg, P. and Jakobovits, L. *Semantics*. Cambridge: Cambridge University Press, 329–40.

Lakoff, R. 1972: Language in context. *Language* 48, 907–27.

Lakoff, R. 1973: The logic of politeness: Or minding your P's and Q's. *Papers from the ninth regional meeting of the CLS*. Chicago: CLS, 292–305.

Leech, G.N. 1983: *Principles of pragmatics*. Harlow: Longman.

Levinson, S.C. 1979: Activity types. *Linguistics* 17, 365–99.

Levinson, S.C. 1983: *Pragmatics*. Cambridge: Cambridge University Press.

Levinson, S.C. 1992: Activity types and language. In Drew, P. and Heritage, J. *Talk at work*. Cambridge: Cambridge University Press, 66–100.

Levinson, S.C. 1995: Three levels of meaning. In Palmer, F. *Grammar and meaning*. Cambridge: Cambridge University Press, 90–119.

Lockwood, W.B. 1968: *Historical German syntax*. Oxford: Oxford University Press.

Loveday, L. 1984: Pitch prominence and sexual role: An exploratory investigation into the pitch correlates of English and Japanese politeness formulae. *Language and Speech* 24, 71–89.

Lucy, J.A. (ed.) 1993: *Reflexive language: reported speech and metapragmatics*. Cambridge: Cambridge University Press.

McCawley, J.D. 1981: *Everything that linguists have always wanted to know about logic but were ashamed to ask*. Oxford: Basil Blackwell.

Matsumoto, Y. 1988: Reexamination of the universality of face: Politeness phenomena in Japanese. *Journal of Pragmatics* 12, 403–26.

Matsumoto, Y. 1989: Politeness and conversational universals: Observations from Japanese. *Multilingua* 8, 207–22.

Mey, J.L. 1993: *Pragmatics: An introduction*. Oxford: Blackwell.

Morgan, J.L. 1978: Two types of convention in indirect speech acts. In Cole, P. (ed.) *Syntax and semantics* 9. New York: Academic Press, 261–80.

Niemeier, S., Campbell, C.P. and Dirven, R. (eds) 1998: *The cultural context in business communication*. Amsterdam: John Benjamins.

Nunberg, G. 1993: Indexicality and deixis. *Linguistics and Philosophy* 68, 1–43.

Nwoye, O.G. 1992: Linguistic politeness and sociocultural variation of the notion of face. *Journal of Pragmatics* 18, 309–28.

Oh, C.-K. and Dinneen, D.A. (eds) 1979: *Syntax and semantics* 11: *Presupposition*. New York: Academic Press.

Palmer, F. 1995: *Grammar and meaning: Essays in honour of Sir John Lyons*. Cambridge: Cambridge University Press.

Peirce, C.S. 1932: Division of signs. In Hartshorne, C. and Weiss, P. (eds), *Collected papers of CS Peirce*, Vol. 2. Cambridge, MA: Harvard University Press, 134–55.

Romary, L. and Reboul, A. (eds) 1996: *Time, space and identity*. Nancy: CRIN-Loria.

Russell, B. 1905: On denoting. *Mind* 14, 479–93.

Sacks, H. 1974: An analysis of the course of a joke's telling in conversation. In Bauman, R. and Sherzer, J. (eds) *Explorations in the ethnography of speaking*. Cambridge: Cambridge University Press, 337–53.

Sacks, H., Schegloff, E.A. and Jefferson, G. 1974: A simplest systematics for the organization of turn-taking in conversation. *Language* 50/4, 696–735.

Sadock, J.M. 1974: *Toward a linguistic theory of speech acts*. New York: Academic Press.

Schegloff, E.A. 1987: Between micro and macro: Context and other connections. In Alexander, J.C. *et al.* 207–34.

Schegloff, E.A. 1992: In another context. In Duranti, A. and Goodwin, C. *Rethinking context*. Cambridge: Cambridge University Press, 191–228.

Schegloff, E.A. and Sacks, H. 1973: Opening up closings. *Semiotica* 7/4, 289–327.

Schenkein, J. (ed.) 1978: *Studies in the organization of conversational interaction*. New York: Academic Press.

Schiffrin, D. (ed.) 1984: *Meaning, form, and use in context: Linguistic applications*. GURT '84 Washington: Georgetown University Press.

Schiffrin, D. 1987: Meta-talk: Organization and evaluative brackets in discourse. *Sociological Inquiry* 20, 199–236.

Schiffrin, D. 1994: *Approaches to discourse*. Oxford: Blackwell.

Scott, M. and Lyman, S.M. 1968: Accounts. *American Sociological Review* 33, 46–62.

Searle, J.R. (ed.) 1971: *Philosophy of language*. Oxford: Oxford University Press.

Searle, J.R. 1965: What is a speech act? In Davis, S. 1991 *Pragmatics*. Oxford: Oxford University Press, 254–64.

Searle, J.R. 1969: *Speech acts*. Cambridge: Cambridge University Press.

Searle, J.R. 1975: Indirect speech acts. In Cole, P. and Morgan, J.L. (eds) *Syntax and semantics* 3. New York: Academic Press, 59–82.

Searle, J.R. 1979: *Expression and meaning*. Cambridge: Cambridge University Press.

Seuren, P.A.M. 1998: *Western linguistics: An historical introduction*. Oxford: Blackwell Publishers.

Silverstein, M. 1976: Shifters, linguistic categories and cultural description. In Basso, K.H. and Selby, H.A. *Meaning in anthropology*. Alberquerque: University of New Mexico Press, 11–55.

Sperber, D. and Wilson, D. 1995 (2nd edn): *Relevance: Communication and cognition*. Oxford: Basil Blackwell.

Steinberg, D. and Jakobovits, L. 1971: *Semantics*. Cambridge: Cambridge University Press.

Strawson, P.F. 1950: On referring. *Mind* 59, 320–44.

Stroebe, W. and Hewstone, M. (eds) 1991: *European review of social psychology*, Vol. 2. Chichester: John Wiley & Sons Ltd.

Talmy, L. 1978: Figure and ground in complex sentences. In Greenberg, J.H. (ed.) *Universals of human language*. Los Angeles: Stanford University Press, 625–49.

Tarski, A. 1944: The semantic conception of truth. *Philosophy and Phenomenological Research* 4, 341–75. In Tarski, A. 1956: *Logic, semantics and metamathematics*. London: Oxford University Press.

Thomas, J.A. 1995: *Meaning in interaction: An introduction to pragmatics*. Harlow: Longman.

Traugott, E.C. 1989: On the rise of epistemic meanings in English: An example of subjectification in semantic change. *Language* 65, 31–55.

Traugott, E.C. 1995: The role of the development of discourse markers in a theory of grammaticalization. Paper presented at ICHL XII, Manchester.

Traugott, E.C. 1998: The role of pragmatics in semantic change. Plenary address, 6th International IPrA Conference, Reims.

Verschueren, J. 1998: *Understanding pragmatics*. London: Arnold.

Verschueren, J., Ostman, J.-O. and Blommaert, J. 1995: *Handbook of pragmatics, manual*. Amsterdam: John Benjamins.

Wilson, D. and Sperber, D. 1993: Linguistic form and relevance. *Lingua* 90, 1–15.

Yule, G. 1996: *Pragmatics*. Oxford: Oxford University Press.

Zimmerman, D.H. and Boden, D. (eds) 1991: *Talk and social structure: Studies in ethnomethodology and conversation analysis*. Cambridge: Polity Press.

Index